I0531787

AT☢MIC BABY BIBLE

MY SIX DECADES OF DIFFERENT

JOHN REDDEN

© 2022 John Redden

All rights reserved. No part of this book may be reproduced in any form or by any electronic or mechanical means, including information storage and retrieval systems, without permission in writing from the author and illustrator, except in the case of brief quotations in the context of critical articles or reviews.

Cover design and interior layout by Aaxel Author Services & Noah Adam Paperman

ISBN 979-8-9858680-0-5 (print)

ISBN 979-8-9858680-1-2 (eBook)

I dedicate this work to my wife, who is barely mentioned in this epistle. She has tolerated my eccentricity and foibles for over forty-two years.

CONTENTS

PREFACE

...

S omeone once told me that because of all the atomic radiation from nuclear explosions around the world that my generation, born post-WWII, are mutants. We affected an upheaval of Western culture, so maybe there's something to that. This epistle is a personal memoir of being a child in the late 1940s and 1950s, when mass culture became a fact of life. In the 1960s, I share my dealings with puberty, emergent sexuality, and then revolution in Western culture. In the 1970s, I focus on devastating loss and subsequent recovery and entrance into the emerging cybernetic economy. The post-1970s are an account of my journey through corporate culture. In the Afterword (Revelation), I am cross examined by an alternate self. The Geek Apocrypha books only interest one who wants a history of technology from a subjective point of view. Unless you have a fair knowledge of computer technology, the Geek Apocrypha will bore you to tears. But I thought it was important to write it and marry it to my memoir.

ORIGIN

●●●

Being an atomic baby boomer born after World War II is not a unique experience. I can imagine how someone born in an Italian city-state at the beginning of the Renaissance and experiencing that transformation, or a Roman citizen-youth experiencing the creation of the Roman Empire around what we call "year one", might compare. But being a toddler and a preschooler in the San Fernando Valley in the late 1940s and in 1950 and 1951 is a similar transformation that I experienced, and what many others experienced on a purely quantitative scale of the mass culture that developed in what is now called the "fifties." This shaped my early life.

Whereas a youth in an Italian Renaissance city-state or in the burgeoning Roman Empire came from a narrow class background, in the 1950s, I was part of one of the greatest working-class transformations in history. I grew up during the creation of the so-called "North American middle class" on a massive scale. The GI Bill and similar government programs ushered in suburban culture and sometimes a real transfer of power to unprecedented numbers of people who in previous decades would have been an adjunct to the eighteenth and nineteenth century ways of life—that is, working in a factory or working on a farm in an agrarian area of North America. This is significant in terms of the political economy. The ability of GIs returning from World War II to gain access to suburban housing was a silent, but a significant transformation. In terms of real wealth, it was one of the most significant acts of class mobility in planetary history to this date.

I can make a convincing argument that economic advantage funded the transformation in North America of a transnational base originating from the early twentieth century. This is an analysis with which I would agree. Regardless, funding of the middle class in the late 1940s took place after the establishment of the nascent "USA-sian empire." The core of this empire was solidified and expanded in terms of a global economy during a period where the perception of the public was one of isolationism and had little to do with the trans-national economic solidification.

My earliest memories in this era are, as you would imagine, sketchy. My grandparents purchased considerable acreage at the west end of the San Fernando Valley. From my perspective, there were vast alfalfa fields. The neighbors had a ranch with horses. Local roads, Independence and Gault, were dirt. A goat man drove his goats down the road to his pasture. They designed the house and property as a hacienda, with three sides enclosing a courtyard of grass, trees, and flowers. The fourth side spread around the pathways, supporting seedless grape vines. There were chairs I used to sit on while looking at the often-clear sky before it later became a sea of smog. Around the edges citrus trees, pomegranate trees, many pepper trees, eucalyptus trees, and edgings of hollyhocks accentuated a tiny child's fantasy. Amid these wonderlands of flora and fauna, I would stare into the night sky. One distinctive memory of my father is when took me on his shoulders and showed me the moon. He asked me, "Do you see the man in the moon or the lady in the moon?" This was a child's introduction to the fantastic.

There were irrigation ditches that ran parallel to the south side of the south wall of the hacienda complex. Once in a while I got to turn the water on, and see it flow through the parallel ditches to water all the vegetables. To a tiny child, it seemed like a jungle of plants, row after row going on forever.

One day my hands mortified me. I looked at what once were my perfectly smooth hands and there were creases! Later I could understand that the creases were knuckles and digits, but it didn't matter. I was noticing my body.

I could hide in the alfalfa field, and turn invisible. My child mind would turn to the next fantastic vision, perhaps of fresh grapes, birds, animals like rabbits and frogs from the channels.

Then there were the trips downtown to Canoga Park, which was an external suburb with a sparse population in the San Fernando Valley, and to all places, Sherman Way, in my dad's 1947 Frazier automobile. It was like a scene out of the movie Back to the Future. At the local Mobile gas station with its huge Pegasus sign, a woman attended to our car, checking all the fluids. Sometimes I would ride to downtown Canoga Park in my grandfather's car, a 1946 Studebaker with itchy velvet-like seats, all in light tan surrounded by a metal frame of shiny light brown. On the bumper was a California license plate with a black background, three yellow letters, and three yellow numbers. My grandfather always went some place different from my dad, since my grandfather hated to drive. His journeys often ended at stores with metals and tools, with which he built things out of copper and leather. He always had a supply of jelly beans, and that's what I named him, "Bean." He would talk about how he was going to New Mexico, and build himself a "mud hut," which I understood sometime later to be an adobe house.

Grandfather "Bean" from my mother's side of the family was nicknamed the "Millard County Genius". He was a self-taught engineer. I heard the stories about his trip to South Africa working for the diamond conglomerate. He admired Cecil Rhodes. When I was baptized in 1947 by a Capuchin monk, using his influence, he designated Cecil as my baptismal name. Later, I learned he helped design WW II bombers for McDonald Douglas. Being self taught, I still have his math books.

Later when I was a pre-teen, my father told me I spent a lot of time with the Latino children (his term for the local Mexican children, whether they all came from Mexico is anyone's guess), and told me I was close to being a bi-lingual little kid. In this child wonderland in Canoga Park, my pets were "Dono" and "Bessie," both tame Mallard ducks. I would carry them upside down and launch them while standing on the red brick barbecue. My father acquired them as ducklings and I think they thought he was a mother figure. Local dogs unfortunately killed Dono and Bessie shortly after that.

These are archetypal visions of a very young child. The symbols are simple and the needs direct. As soon as I was paying attention to the surrounding icons, the mass culture of the 1950s, while filtering through my inexperienced eyes and ears. My first vision of a Monopoly game board was scintillating.

What are these people doing with all these colors and letters?

Later, when I was older, about five years old, I fixated on a Time Magazine that had on the cover two airplanes, a Mig and a Sabre-Jet boxing in air.

What was this, I wondered.

But the real injection of mass culture came with television, which transformed the culture, first nationally and later on a global one. This is the archetypal 1950s icon. Our black-and-white set with its huge cabinet sat in the family room. Pages and pages have been written about TV and fifties culture, but we might neglect some programs in the prior history of television. Prominent in my memories are ones my grandmother liked very much—travel logs, where a camera was mounted on the side of a car fender to show the scenery plus a moving white line on the asphalt in black-and-white. And a narrator would talk as you moved along. Then there were the commercials featuring stop-motion animation, like the one with rolls of Scotch Tape marching down the street. It was also a world of cartoons, Beany and Cecil and Howdy Doody, often with subtle political criticism that a five-year-old didn't understand. I have some vague memories of watching the McCarthy Hearings on a 1950s TV, and the disgust of some family members at the process. We also had Friday Night Fights sponsored by Gillette, and the Roller Derby, great sleaze fun to watch all these skaters going around in a circle bashing each other. Then stations would go off the air with the Lord's Prayer and a circular pattern that looked like the state flag of New Mexico.

My grandfather introduced to music at a very early age. My grandfather, who was working for McDonnell Douglas in San Diego as an engineer, showed me his guitar and taught me some chords. I have long fingers and at a very young age could press down the strings on his not-so-good Stella steel string guitar. He taught me Pancho Villa's marching song and Over the Waves. He also taught me how to count to ten in the Ute Native American language.

Another musical influence occurred when a friend of my parents who also attended Occidental College brought along a portable 45 RPM record player and put on Les Paul and Mary Ford's "How High the Moon." I thought it rocked, and it endured as an archetype of rocking-rolling music in my mind.

While in town at Canoga Park, my father took me to the movies. I remember one of the Disney nature movies, maybe the Living Desert. Before the movie started, there were previews of a science fiction movie that had a stop-motion, medium-sized bug chasing people. It looked something like the "Cootie" in the Cootie game, which I later owned and played, but with an enormous head. I called it the "Bowda Bug," and for several years after that I periodically had nightmares that this bug was after me.

Before the skies were too full of smog, yes it did roll in about this time, I sat in a small pepper tree with a board serving as a micro-tree house where I watched aircraft soar through the sky. I wonder if these were experimental aircraft from Edwards or Lockheed in Burbank. Regardless, they would feed the imagination of a young child.

I traveled dirt roads, looking at reeds and plants in the Los Angeles River, crossing bridges, and gazing up at eucalyptus trees.

My childhood wonderland continued until the day I arrived at the school-yard door, and a small complex of light brown buildings. They had me do a test comprising shapes and symbols. I must have made the grade. Afterwards, my parents received a glowing report from the elementary school. I remember little about this school, except being told we were going to have a drill. I followed the teacher's instructions and crawled under my desk. That drill was my initiation into being an atomic baby.

Grandma from my mother's side was always simply "grandma". This grandma told me that when I was very young, that she raised me, not my mother and father. Even at a young age, I heard tales about "Grandma Fern". Her father, George Bartholomew, ran the Bartholomew Circus and my grandmother would ride on the back of a pony and shoot the ace out of an ace of spades. She grew up in the countryside of Utah. My mother would complain since she was a western woman with little education, she had terrible English language skills. And she told me since grandma had "raised" me, I had poor English skills. Keep in mind, my mother was an English major at Occidental college.

TRANSIT

•••

I n 1950, for an unremembered amount of time, we moved to a three-story house that had at one time probably been a large farmhouse and was part of a Spanish land grant in Highland Park, a neighborhood in northeast Los Angeles. Highland Park was the first place I lived that was not in the rapidly diminishing rural area of Canoga Park where my grandmother on my mother's side lived. The rural area around Canoga Park was diminishing due to sub-urbanization. Highland became my introduction to urban life.

The Realtor that rented it to us had the name of "Throop," so everyone in the neighborhood called it "Throop's Coop." Throop had a real estate on York Boulevard and owned several houses in Highland Park. The house was divided into two rentals, a downstairs and an upstairs comprising two floors.

My parents told me never to bother the person downstairs since he was "crazy." I realized what the issue was later when exploring the basement below the first story, where I discovered many empty vodka bottles. I don't remember ever speaking or meeting with the downstairs tenant.

It was a vast house with secret closets, stairways, and the like. I stayed on the third floor, where there was a screened window that, in theory, could be opened. My father told me that a child of the previous tenant had rolled out of it from the third story and been killed. I don't know whether this was a parent trick or a fact.

Growing along the side of Throop's Coop was a huge old apricot tree, and one year it produced a massive number of apricots, which I ate until I almost got sick. There was also a huge, open field to the northeast that existed unmolested from 1950 to 1957, and that was a substantial source of adventure.

For a short while, I attended kindergarten at Aldama Elementary School on Avenue 50 in Highland Park. I remember little about it, except that I panicked, crawled out of the first-story window of the school, and ran home. This, of course, got me into trouble. Los Angeles was not to be the cornerstone of the West Coast sprawl. It was relatively small and still somewhat rural. People kept chickens and folks still burned trash in an incinerator before this was all put a stop to around 1952 when the first smog alerts occurred.

Like many young boys in the early 1950s, trains were a significant source of fascination with me. From Throop's Coop, you could hear the trains coming into the rail yard near downtown Los Angeles. During this period in my young life, my grandparents would arrive from Arkansas, a mysterious place to me. My dad would take the Frazier to pick them up at Union Station, which became my first remembered transit center. This was before the heyday of buses and transcontinental flights. The station was this fantastic complex, with archetypal arches, high ceilings, huge wooden benches, sizeable gardens, and vast tunnels leading to the train yard. These memories which are tinged with, of all things, the aroma of mint. When my grandparents opened their suitcase, it had the overwhelming smell of Wrigley's gum. They always brought their own food, and it was almost gone by the time they reached Los Angeles, but if I was lucky, I would score a piece of candy or gum. When my grandparents from Arkansas visited, they would stay about a week and then return to Arkansas on the train.

Candy is prominent in my earliest memories. When my parents rented an apartment for a short time in Eagle Rock on Yosemite way, close to Highland Park in north-east Los Angeles, the landlady gave out candies to the kids for good behavior. During this time, I attended kindergarten at Toland Way Elementary School. I don't have many memories when attending kindergarten at Toland Way, but the ones I remember are of me gazing out the school windows to look at the odd structure of the Sparklets Water bottling plant with its strange middle-eastern architecture and the recognition of fall colors and trying to reproduce them in Crayon drawings, and, finally, consuming wonderful British licorice.

My world grew larger when my Aunt Kitty and Uncle Leslie returned from Europe to Canoga Park. Of course, my mother, father and I would return to Canoga Park for a visit. Leslie was a socialist and a former member of the British Labor party before becoming a US citizen, graduating from UCLA with a master's degree in history, and going to work as a historian for the United States Air Force. We used to sit at a huge redwood table in the dining room adjacent to grandma's kitchen. During a particular spaghetti dinner when I was five, they gave me a glass of watered-down Famiglia Cribari wine, my introduction to alcohol. According to what my mother told me later, giving children watered down wine was common in Europe. What followed, I remember, was a huge political discussion concerning Trotsky and Stalin. My uncle would have an enormous influence on me later when I entered college at seventeen years old, and I majored in history.

In 1951, we moved back to Highland Park and rented a two-bedroom house, with a living room, garage and yard on Shipley Glen Drive within walking distance of Throop's Coop and Aldama Elementary School. When we moved in, there were hardwood floors that my father refinished. It had a fireplace and a not-so-good peach tree in the front yard. Unlike the apricots at Throop's Coop, the peaches were mostly white with no taste. Thinking back on it, I question if the trees were ever properly watered and fertilized.

My bedroom was in the house's front, maybe something on a compromise of bungalow architecture. And in the backyard there was a soon-to-be-outlawed furnace. The backyard was mostly a mass of licorice-smelling plants, weeds, and bugs, but it was to be my home for the next six years.

These are the quintessential recollections of an atomic baby boomer, not just family and home, tastes and aromas, mysteries and adventures, but burgeoning technology, nascent mass media, and the seeds of upcoming political unrest associated with desired social equality. What are these seeds that I, a five-year-old, am oblivious to? One is the integration of the military during WWII and Jacky Robinson breaking the color barrier in baseball. Another is amorphous, but housewives gathering while their husbands worked, sharing cock-tails and sometimes playing "Peyton Place", set the stage for women's behavior in the 1960s. The instant dinners and "quick food" of the 1950s set the stage for the healthy food movement that started in the 1970s. You get the idea.

ELEMENTARY-1

•••

I n some ways, I didn't experience the vintage 1950s, not like the kids in the newly constructed suburbs. The Highland Park area was still so rural that people kept chickens and we generated refuse smoke before it was illegal. Backyards had furnaces where we burned trash, but after several first-stage smog alerts, the furnaces were no more. This was a fading working class urban culture before the suburban influx after WWII. There were families across the street from my house that had barely made it through the Great Depression. For at least one of them I was told, and I didn't forget, that the father had worked for the Civilian Conservation Corps (CCC), a public work relief program that operated from 1933 to 1942 in the United States for unemployed men. But the cultural apex of the 1950s, which was television, made its way to my poor, but mostly Anglo neighborhood of Highland Park.

In the driveway at the Shipley Glen house, when we first moved there, sat a Ford Model T car (yes, it was black). Someone, probably the previous owner or renter, started the ancient voiture at about five in the morning and delivered things. I would get in the vehicle and explore it, but at such a young age, I just didn't understand how you could get it started.

As I went to school each day, I realized that there were kids around me just like me. Lots of them. One thing I have to say about the Great Depression-WWII generation made up of my parents and my peers' parents. They were making babies. For my generation, the term "Baby Boomer" is appropriately chosen. That we lived in the best society possible, even invincible and untarnished, was a common theme in all the very young "Baby Boomers" minds.

With all the kids in the neighborhood, the conversation would center on candy, television, and maybe movies and petty differences. The kids had local candy stores within walking distance on Avenue 50. There were jujubies, bubble gum cigars, and a whole plethora of candy bars, all for five or ten cents each. Like all kids in the expanding Southern California region, my earliest memories of school comprised Dick and Jane (the subject of many childish obscene jokes when I was a teen), basic math, coloring "inside the lines," recess, and visits to the school by Monty Montana, the Hollywood Cowboy and his horse with his amazing rope tricks. It made us kids feel special, that an actor who could actually do cowboy tricks would visit us.

My first piano teacher, Mrs. Duval, lived right next door. She had at least twenty chickens which made noise, but were obviously a source of food. Mrs Duval enjoyed listening to a radio station in the wee-hours of the morning called the "Night Owl" show. I believe it was a talk show possibly interspersed with music. Unfortunately, about a year later, my mother let the brake slip on the brand new 1953 Pontiac, and it backed into Mrs. Duval as my mother was helping Mrs. Duval shop at Boys Market in Highland Park. She went to the hospital with a cracked rib where she died of pneumonia. My mother killed the piano teacher. So I needed a new piano teacher. To fill in, a Polish woman down the street who had a child about my age named James and a dog named Blackie, who, when on the loose, will get into trouble, as you will see. So Mrs Blaszczyk taught me the piano.

Those were great times! After digging a mud-hole and getting covered from head-to-foot, James and I would then jump off a shack about five feet from the ground, and land in the mud as if nothing had happened. Constellation airplanes flew over our house in Highland Park periodically in the morning, heading to what was a very new Los Angeles International Airport. What most people don't know is that the original Los Angeles Airport terminal, which was on Imperial Boulevard, southwest of central Los Angeles, and is where the movie Casablanca supposedly did the air hanger scenes. I loved to look at the splendor of the Constellations. They were noisy and did not have the altitude of jet airliners in the 1970s and the years after. For a kid, this propeller driven passenger craft embodied a wonderful fantastic image with their long slim body and triple fins on the tail.

Key elements in the atomic baby's schooling also included a semi-communal dance called the Hokey Pokey. There were actually dance and body steps, including your arms, legs, and head. Also during these years, elementary schools had May Day celebrations, including a May Pole. (Of course, us kids did not know that the May Pole was a fertility symbol.) Later, these May Day celebrations quickly vanished. During the May Day celebrations, all the kids lined the edges of the playground, often dressed in bright clothing. Happy-time music played over the small speakers connected to a low-fidelity record player. And we would dance.

ELEMENTARY-2

•••

Before 1953, I wandered around in a world of archetypes. I encountered one fantastic symbol after another. They were all archetypes outside environment, cars, airplanes, animals, essentially items animate or inanimate. This was about to change because of the emerging mass culture.

Every kid in the neighborhood knew every new program on television. If the young kid so happened not to have television, there would be a visit to a family who had one. At that time, there were only a few new shows, not like the ever-changing line-up seen in post-modern times. The new mass culture engulfed me. In 1954, the World of Disney aired on public television. This imbued the Boomer generation with a bond. For males around my age, they gravitated towards the saga of Davy Crockett. For females, they were likely attracted to Mickey Mouse Club. Of course, my recollection is this perception.

Johnnie Correa was my next-door neighbor, and a consistent friend during my elementary school atomic baby years. His parents, Dave and Louise, were both engineers. His dad and my dad made Shipley Glenn Beer in the garage of our house. It wasn't very good by modern, micro-brew standards, but they liked it, and I took the leftover beer bottles to Barney's Liquor Store at the corner of Avenue 50 and Monte Vista Avenue in my wagon to cash in so I could buy Revell models of various model aircraft. I think Louise's career in engineering was cut short when she had back-to-back sets of twin females, giving them five kids in a compressed time frame.

During this period, I became much more aware of kids around me. Not only did I spend time with Johnnie, but I met Terry, who was building a fictitious army. We would go to the vacant lot next door to Throop's Coop and fight fictitious wars. I met Kenny, who lived just down the street from where I lived, who later would knock out part of my front tooth with a marble. And I met Penny, the girl up the street who lived directly across from Throop's Coop, at whose house I listened to some of the last Space Cadet radio shows on her parents' radio.

By this time, at semester start, September 1954, I walked to Aldama Elementary School in Highland Park. The result of this new mobility and freedom, my after-school activities spanned a much larger area in the neighborhood. We remained good friends with James' mother, Mrs. Blaszczyk, when I gained another piano teacher, Mrs. Stevenson. Maybe my parents thought she would be a better landing place for the atomic baby. Mrs. Blaszczyk had several quirks. She would not register to vote, so they would not select her to serve jury duty. Perhaps some of this was because of living in

Poland behind the "iron curtain". Mrs. Stevenson lived in a large, two-story house, where I never saw the second story. Up there lived a mysterious person, her father, quite old. She would bring him his favorite snack, Twinkies. Of course, all the kids that came to Mrs Stevenson's house coveted this unhealthy food.

Next to Mrs. Stevenson's house were a series of small square styled buildings, all flowing down the hill, very much in the style of a Hollywood bungalow. My family labeled the area up the hill from us "The Courts." Several kids lived in the "Courts" with their parents. Many of these kids were older than me, but there were a few around my age.

Besides piano lessons, both Mrs. Stevenson and her father were Christian missionaries, probably of a Protestant flavor, that had escaped from China during the revolution. Her lessons were fascinating. She stuck felt figures on a board and lectured about them in simple terms. But other than trying to teach us her flavor of Christianity, she was an excellent music teacher. I would see some courts kids at Mrs. Stevenson's house for Bible lessons and also piano lessons. Mrs. Stevenson had a beautiful baby grand piano, on which she gave us lessons. In retrospect, I think she was a positive influence on the neighborhood, her religious views notwithstanding. These were working-class kids getting more, or less, what is good behavior outside the conflict of their own families. And those that studied the piano had a tremendous boost in life skills. I know it helped me. Being able to read and play music on the piano taught me sequencing and logic I would use much later.

I met Stanley at Mrs. Stevenson's house. Stanley also took piano lessons. His father worked on the railroad, and he came from a very modest, blue-collar, working-class family. Stanley had comics. Batman comics. Green Lantern comics. Superman comics. Archie, Veronica, and Jughead comics. Stanley collected them all, and I read them at his house. I had a few myself, but not like his collection. However, I had some Space Cadet comics. Mrs. Stevenson's house turned into one of the young kids' hangouts. She had this large black-and-white television where we all watched the original 1930s version of King Kong, more than once. That was great! Dinosaurs, the huge ape, a screaming female, and airplanes fighting the beast. It kindled my imagination for adventure.

Highland Park was a tough neighborhood in the 1950s. Perhaps it is currently tougher, since it is now essentially a barrio. The underlying tough nature of the neighborhood made its way into Aldema elementary school. I developed a continuous conflict with a kid in my class. It had to come to a head and needed to be resolved. He was smaller than me, but something of a bully, and his name was Frank Schmedwick. We knew if we got into a fight on the school campus, we would both get in trouble. So we agreed to fight at the other end of the underpass that went from the entrance to the school to the opposite side of Avenue 50. I didn't know martial arts or how to box, so I used my size and reach and nailed Frank with a head-lock grapple. I punched him twenty-five times in the nose, counting one by one. When let go, and he got me once in the jaw. Ouch! After that there were no more fights, and we became friends. Evidently, this is a common kid male ritual where adversaries end up friends.

A true Latino family moved across the street, and one day I had my very first taco. A venison taco. I remember little about the family, but I remember that very distinct taco. After that, Paul moved into the same house. When we raced, he could always run faster than me. Both of us really liked model trains. We would compare our collections and imagine what we would add next. Paul's relationship with his stepfather was terrible. It bothered me and I was just a fifth-grade kid. Paul was berated and never complimented. His mother seemed to never interfere. However, by the time we were in the seventh grade and living in Eagle Rock, his parents were divorced. His aunt was just the opposite. He had nothing but good things to say about her and was a guiding light. I distinctly remember his aunt taking us to see the printing presses at the Los Angeles Times where she worked. Those presses were amazingly noisy and fast.

One summer Paul and I both went to catholic school in Highland Park at the end of Monte Vista Boulevard. The nuns there were scary, just like in the Blues Brothers movie. But the nuns weren't really scary. The nuns just looked scary. Teaching was their sole activity. The orderliness of the class was impressive even for a fifth grader. Paul loved scary 1950 movies. Them, It, Godzilla, Rodan, The Blob were conversation pieces we had for several years. In the sixth grade, Paul and his family moved to the hills to the just west of Mount Washington, hills skirting Highland Park. There were several dirt roads, and being uncontrolled preteens, we attempted to trap pet tarantulas and bombed everything we could with dirt clods. Paul and I remained friends even when we both moved to Eagle Rock in junior high school. But let's get to that later.

Animals always figured prominently in my childhood while living in Highland Park. Once the family gained a bantam rooster and hen. They lasted about two years, and then succumbed to a bird disease. The rooster always attacked me when I tried harvesting the eggs. He was a real bad-ass little rooster. About the same time, my parents gained two rabbits. They were a male and a female, and each had its own separate cage. One day, I decided they were lonely and put the rabbits in the same cage. To my parents' chagrin, they came home and found the rabbits together. A couple of months later, I had eleven more bunnies.

One day while hanging out with the "courts kids", found around the bungalow houses, next to the open field to the west next to Mrs. Stevens' house, I started talking to a young girl who also lived in the "courts". All the square houses there had a fairly large crawl space under the first floor, since they were all built on a sloping hill. I convinced her to "play doctor" with me in the crawl space. She took off every piece of clothing for me. She seemed amused. Perhaps she thought it was a funny game. I had brought along a bucket full of snails. I covered her with snails and declared her "cured." Then I took all the snails off her and put them back in the bucket. She put on her clothes and left. This is the first and last time I "snailed" a member of the opposite sex. Who knows, I may have warped her for life. I didn't get in trouble for playing doctor, but what to do with the snails? I took them home and decided the easiest way to dispose of them was to flush them down the toilet. The trouble was they crawled out of the toilet, so when my parents came home, there were snails all over the bathroom. That's when I got into trouble.

Penny was a young girl who I visited often until I moved from Highland Park to Eagle Rock in 1958. Understand by now, I was an eight, nine, ten-year-old kid roaming the neighborhood, looking for friends until my mother got home after teaching in Pasadena. Often I would sit for hours and just entertain myself. So I actually hung out with girls more than most kids my age. Penny would have been the type of female that I would have played Dungeons and Dragons with if I were a pre-teen in the 1980s. We played games, mostly card games. Canasta, which her parents played, was beyond us, but we played simpler card and board games. Since she played the games I wanted to play, to keep the friendship, I played the games she wanted to play, which were "dolls" and "house." Penny hit puberty earlier than any other girls in the neighborhood, which caused something of a strain on our friendship. We still hung out together, though not as often. I have fond memories of listening to the radio with her. This was the last place I ever heard the Space Cadet show on the radio airways.

A very poor family moved into Throop's Coop, and I became an instant friend of Linda, which more strain on my relationship with Penny. My mother had had a miscarriage and there was left-over baby formula, so I took it all to Linda's house, Throop's Coop. I believe that got me in the front door as a permanent friend and it sure put me in a favorable light with her mother, who had recently given birth. Linda was the first person other than Paul that I had real deep discussions about the Universe, Life, and Everything. Linda was a medium-sized skinny girl, something of a tomboy, very athletic. Once in a while I would stay overnight at her house, but her mother made sure that we slept in different beds. I didn't understand, but I slept on the couch. It wouldn't have mattered. I had not reached that puberty stage yet. She was the oldest child in a really poor family with several small children. I spent a lot of time with her until I departed Highland Park for Eagle Rock. We were like brothers and sisters. Linda was a delightful friend.

On Saturdays on Figueroa Boulevard, a theater with fantastic, almost religious, art on the ceiling put on a kids' show. All the kids showed up. Thirteen cartoons plus a major feature for only twenty-five cents! There is a large amount of documentation on the litany of 1950s television shows and I think I engaged with all of them. Included were classic cartoons on our black-and-white television, like Felix the Cat, Betty Boop, Looney Tunes, and more. There were shows I didn't really understand, like Hallmark Theater, You Are There, and others. During the fifth grade, I was really ill. I contracted measles and then chicken pox pneumonia. It almost killed me. But while recovering, I got to watch television. My mother encouraged me to read, which I did, but I still absorbed a lot of television. When I recovered, my mother took me to see the classic science fiction movie, Forbidden Planet. I was stunned and amazed. It cemented my passion for science fiction that has never left me.

I wanted to engage in real-world activities. I wanted to play baseball, but my mother had a strong dislike of sports for whatever reason. So I joined the Cub Scouts. This was okay, but it wasn't baseball. However, it gave me a feeling of belonging to an external group, and some activities were entertaining.

More entertaining, though, was the excellent vacant lot next to the courts, which were next to Mrs. Stevens' House. The big kids, sixth and seventh graders, built a whole series of tunnels in that vacant lot. Some were real tunnels, others were big excavations covered with heavy plywood with dirt on top. They were great dungeons, with enclaves for candles. I went in even though I wasn't supposed to. But the big kids wouldn't let the fourth and fifth graders into the deepest caverns, which I never got to explore. What was above was even better than the tunnels. The older kids had built a tree house, basically large planks of plywood reinforced by 2x4s. Not the safest structure in the world. I remember one kid fell out of the tree house, and broke his arm. From the top layer of the tree house, there was a big rope that some of the big kids had tied to a high limb. You could swing out over the tunnels on the rope.

Johnny Correa and his dad built a great fort next door. Two stories, a downstairs and an upstairs plus a ladder. Not as good as a tree house, but still great. I do not know how many imaginary monsters we held at bay in that fort. After the bantam chickens died, I cleaned out the shed that they lived in. Here I built my private club house. I drew a space cadet-style rocket on the wall and named it Fuck42 (my parents must have loved this when they finally found it. I was well into "colorful language").

I met Geraldine while in the sixth grade. This is the first girl I had any real puppy love interest in. She had a Southern accent and lived in a distinct set of courts on Avenue 50, very close to Aldama Elementary School. Her father got wind of a boy (me) and told her "not to go near him." Also Dennis LeDouxe, the primo school bully, liked her, and told me that if I went near her, he was going to "beat me up." Well, I hadn't quite completed the mental pattern yet, but basically I thought "F Him (and her father)." So I met Geraldine outside of her court bungalow after school and we talked like two ten-year-olds. But things took a terrible turn for the worse when Geraldine actually visited MY HOUSE! My friends and I were in the middle of the Great Dirt Clod War, and she appeared around the corner of the garage where the 1946 Frazier used to be parked. A wild throw got her right in the middle of her beautiful chiffon dress—love lost forever!

After the incident with Geraldine, I continued to find trouble. Myself and all the "courts" kids started making homemade rockets. I made one that set our clothes line on fire and set several dried towels on fire. Once again, I was in big trouble.

I had a sixth-grade teacher with the unfortunate name Mr. Glasscock. He tormented me endlessly in class. My mother went to the principal of the school and complained. Supposedly, he had graduated from West Point. By now, I was developing a great distrust of certain male figures. And also by the sixth grade, I was having vague fantasies about females in my sixth-grade class. Two in particular, Karen and Marty, were the subject of my fantasies. Karen had a medium build, neither obese nor skinny, with sandy blond hair. Marty also had a medium build, neither obese nor skinny, and had flaming red hair. Many of the male classmates in the sixth grade class considered these two young girls to be the "cute ones" in our class. Also in the sixth grade, I had a repeating nightmare similar to the "Talking WWIII Blues," with me walking around all by myself after the atomic war. There were vivid memories of melted landscapes, Swiss cheese, mountains. By then I only had a vague idea what radiation was. In one dream, Karen and Marty made an appearance. I took both of them to my little club house in the early hours of the night and thus providing protection and a haven from the impending nuclear attack.

We had a graduation party at Marty's house to close out the era. Forty-five RPM records comprising 1950s rock-and-roll played while we danced. It was one of the few times I could socialize with all my classmates while not in school. Almost all of them would attend Franklin Junior High School in Highland Park. I was also supposed to go to Franklin Junior High School, but that was not to be. I had trouble believing we were moving to Eagle Rock, the community north of Highland Park in northeast Los Angeles. Paul was the only friend that also moved to Eagle Rock. I almost saw none of the kids in 1957 Aldema graduating class. I had to start from scratch to establish friendships in the seventh grade at Eagle Rock Junior High in 1958. Thus, the goodbye at the graduation party is the close out of Elementary-2.

PUBERTY I

•••

My father always wanted to be an architect. He designed a beautiful hillside house comprising descending stories in Eagle Rock near Occidental College, where both my mother and father received their diplomas. With his friends and with both of my grandfather's help, they had nearly finished the house by the end of 1957. I helped him from time to time when I was old enough, but most of my real help was when I was in the fifth and sixth grade.

In 1958, we moved to the mostly finished house. There were some half-finished interiors, but the heat worked along with the plumbing and electricity. I completed enrollment in a new school as a seventh grade junior high school student at Eagle Rock Junior and High School, a medium-sized school in Northeast Los Angeles. The first day at a combined junior and senior high-school in a 1958

September was terrifying, but exciting. There were periods, with many teachers, and you had to find the classrooms. Upon entering the seventh grade, the hormones of puberty were just starting their power to effect on my behavior.

Until the move to Eagle Rock when I entered junior high school and started the seventh grade, I had almost always spent my summers in Santa Barbara with my mother's mother and father, all from the Chesley side of the family. The grandparents used to live in Canoga Park, one area in Southern California, but moved to Santa Barbara when I was in the fifth grade. I made one more trip in the summer of 1958. When there, I spent time with a next-door neighbor, Tommy. He introduced me to rock-and-roll music. So another release quickly became a transistor radio. We listened to songs like "At the Hop," "Revelry Rock," and "Behind the Green Door." The introduction to pop music by Tommy is significant. Listening to the twang of electric guitars would cause me later to gain one. Music with electric guitars would be a pleasure that would be with me for the rest of my life. My grandmother's cooking and treats added to these fond memories. I would eat my grandmother's homemade taffy, which we pulled, and her lemon meringue pies. My grandfather, Bean, would tell me stories about the Old West and how one day he was going to build himself a mud-hut (an adobe house).

I had two cousins on my mother's side that attended Eagle Rock High School, both I remembered vaguely from their visit to Canoga Park and to my grandparents' house in the early 1950s while I was a little kid. My mother took us for a visit to the cousin's parents' house. From the two cousins, I got a good dose of late-1950s culture. One cousin was a talented artist, and the other played electric guitar. For a time, I decided I wanted to be an artist. The two cousins gave me a feeling of status and someone to look up to. They were on the football team and I could say to my peers, "I know these two guys. They are my cousins, the Chesleys." My mother and I were never close to the Chesley relatives from Utah. There was a subtle divide because of religious differences. My mother's side of the family was Roman Catholic and the Chesley relatives were Mormon. After the two cousins graduated from Eagle Rock High School, I never saw them again.

I also met Douglas, or just Doug. We were both members of the same Boy Scout troop until the eleventh grade, but during the tenth grade, when I was living in Arkansas. He was in my art class. That was my favorite class in the seventh grade. Both of us idolized the artists who drew realistic and futuristic vehicles. I also enjoyed drafting, the drawing of straight lines, the projections of three-dimensional objects on a two-dimensional paper.

Typical Eagle Rock High School students consisted mostly of white Anglo's of various backgrounds. I often considered Hispanic kids outcasts. Typically, they came from Morningside High School towards downtown, and wore long, khaki, bellbottom pants that covered their very shiny black shoes. Discrimination against them was subtle. They were the Latinos, the "Vatos" and the only persons of color in the school, janitors notwithstanding.

On each typical day, junior high school terrified me. There were big kids and nasty kids everywhere. When I asked for a potato chip from one of the big kids,

"Hey can I have one of your potato chips?"

"No!"

And then the kid would throw the chip on the ground and squish it.

"If I can't have it, no one can."

Gymnastics was also terrifying to a seventh grade eleven-year-old. You had to get naked and teenagers really were nasty to each other. This was 1958, so the coaches still practiced corporal punishment. For junior high school kids, we got a ping-pong paddle as the instrument of pain. There were larger paddles on the gym office wall that were used for who knows what. We found out. Junior high school was my introduction to a real regimen, whether restrictive or structural.

My grandparents on both my mother's and father's sides made extended visits, and helped finish the house. They built our Escarpa house on a hillside, with the garage was on the top. The living room, kitchen, small bathroom and small bedroom were below the garage on the second floor. The first floor had three bedrooms and a bath. Under the first floor was something like a basement, except the floor comprised somewhat irregular natural rock. In terms of basic functions in the house, it was complete. Work on the floors, both upstairs and downstairs, plus various interior projects needed to be completed. Even a few families from my old neighborhood in Highland Park visited and assisted. The Polish piano teacher that lived down the hill from us in Highland Park, my former residence, had her husband build some beautiful handcrafted cabinetry, of course, which we paid for. We completed the remaining interior work by the end of my seventh grade in 1959. Maybe that was prophetic. The street number of my house on Escarpa Drive is 1959.

For all intents and purposes, it was a new life. To get to school using the direct route, I had to pass through the neighbor's yard directly below us, which is where Mr. Wilson and his family, including a son and daughter, lived. His son, Ron, was close to my age. We quickly became friends. Ron and I would design imaginary scenarios, often imitating Disney adventure movies. I believe my mother convinced Mr. Wilson to allow passage through his property to school, and not only did he let me walk on a sidewalk he built on the north side of his house, but any of the teenagers that lived on Escarpa Drive and had to walk to Eagle Rock High School from above his property. He was an excellent teacher, who taught one of the few classes in agriculture you could find in the Los Angeles School District. His class prepared me for an unlikely future such as working for an organic truck farm when I graduated from college in 1970 and farming in Hawai`i. After walking the outskirts of Mr. Wilson's yard on a nice cement path, I headed maybe fifty yards on a dirt road, walked across Yosemite Park (not to be confused with the large national park about three hundred miles to the north), with large, beautiful sycamore trees mixed with a few local evergreens. There were two baseball diamonds with well-kept grass. More to the northeast side of the park was an honest-to-god croquet pitch. You could rent the set and play by leaving an item of deposit, not money, at the park office. After crossing the Park, I was at school.

Junior high school kids and senior high school kids all had lockers. I would run to the locker, stash my particulars, and make first period. So for me it was a slam-dunk to make it to first period on time as long as I could get a move on, since where I lived on the hill is where I had line-of-sight to the school. I had to adjust to the new strange regime of periods lasting approximately one hour. When entering the seventh grade, my initial first period class was drafting. I enjoyed that class. Other classes, like math and English, required discipline. I could not develop a discipline for classes that required large amounts of homework. My mother provided minimum help. By now, my father had effectively disappeared. He had graduated from Occidental College, and was going to graduate from the University of Southern California medical school. Subsequently, I really had little a parental guiding light and mentoring when dealing with seventh-grade classes and did not get support on how to be an excellent student. So learning was up to me. I just didn't do sections of homework. The classes that I did best in were art, social studies, history, and drafting. I was capable of math, but didn't apply myself. I performed poorly in English class. This drove my mother, an English major, crazy.

A professor, Dr. Ferrson at Occidental College, lived next door to us on Escarpa Drive. I took part in the school chess club, but not a capable player. I told the professor I was learning chess when visited the family. He was also Sarah's father. You will hear about her later. The professor taught me the fundamentals of chess. Then I looked up classic games in an old edition of Encyclopedia Britannica that belonged to my parents published in the early nineteen twenties and learned enough to play other players in the gaming club at the Junior High School and win the matches.

From the time my father began medical school, until when we moved, he was not an active parent. By that I mean we rarely took part in events that occurred during the week, like other kids did with their dad. When I saw him, it was more of a status check. He became an abstract figure. I did not sense what was going on in my family. My mother kept in minimal touch with some of her peers from my old neighborhood in Highland Park, but she directed her attention to her group of teachers in Pasadena where she worked. From time to time, I saw several Pasadena teachers when they visited my home on Escarpa Drive. Even to a launching teenager, I must admit the faculty and administrators that my mother introduced me to were entertaining and amusing. They would tell stories about what was taking place at the schools where they taught. Should I become a teacher in the future? For me, it was an open question.

My mother often would stay late working with her associates at the Pasadena City School System. Most of the time, if I desired an after school activity, I was on my own. Even as a seventh grader and only eleven years old, I took an interest in girls. I would watch certain ones, though I knew I would never talk to them, let alone dance with them. I was a socially under-performing student even in the seventh grade. My mother took me to the Women's Twentieth Century Club to learn how to dance. There we learned traditional dances like waltzes and the foxtrot. What we didn't learn was the popular dances that older teenagers danced. No shaking like Elvis at the Women's Twentieth Century Club. Sometimes I attended with Marilyn, another Occidental College professor's daughter, up the hill from where I lived. Marilyn was tall, dark-haired and skinny like me. If I attracted her, she didn't show it. Later in life, I realized that kids our age the females typically had superior social skills when compared to males. This deficiency was obvious by my behavior at the Twentieth Century Club. I would only approach the young girls when requested to do so by the instructor. I tried to dance with the young girls to some avail. At school, I would see Marilyn in the halls of the junior high, and the greetings were pleasant, but formal. It is as if we tolerated each other. Females older than me were the object of my fantasies. For example, my social studies teacher, probably in her early forties, with her fully developed woman-looking physique, captured my imagination. In the eighth grade, I even volunteered to work on her projection crew. So, at a very early age, I turned my attention to older women.

Sarah, the pre-teen next door, would scream and have a fit when she didn't get what she wanted. I would hear her. When my mother was home, she would hear her. Her parents, her kind mother, and her father, the professor who taught me how to play chess, were the brunt of Sarah's abuse. She had a younger brother, usually remaining silent in the background.

Sarah was a spoiled brat among spoiled brats.

Sarah was my neighbor, and subsequently I attempted to establish something of a friendship. She did not treat me the way she treated her parents. Deep down, perhaps she was as lonely as I was. Often our conversations turned into a game of one-up-man ship. "My dad does this... ", "Oh yeah, my dad's doing this..." We met a few times in the private area under the first floor. The two by fours provided primitive shelves to place objects in the dim light. There boxes sturdy enough to sit on Here the parents could not hear us or bother us. She would not play games like Penny, or have deep conversations like Linda, the two young females from my former neighborhood. Conversations were short and curt. Talking with Sarah was nothing like the conversations I had with Linda or Penny when I lived in Highland Park. Sarah had no interest in any games, board, or cards.

It was a failed friendship.

One day I decided that if I did what she did, I would be paddled or worse. Then I transformed into something of an avenging angel. I gave her something to remember. I punished Sarah for her behavior. It was easy to invite her to a private area in the crawl space under the first story of our house, since we had met several times before to talk in private. I pulled down her pants, spanked her and told her why. She departed, crying bitterly, and ran to her mother. I was in trouble after her mother talked to my mother.

"John, you can't spank Sarah, even though she is a spoiled brat."

I don't know if it had any permanent effect, but she did not come near me after that, and I never spanked her again. After the spoiled brat's mother's scolding, who was a gentle and sweet person, and I was told not to spank her spoiled little shit of a daughter (my words). She was so rotten; I wonder if the spoiled brat ever made it out of Dodge alive. By the time they moved away, the little princess was already causing the parents a world of trouble. Of course, in retrospect, from an adult perspective, I feel sorry for all the family, especially Sarah.

What I learned—never, never, ever spank or strike a female. Much later in life, I would again make the same mistake. Only two times in my existence did I spank a member of the opposite sex.

By the time I was in the eighth grade, I loved my art class, had been to summer camp, and had made a few friends, many in the Boy Scout troop. In art class, I took an interest in cars. Not that I ever was a "car boy," but they were shiny and fun to draw. And all the young teens looked up to the artists that drew fine and futuristic cars along with the "hot rods". I also took another of Mr. Wilson's agriculture class. He taught us how to grow vegetables. It is possible that what I learned in agriculture class laid the subconscious basis for farming experiences later in life. I even had a little hillside garden with a perfectly trapezoidal row filled with radishes. Near the garden I wanted to build a tree house where I could view the garden, but the eucalyptus tree did not lend itself to the required construction.

But I was a thirteen-year-old with amplified sexually developed hormones and all that baggage that went with it. As teenage adrenaline and hormones dominated my psyche, I forgot the specter of WWIII and all the advanced atomic weapon delivery systems that were emerging in the world. About this time, I reconnected with my friend Paul from Aldema Elementary School in Highland Park, where both of us used to live. His mother had separated from his step-dad, a real asshole because of the manner he treated Paul, and lived in an apartment on Yosemite Drive, with Eagle Rock High School on the same street. As an emerging sexual experience, when "his dick got excited," this frightened him, so he called up his aunt, the same aunt as mentioned before that worked at the Los Angeles Times, and she told him, "Don't worry; it's only a sexual experience".

Paul visited my house where we lived on Escarpa Drive, in Eagle Rock overlooking the school we were attending, and I showed him a book in my mother's library called the History of Sex. He looked at it and said, "Oh, I gotta get my dick excited". To us, it was exciting. There were seventeenth century wood-cuts of people fucking. Paul, who also has a friend Vern, still living in Highland Park, whom I'd met once or twice. Evidently, he had some extended conversations with Paul about arousal and incipient sexuality, and Paul reflected on some of his conversations with me. Paul told me regarding arousal, "the same thing happened to Vern. He also became hard. He says it happens all the time." "Wow", thought to myself. I must go through life with this ...? I left the History of Sex with Paul and left my mother's bedroom to experience what he was experiencing in private. Neither of us cared, since my mother wasn't home. As I considered this sexual experience, I was connecting the dots. When I was eight years old I asked my mother "where do babies come from?" She drew two stick cartoon figures having intercourse and told me "like this".

I did not know it, but that was my introduction to pornography. The History of Sex was also arousing for me. I actually ended up reading some of it. The book was not only history but also a sociological and anthropological work, in terms of scholastic disciplines, that I did not know. There was one woodcut image, a man with a naked bottom on top of a naked woman being spanked by a second woman. That puzzled and confused me. What does this have to do with sex?

Masturbation frightened me at first. How could this physical stimulation literally take over my body for several seconds? And I was a freaked out by little bubbles being emitted by my penis when this overwhelming feeling occurred. Not long after that, it always became a mess to clean up. Thus, this experience is one of entering "Puberty I."

Since my mother detested sports, except for tennis, my out-of-school activity was Boy Scouts. Scouting would be my consistent out-of-school activity until the beginning of the eleventh grade. In the sixth grade, while living in Highland Park, I had been in a Scout troop for a short while. I remember going on one camping trip with that troop. The troop in Highland Park seemed disorganized, so during the seventh grade I joined a different organized troop in Eagle Rock. There was camping all year around. In the winter and the summer, we went to a camp near Wrightwood in the Los Angeles National Forest.

During the summer at Wrightwood, we would work on projects like woodcarving, rope handling, fishing, and campfire singalongs. The winter was more pure fun like snowball fights, sledding and listening to scary ghost stories at night. In either environment, Scouts were not above a little mischief. One winter, one scout brought some Playboy magazines that the scout master did not know about. I got in trouble for writing on an outhouse wall, something like "While you are reading this, you are peeing on your foot". Other times, the troop stayed at sites closer to home, like the mountains near Sunland-Tujunga, a simple drive from Eagle Rock.

In scouting, you earn awards, known as merit badges. Each merit badge has an activity focus. For example, if a Scout earns a merit badge in first aid, he then has the basic skills of a first responder. To gain the badge, you had to take a test. This usually meant showing a skill or producing an artifact associated with the badge. To gain a badge, a qualified adult with the skill certified you. One of my more useful merit badges I attained was cooking. I had to prepare a meal, on a campfire, for an adult certifier. Learning to cook ended up being important, since I ended up often cooking my own meals with no mother at home.

Scouts replaced what should have been a family. In some ways, I was the odd man out, since I had no father or mother taking part.

I tried to organize a patrol with me as the leader. That didn't work out as planned. First off, I picked a mythological character, Pegasus, as the icon for our patrol. But the closest off-the-shelf patches that existed was a horse. People would ask, "You are the horse patrol?" My stint as a patrol leader didn't last long.

Besides Boy Scouts, while I was in the eighth grade, my mother sent me to a spring camp with the YMCA at Death Valley. They put us in the back of a big pickup truck, along with camping equipment. The first few days of the trip were fun. The group did not have the regimented feel of the Boy Scouts. When arriving at Death Valley, the adult leader took us to various places like The Devils Golf Course and Badwater, the remnants of an inland sea many feet below sea level. The hills, with its desert colors in April, were impressive. They easily captured my imagination. If you have never been to Death Valley and have seen Star Wars IV, "A New Hope", they filmed the outdoor Tatooine scenes in Death Valley. I had a pocket full of money, more than I have had on any trip. We stopped at Calico Ghost Town in San Bernardino County. Here I blew a wad of my money on a "thunder egg," an agate formation. Oh, what a mistake. By the end of the camping trip, which slowly deteriorated in terms of fun as it went on, we literally did not have enough food. Kids were buying food at Furnace Creek Inn instead of souvenirs. I was so hungry I started eating tooth paste. Other kids were also hungry. So I helped hatch a conspiracy. "Let's break into the pantry where the leader keeps the remaining food." "Are you in?" "So am I. Let's wait until everybody goes to bed." So we broke into the food wagon to steal food from the store managed by the camp counselors. I consider this incident a failure in planning by the adult leader.

By the end, it was an awful trip. When I returned to Eagle Rock, I was really ill. I contracted pneumonia. My mother called up the Highland Park YMCA and gave them a piece of her mind. Then I ended up in Children's Hospital in Hollywood, and missed not only two weeks of school, but an award for my rendering of a hot rod in colored pencils. After that, I stuck only with Boy Scouts.

Our scout master drove a red, round Portia, and guided the troop on several camping trips into the Angeles National Forest. He would fly around the curves in his Porche. None of the Scouts ever got to ride with him. He allowed me to visit his house in Eagle Rock, where he had an excellent collection of science fiction novels, many of the Ace double-book variety. One of the earliest I can recall was the Three Suns of Amara. So it started my interest in reading science fiction.

Listening to the Los Angeles Dodgers was one joy of that junior high school time frame. Sandy Koufax was one of the dominant pitchers in the National League. Most of the time, my father had disappeared, but I remember him taking me to a game in the Los Angeles Memorial Coliseum where I could witness Lew Burdette, Warren Spahn, and Sandy Koufax pitch. My mother had no truck with baseball or football, so without a choice, I stuck with Boy Scouts.

Since my father was away from home even more often, compared to when I was younger, I held this false notion that he was becoming a doctor and after he completed his residency and set up a practice, he would be with us all the time. Then all these dreams came crashing down.

While in the ninth grade and a dysfunctional student in a

collapsing family, the life drama finally came home. Less and less did my father appear at the house in Eagle Rock. And from time to time when we went places, like to the house of his new good friend, a fellow doctor, in the Malibu colony. During the visit, the situation was uncomfortable. My mother consumed large amounts of alcohol at each night and had trouble getting to work in the morning. To make it to work, she had orange juice and one or more bottles of Coca-Cola. The people she worked with would visit our house, but the atmosphere had changed. They could tell she showed up for work as a wreck. Fortunately, the leader and principal of her group, Leo Buscaglia, later known as "The Love Doctor" on television, covered for her. The truth finally came out. Her marriage was breaking up and my father had gotten one of his nurses pregnant. That woman later became "step mother number one".

I did not meet step mother number one face-to-face until at some point when I was in the eleventh grade. What I knew about her was what my mother told me. My father said little about his new wife. Most of his conversation centered on how, during the divorce, my mother had taken everything from him. The only direct reference to Shirley occurred when my father told me that his new wife had gained a baseball from Dodger Stadium and it was a gift for me. I kept it for a day or two. It simply became an object that mentally tormented me. Finally, I went outside with the baseball in my hand and threw it as far as I could in the downhill pasture on the north side of the house. I watched it vanish in the weeds several yards away. My unhappiness did not vanish with the baseball.

During this time, I had terrible fantasies. As a minor, if I killed the other woman, I could get off free. This torture reached a culmination one evening when my y mother woke me in the middle of the night and asked me to confront my father. I looked at him and simply told him, "you are a poor father". Then I went back to bed, obviously depressed. My father later claimed that my mother was also having an affair, but I saw no actual evidence of this. When I was much older, as I got to know my mother, it was in the realm of possibility.

My friends in Scouts and at school were oblivious to my family troubles, so when I was with them I would also put the confusion and bad feelings behind me. Through all of this, my attention at school suffered.

My grandparents tried to help me all they could, and would visit and try to inject some joy into what was an unpleasant situation for a thirteen-year-old kid, now living in a completely dysfunctional family at the age of the atomic bomb. I wanted to live somewhere else. My mother also wanted me to depart so she could attempt to rebuild her life. She asked relatives to take me in for the summer. I suspected she did not want me living with her. This proved to be true when later I graduated from high school. She told me "you can join the military, get a job or go to college. You can't stay here." Sending me to Santa Barbara in 1960 after graduating from junior high was out of the question, because of logistical restraints. Both parents were searching for my next landing spot.

DIXIE

•••

In the summer of 1961, my father attempted to send me to Ankara, Turkey, to live and go to school with my cousin Robin, her father, a colonel in the United States Airforce, and my aunt. That did not work out because of a legal technicality. They sent me to Pine Bluff, Arkansas, to spend the summer with my father's mother and father.

As September 1961 approached, I pleaded with both my mother and father to allow me to stay with my father's parents for the rest of that year, until the summer of 1962. I accepted the fact that both of them wanted to build, or should I say, rebuild, their lives. Both my parents and my grandparents came to an agreement that I would spend the tenth grade in Pine Bluff, Arkansas, not visiting for the summer. I believe the exotically different life that I was experiencing motivated me to make the request. And also it was an escape from a depressing situation in Southern California.

The core of this Dixie life comprised fishing, hunting, a high-fat diet, and church. Southern Baptists liked to save you with their Bible and bury you with their cookbook. Of all these recent activities, fishing was the one I enjoyed the most. I would wake up at four AM, ride to a beautiful lake. I could operate the motorized fishing boat through the glassy water between the cypress trees, with the cicadas ringing in your ear. My grandfather and I had to be on guard for poison water moccasin snakes that could drop into your boat.

One morning, my grandfather drove me to Sheridan, a town to the west, and fish in my Uncle Evans pond. This was a prize in my mind since he was the mayor of the town and had the emergency air strip for planes on his property. I noticed that some of the fish were breaking the surface of the water, likely catching insects. I cast an artificial into the pond where there was feeding activity and I would catch a large bass fish, a real whopper. It was my premier trophy during the entire Arkansas fishing experience. I wanted to have a taxidermist mount it as a prize, but my grandfather rejected this idea. Instead, a photograph captured the trophy.

In retrospect, fishing, hunting and planting food is or was a core Dixie value. I suspect this was due partly to the necessities that resulted from the south losing the civil war. The southern forests became a prime source of food. So they introduced me to hunting. My grandfather took me, a relative and a "squirrel" dog, to a forested area west of Pine Bluff. My grandfather carried a 12-gauge shotgun loaded with squirrel shot, and the relative, whose name has I forgot, carried a 22 caliber rifle, since he was an outstanding shot. "Learn how to hunt," my grandfather told me as he put a 410 gauge shotgun in my hands and handed me a pocket full of shells. It was a chilling feeling. I had never handled a firearm in my entire life. The butt and the steel barrel felt cold in my hands. I placed a set of empty cans on a log and stepped away, putting a reasonable distance between myself and the cans. The 410 gauge shotgun is a single shot firearm, or at least this one was. I put a single shell in the chamber and pulled the trigger. I squeezed the trigger quickly. That was a mistake. Later, I learned to squeeze the trigger with a steady, slow grip. When I did that, I could usually hit the can.

My grandfather was a much better shot than I was, so he killed the wild game. During my stay for a little over a year, I killed no wild game other than fish. It was my job to butcher and clean the squirrels after the hunt. Yuk. I'm amazed that I'm not a vegetarian these days. I had to always clean and butcher the fish and squirrels. They considered it my job to assist the family. I guess I was lucky that I didn't have to deal with possum or racoon road-kill.

As fall rolled around, it turned cold, much colder than what I felt in California. It was now huntin' season. By that I mean hunting deer. I "graduated" to a 12-gauge shotgun. My grandfather took me into the woods and had me fire his twelve-gauge shotgun. It had a nasty kick and made my shoulder hurt. So I went out with the deer club, wearing a large red hunting jacket, freezing my ass off, with a twelve-gauge shotgun. "If a deer runs by, shoot it" was my grandfather's instruction. I heard the dogs, but never saw a deer. After a very cool morning, the hunt was over. The club had their quota of deer. I loved the venison steaks even with their gamy taste.

Hunting was exciting in some ways, but terrifying in others. Youthful fantasies of playing "army" came to mind, but then you realize, I'm holding a weapon that kills. It seemed a requirement to hunt as a male conforming to that role in Dixie culture. During deer season, which was about a week long, I would say that at least half of the males, including teachers, were absent from Pine Bluff High School. For myself, going on a deer hunt was a one time only event. I continued to go on the squirrel hunts. As before, I had to pull the skin off with pliers, butcher them and hand the cleaned squirrel to my grandmother. Typically, "squirrel stew" was the result. It had a lot of black pepper to cover up the gaminess. In some concoction, I would identify as similar to "red eye" gravy. I got used to it, since it often was the food on the table for lunch and dinner.

Religion permeated all the surrounding institutions. Both of my grandparents attended South Side Baptist Church. Me being the good grandson I was trying to be, I always accompanied them. To talk to Jesus, dress up in a suit, with a tie. So for one year, one center of my social life turned out to be South Side Baptist Church. I enjoyed the music and the musical education in the choir. It so happened that the choir director at South Side Baptist was also the choir director at Pine Bluff High School, which I was also part of when attending high school.

I registered in the tenth grade at Pine Bluff High School, being accompanied by my grandmother, who knew many people at the school. I started this new school on September 1961. Physical education started at 07:55 every morning. Then the coach, who I could swear was also one of the football coaches, would read a verse out of the Saint James English Christian Bible, and then we would run up and down the bleacher stairs in the gym. It absolutely exhausted me. I was one of the slowest kids and not used to the severe exertion.

Perhaps I was identified as an outsider, a "Westerner". Any of the students at Pine Bluff High School that were slightly outside of Dixie norm got my attention, me, the "LA Alien." One such student, Sammy Weeks, would talk about Nietzsche. If I would speak of Los Angeles and how none of the tenth graders drove vehicles, he would quote some random passage out of Nietzsche about a loss of freedom. I told him how much I liked the Dodgers baseball team and he would tell me "that's you, and your fate". Sammy liked to delve into philosophy. That differed from the standard tenth-grade ilk, especially in Pine Bluff, Arkansas.

The teachers I had in the tenth grade were from an aged era or were so young, it was difficult to tell them from the students. There were notable teachers, among them a very sexy teacher that lived next door to my grandparents who lived an active social life, and an English teacher in a tight dress who couldn't have been over twenty years old, and my Spanish teacher from a local four-year university. While at school, I noticed several tenth graders the same age as myself who drove vehicles. I believe they had some type of dispensation for a driver's license. It also amazed me at how many students, including students in my grade, drove motorized scooters similar to scooters that you would see in city scenes of European movies.

But I was still a male with raging hormones, and didn't know how to react to young women yet. One time a group of female class members offered to "take me for a ride in their car." I declined. Where were they going to take me? What would happen if they left me somewhere? I recognized the young women from the high school, but I didn't trust them. "No thank you, I need to go home and work on my schoolwork", replied to them politely. Part of me wanted to go riding with them and part of me didn't trust them.

I had trouble assimilating into this culture along with what you would expect in Dixie in 1962. I could not understand the intolerance, bigotry and general disdain for "Negroes" and other peoples of color by my family members, relatives and peers at high school. My uncle, the mayor of Sheridan, who in almost every instance was a paradigm politeness, would complain to my grandfather about "uppity niggers". Another uncle who raised horses and lived in the countryside when asked how he was going to get his septic tank cleaned out. "Oh, don't worry about that, I have a nigger that will clean it out." He behaved as if he owned this lowly African-American. At most other times, the uncle also behaved with a paradigm of politeness. Some students at school would brag about how they were going to go out at night needlessly to attack someone because of the black color of their skin. I found these behaviors and attitudes deeply disturbing. It affected my view of the southland the rest of my life.

Everyone I interacted with was a white Anglo. Desegregation and "white flight" did not exist in 1961. All the views and attitudes of all these people contradicted all the Christian teachings in the biblical new testament. The juxtaposition of these Dixie "norms" against the basic teachings of Christianity really got to me. My grandmother actually told me one time, "if you see an Italian walking on the sidewalk headed your direction, cross the street to the other side". So intolerance was not only directed against people of color, but any foreign culture. I sensed suspicion in several other people, with me being from California.

My grandfather, a lifelong Democrat in terms of politics and a union man, had all the same prejudices. He would ask me, "are you a Yankee or a Rebel? I answered, "I'm a Californian from the west". I knew where the sore points were from the Dixie viewpoint. When becoming angry with my grandmother, instead of swearing, I told her, "I'm going to marry a Negro Roman Catholic."

I knew my time in Arkansas was ending with a return to an uncertain future in California. In reflection, fishing, Boy Scouts, music, reading science fiction and collecting stamps all became a refuge from what I disliked around me. I knew my grandparents truly loved me, but it was time to return to what was now my mother's house. And that Dixie exit day came in August 1962. My grandfather and grandmother took me to the bus station. They made sure that I had enough cash to eat properly on the way to my destination. My grandmother emphasized repeatedly how my father loved me. I believe she worried I would reject him. I boarded a Greyhound Bus by myself and returned to California. To pass the time, I, a horny young male who thought less about religion and more about girls, purchased a nice stack of Playboy magazines to peruse on the way home. A young couple older than me saw them and wanted to borrow them. After that, they gave them back, and they started to "make out" on the bus. I had a lot to contemplate regarding my future during the bus ride across country.

The relation to my mother and father changed while I was in Arkansas. My mother had put my father through medical school and then my father left her. I paid little attention to it, but she told me about her new male friend, Greg, shortly before I departed Arkansas for California. Greg was now an insurance agent but formally a Methodist minister whose wife, leader of the choir in his church, ran off her gynecologist. The two had a common bond of disliking doctors. They picked me up at the bus station in downtown Los Angeles and all of us returned to Eagle Rock. My mother never was the huggy-kissy type, but she seemed pleased to see me. My relationship with Greg was formal. I found out that my mother and Greg had gotten married, making Greg step-father number one.

So they welcomed me back to my former home, ready for the continuation of my education in the 11th and 12th grades. I also talked with my father, though it conveyed a somewhat terse and uncomfortable tone. My father had started a practice as an orthopedic doctor in Beverly Hills, California. He set up a home in Brentwood with step mother number one where the two of them had a son, my half brother James Redden. He wanted me to meet my stepmother Shirley and half brother Jim, who was a toddler. I had already accepted the fact meeting my father's new family was going to happen when I returned to Southern California. I missed my grandparents, but I did not want to spend any more time in Dixie. It was time to restart my life in Eagle Rock.

PUBERTY II

•••

Upon returning to Eagle Rock, Southern California in the summer of 1962, I arrived at a Boy Scout meeting hoping to continue where I left off in the ninth grade. The scout master of my former troop did not approve the massive quantity of merit badges I had collected while in Arkansas. He told me "these are for your hobbies, not a collection of medals." Another scout I knew and had been with the troop since I was in the seventh grade looked at me and said, "John, you look like an admiral in the Swiss navy." Continuing with Boy Scouts that year, I was on the verge of becoming an eagle scout. Met all the requirements except I didn't have a written reference from a priest or minister. I delayed my election and then finally just quit scouting. I wasn't interested in completing the eagle scout rank.

Life at home continued to deteriorate into a personal disaster. My mother was a mess. Greg, step father number one, now worked as an insurance agent and usually arrived home late at night. My mother would often walk around inebriated, clinging to the family cat. Often I ended up cooking my own meals when not taken to happy hour at the Barristers Inn Restaurant near the border of Eagle Rock and Glendale in northeast Los Angeles. By late 1963, I had memorized the menu. I had little school support from my mother or my remote father, so my grades deteriorated. My mother did have concern about my wellbeing in her own way. She sent me to a Roman Catholic priest she had received counseling from. The same priest taught him me Baltimore #3 Catechism, a pre-Vatican II document. I enjoyed the Latin in the missal. I disliked "no-sex" what so ever. Note, after Vatican II all that changed in the church. The sequence of lessons by the priest had a permanent effect. From that time on, I considered myself a Roman Catholic and certainly not a Southern Baptist.

In the eleventh and twelfth grade, I spent a significant amount of time with Dave Carlson. Dave and other Boy Scout peers were no longer interested in field trips and camping. Now all the former scouts talked mostly about surfing and finding girl friends. This included Dave. Dave could purchase a vehicle as a sixteen-year-old in the eleventh grade. He landed a job at a print shop. Offering to drive me, having a social security card, I could also land a job at the print shop doing clean up for minimum wage. This print shop was in Highland Park on Monte Vista Boulevard, in the realm of my old neighborhood, prior to moving to Eagle Rock. The print shop experience changed my attitude towards the curriculum at high school. I began rebelling against the "college track". I wanted to take print shop and wood shop instead of advanced math.

Dave took me to a small concert on an outdoor dance floor in Glendale. The dance featured the Beach Boys, who would later become an iconic "surf band". I got it. Dances like this are where you scoop the opposite sex. I had enough money, given my part-time work, to explore more dance venues that would attract teenagers. Dave and I journeyed to the Pasadena Civic Auditorium for Saturday night dances. The auditorium is large and has a beautiful wooden floor ideal for dancing. High school students would flock therefrom several nearby schools, most notably the nearby Catholic girls' schools. There were two performing stages in the auditorium. The secondary stage had a visiting band that would change each Saturday. The primary stage held the house band that could have easily stepped out of the film "Back to the Future". I have vivid memories of their up-tempo version of "Night Train". In reality, attending the dances presented itself as a rite of passage. I now felt I had to have a girlfriend, since most of my friends had girlfriends.

The spring of 1963 was germinal. My mother bought me a used surf board, a brand new Fender Stratocaster electric guitar, plus an amplifier. Dave Carlson also purchased a surf board around this time. My father's good friend, a fellow doctor, had a beach house on the beach at the Malibu Colony. So we took our surf boards loading them into Dave's station wagon and headed to the Malibu Colony. Entering the water and attempting to catch a wave for this beach break was a lot more difficult than first imagined. The best we could do was riding on the board prone face up. Eventually, we both learned to surf. For myself, it did not come easy because I was tall and relatively nonathletic. By the time I learned to surf, I was never much of a "hot dogger". Surfing in Southern California became a subculture. The subculture defined who you would hang out with, where you went, what you wore, and gave you an advantage when attempting to attract the opposite sex.

Towards the end of summer 1963, I bounced between girlfriends. Marla and Stacy were their friends with each other, both of whom I met at Yosemite Park, next to Eagle Rock High School. I quickly found out that if you messed with both, you ended up with neither. Marla is noteworthy. She was the first young girl that I experienced some "light" petting. This was the first time I felt real breasts inside a bra. The last time I saw Stacy, she was riding around in a car with her new boyfriend. I realized I was at a great handicap not knowing how to drive. Even though teaching had been her profession, my mother was useless as a driving teacher. She could barely drive herself.

While attending the Saturday dance at the Pasadena Civic Auditorium, I made a new friend, Don Wiley. Don and Dave were the two buddies that I would spend the most time with until I graduated from high school. Don had a surfboard, but he was more of a want-to-be surfer. He lived with his father and his sister in Highland Park, the same community where I used to live, where he attended Franklin High School. Don came from a blue collar family. His father worked as a parking lot attendant at the beach in Santa Monica. We would drop his dad off at work and then travel to Santa Monica Pier. This is where Don liked to sort of surf. The beach break at Santa Monica Pier was poor for board surfing. It was not crowded. They fascinated Don, the beatniks. He was also a want-to-be musician and had a beat up saxophone and took music classes at high school. The sax was one of his beatnik icons. Another one was his tin foil ball collection. When we were at the beach at Santa Monica Pier, Don would convince me to walk down to Venice Beach and go to one of the beatnik coffee houses. He told me "if we're lucky we can see girls kissing each other". Upon entering the coffeehouse, the beatniks would tell us "go away hippie".

Prior to the summer of 1963, my father had taken me to meet and be with his new family two times. I had seen enough of life and had the wisdom to be polite to step mother number one, Shirley. I met my first and oldest half brother, only a toddler, Jim. Shirley had a second son, Tom, who was an infant. The conversation during the visits was guarded and polite. My father wanted to know what I was doing and I would respond with deflected answers regarding school. During the second visit, I had a lot to say about surfing. As a result, Shirley suggested that in the future, I bring a friend and we could stay overnight before going to the beach. I spoke with another friend, Jeff Hawk from my high school, who I did not hang out with regularly, that we could stay at my father's house in Brentwood and then travel to the beach. We stayed overnight with my dad and the new family. Jeff told me "we need some gas for my car, let's go siphon some gas from a neighbor's car." We did just that. Jeff had a mischievous streak, but step mother number one liked him. He was very sociable. Later I discovered he stole someones new surfboard from end of Sunset Boulevard where it ended at the beach. Several years later, I ran into him at a supermarket. He told me he was a cop in the Los Angeles police force. Perfect.

The activity of attending classes, going to dances and surfing masked the great anxiety of this immediate time. The prime point of the Cuban missile crisis was a constant in the background of my thinking. During this masking, I continued to catch rides from Dave and Don, while focusing on surfing, dancing, and young females. Jane, one young females Dave introduced me to, I befriended not as a girlfriend but as just a friend. Jane, for a short period, became my guide and councilor to help me through Puberty II.

As I entered the twelfth grade, I continued to rebel against the college preparation path. I enrolled in wood shop and print shop. In the eleventh grade, I took such a beating in English I had to go to summer school to make up a "D". I made a good grade in the summer school English class because it was mostly writing and not spelling and grammar. In summer school, I met what we knew as a "surf bunny". She had a good tan and bleached blond hair and was visiting from Mira Costa High School near Redondo Beach, which is in the south bay region of the Los Angeles area. I flirted with the visiting girl and could get her phone number. Jane told me "stay away from her, she's looking for older guys." Jane was correct. I struck out.

My adventures in the twelfth grade centered on surfing, focusing on young women, and sometimes on school subjects. I met three young women at the Pasadena Civic Auditorium that molded my passage through the later stages of puberty. The first was a very cute young woman from a local Catholic School, whose parents had come to the United States from North Africa. Her name was Elizabeth L'Coer, or just plain Liz. It was an off-and-on relationship for the twelfth grade. She had an older sister, who at one point went out with Don Wiley. Don had a way of buying illegal alcohol. One night we took Don's car into the Pasadena foothills and drank what may have been vodka or some other clear hard-liquor, a dangerous thing along with Liz and her sister. This was the first time I removed a young woman's underpants and actually felt the pubic area of her body. Fortunately, I was too naïve and intoxicated to get into real trouble. Somehow, I maintained contact with Liz up to the point when I was a freshman at Long Beach State University.

The second girl was a cute girl-next-door type who also attended the same Catholic school as Liz. As you can read, there is a theme developing here. Her name was Carla Motto, and she liked music and dancing. It was an on-and-off again relationship that continued for three or four years, even when I was a sophomore in college, continuing into the summer of 1966.

On Valentine's Day, I had promised to meet another new girlfriend, Susan Jackson, at a dance in a church hall in Eagle Rock. Later that year, we would also meet at the Pasadena Civic Auditorium. But this time, it did not work out so well. My mother, on Valentine's Day, and me being a sixteen-year-old senior, tells me, "It's time you learned how to drink." She placed a full bottle of red wine in front of me and a glass. I drank the entire bottle and walked to the dance a few blocks away. If Susan showed up was unknown to me. That night, I spent most of the dance puking in the men's room. Liz was difficult to date because of parental restrictions. After the unfortunate incident at the church hall, I could reconnect with Susan. In some senses, she became my steady girl. Susan was a thin, almost bony natural blond with blue eyes and had something of a "roman" nose. To begin with, we met and then danced at the Pasadena Civic Auditorium. Later in the night, we would go into the dark parking lot next door, smoke cigarettes, an addictive habit I would later regret, and then the two of us would make out. The kissing and necking caused me to be aroused. Susan would then make a comment, "you seem to have a third leg". We also went to the beach, another activity of mine that disrupted my mediocre endeavor as a student. Given my own flaky sixteen-year-old behavior, I became enamored with one of her classmates, Laura. I then broke up with Susan. The relationship with Laura failed, so I made up with Susan. I ended up taking Susan to the senior prom, but after that, it was a tarnished relationship. After I graduated from high school, my relationship with Susan continued to be tenuous, and after one night in the front of my friend Don's car, she became sexually stimulated and crawled on top of me, probably having an organism with her cloths on. She was quite embarrassed afterwards, as was I, to a certain extent. Given her Roman Catholic religion. the young woman was very much a product of the pre-Vatican-II Roman Catholic Church. That was the last time I saw Susan.

As a senior in high school, I continued to focus on fun shop courses, and ignored studies. This was true, but I focused on a few academics. I found my twelfth-grade civics course engaging. We organized elections in the class. I ran as a "socialist", nationalizing everything in sight (oh, how I was the perfect twenty-first century "socialist" by definition of the USA-sian Republican Party of the future.) I actually won the election, likely because I was the most vocal in the class. My imagined position was because of the influence of my mother's family, especially my uncle, who had been a member of the British Labor Party. Lurking silently in the background were news releases about the conflict in Indochina, Vietnam. The civil rights movement gained national strength, but neither of these had yet entered my center of focus. I directed my interests towards surfing, beach, pop teen music, and young women. There was a national election of Lyndon Johnson versus Barry Goldwater. The left-liberal influence of my mother affected me, so I put a Lyndon Johnson sticker on the fin of my surfboard.

Don Wiley joined the army after graduating from Franklin High School. Don, in his new uniform, took me into a bar in Highland Park. They served us beer; illegal, but since he was in uniform... After that, he disappeared from my life. Before this, he introduced me to Kayla Marsdan, another young Catholic girl. When my mother wasn't home, we took off our clothes, and we attempted to have sex. It just didn't work. I didn't know what to do with both of us naked. We physically didn't connect. For many years after that, we were simply friends, never lovers.

I continued to be a close friend of Dave Carlson. He had the car and the job. We continued our runs to the beach together, even when I started college. About this time, my mother told me I had to vacate the house where we lived. She gave me only three choices. I could join the military, get a job and support myself, or go away to college. Of course I could come visit on weekends. By now, I paid more attention to this "small conflict" in Vietnam. Now my goal was to get into a four-year college. I applied to and was I accepted three state colleges. I chose Long Beach State College, later to become California State University at Long Beach.

So I graduated in the late spring of 1964. It was my last summer living at my mother's house. With no previous commitments, I headed to the American Legion Hall for the local dance within walking distance of where I lived. This time, I was completely sober. A large, busty young girl named Jill attracted my attention, but she wanted nothing to do with me. Towards the end of the dance, I noticed a young girl with brunette hair, a "roman" nose and brown eyes. I thought she was a tenth or eleventh grader, but after a conversation, I found out she was in the ninth grade. Her mother would pick her up at the end of the dance. But, it turned out she lived down the hill from my house on Escarpa Drive. So there it is, me, a seventeen-year-old with a fourteen-year-old girlfriend. Her name was Ann Jensen. We immediately hit it off, me the generic California surfer type heading off to Cal State Long Beach and a young girl in the ninth grade. I visited her at her house, and we immediately ended up making out with some light petting near the bowl at Occidental College where I had just graduated from high school. For me, it was instant teenage love. No one had responded like this young girl. I told her what I was doing, and she explained that her mother was worried that she had matured socially too early for her age. I might agree in hind sight. Ann's mother was a practicing psychologist, an amiable woman, and she was tolerant of typical teenage angst. For the next two years, off and on, Ann became my steady girlfriend.

Cal State Long Beach was bewildering at first. I lived at a boarding house in Belmont Shores, just south of Long Beach, and shared a room with an entomologist whose name I don't remember apart from he gave me some rides to school, and he had an ominous sign on the back of his car—Ronald Reagan for Governor. The other boarder, Payam, a Persian who had gone to school in The United Kingdom, offered a different perspective. An older woman owned the house and lived downstairs. The students lived upstairs. As part of room and board, she cooked us breakfast and dinner. The cuisine was typical middle American, with bacon and eggs for breakfast and meat and potatoes for dinner. My attitude towards school changed. I wanted to become a serious student, but didn't have the correct habits. I became a history major given the influence of my uncle. By late 1964, I realized the conflict in Vietnam was turning dangerous, and it was in my interest to stay in school.

When in Eagle Rock during weekends, my relationship with Ann continued. We were quite sneaky with our trysts. At night in the garage aside her house, we both were completely naked in a sleeping bag. A great deal of heavy-petting, took place in the bag and several other concealed places after that. In the absence of my mother, heavy petting took place in my bedroom, or if she was there, in the bushes along the side of the road near Occidental College. In all senses, this was my first actual teenage love.

I continued my life at school with exploration. I took a class in the art department, life drawing, with real nude models. Then continuing with Latin on the word of fellow students that the teacher was gay, and gave all the males A's and B's. I got a B, but I loved Latin, and ended up taking sixteen units, even though later taught by a retired military officer. My later student activism shocked this teacher.

My boarding-house roommate, the etymologist with the Ronald Reagan for Governor bumper sticker, moved, and a Midwesterner from Illinois named Harry who drove a large red Dodge replaced him. Harry convinced me to take a class in economic geography, which I found interesting. While hanging around the school cafeteria, I met Bill and Bill. The first Bill was from a Russian Molokan culture and lived in Bellflower, a community north of Long

Beach. The second Bill, who lived in the on-campus dorms, was a music major nicknamed "Animal." Both Bills ended up forming a rock-and-roll band that covered favorite songs of the time, including those from the Rolling Stones and the Beatles. We would meet in the dorms, listen to the Rolling Stones' first album, and drink Country Club Malt Liquor, an awful drink bought illegally by who knows who. Then we would go to the state college-sponsored dances, and me, at least once, getting ill in the men's bathroom. Often in the morning before class I would meet Russian Bill, simply nicknamed "Puff" because of the post-fix of his last name, in his 1957 Chevy with a forty-five record player in the dashboard. We would listen to the Rolling Stones' "Heart of Stone" with "Time is on My Side" on this dashboard player.

Towards the end of my freshman year in college, Ann and I temporarily parted ways. Ann was now fifteen years old, and I was eighteen years old. Perhaps she thought her relationship with me was "too serious". Ann was now in the tenth grade at Eagle Rock High School, with many more peers. Perhaps she wanted to avoid being restrained by a steady relationship. Once I returned to the Pasadena Civic Auditorium to dance, but it wasn't the same. After that, I didn't return to my favorite high school dance hall. Without Ann, I spent more time at school with Animal and at the beach with Dave Carlson.

That summer, I met a "beach bunny" at Sunset Beach. After some surf riding, I focused on a tan, well-built young woman named Nancy. Dave took an interest in one of Nancy's girlfriends. This resulted in something of a group bonding. Nancy was four years my senior, lived in an apartment on Gower Street in Hollywood, and worked as a secretary. She had sun bleached hair, an athletic build and filled her bathing suit as a good-looking young woman. She was twenty-two years old, so she could buy alcoholic beverages, in my case, mostly beer. I only went with her for about eight weeks. But in those eight weeks, she showed me what was really going on between the sheets. There is nothing like an older, experienced woman as your instructor. Her apartment wasn't much, basically a room with a Murphy bed, a kitchen, a bathroom, and a closet. We would sit in the apartment, talk and listen to top forty radio. The first night I slept with Nancy, her current boyfriend, a Hawaiian in California named Gaylord, called. He said he was going to come over and kill me. That didn't happen, considering there was a secure lock on the front door that could only be activated from inside the apartment. This incident taught me that some of the crowd at Sunset Beach were part of a rough group.

Nancy was odd in that she liked little mushy foreplay. It was "get an erection and off to the races." One night, while buzzed nicely on brew that Nancy purchased, she tried to convince me to run off to Vegas and get married. I declined, with good sense trumping my libido. Nancy was into some aspects of Hollywood culture. She had a favorite card shop on Hollywood Boulevard. From that shop, she bought me a card and gave it to me. It read, "Friends may come and friends may go and friends may peter out, you know. But we'll be friends through thick or thin, peter out or peter in." After eight weeks, we parted ways, and she was off with the next guy, but I must admit, she turned me from a boy into a man.

By the time of my sophomore year, and given my experience with Nancy, I spent more time hanging out with Animal. His band continued to play gigs. Growing up in Riverside, Animal came from what was essentially a desert community east of Los Angeles. Animal made many trips to Riverside, where his mother and his cousin Lonnie lived. Animal, Lonnie and I would get cheap wine for one dollar, fifty-five cents a gallon. It was Red Mountain Wine, which might be categorized as paint remover. In actuality, it was wine made from the grapes that were vacuumed off the processing floor. We would get drunk and end up with awful hangovers. On one trip, Animal set me up with a blind date that was a friend of his current date. I met her, and we seemed to hit it off. She had a brother in the Marines, was a dancer and taught Sunday school. Her girlfriend had previously described her as "a fun girl who doesn't smoke or drink, but there is one thing she really likes to do." And boy did she ever, in the back of Animal's 1953 Studebaker with me.

During this sophomore period, while visiting Animal in the men's dorm, I met more people who were to be near me at a pivotal point in my life. Russell Sheen was a wiry, high-strung guy who owned a vehicle. Another was Barry Dent. Barry lived in the first of a trio of small houses on twelfth street in Seal Beach, California. Seal Beach is in easy riding distance to Long Beach State and barely inside the Orange County border. This trio of houses was about two blocks from the beach. The rent was inexpensive at eighty dollars per month. Seal Beach was transforming into something of a student ghetto. When Barry dropped out of school, Russell rented the first small house in the mentioned trio of houses.

In the middle of my sophomore year, when visiting Eagle Rock on weekends, I insisted I learn how to drive. My mother hired California Driving School. At the end of the course, I barely passed the driving test, which included parallel parking. As a result, I had a California driver's license. Ann and I reconnected, continuing our romantic affair, lovey-dovey as ever. My mother had a British-style sports car she had gained in the divorce. The vehicle, a four speed stick shift Austin Healey, was difficult to drive, especially for a neophyte driver. I took Ann to the movies in Glendale, California, the neighboring "town" next to Eagle Rock. This is the first date we went on where I was the driver. When returning home near Occidental College, I almost got in an accident making a left turn. We were both terrified. No harm, no foul. My driving improved after that.

One afternoon while at Ann's house, with her mother gone, all the heavy petting stopped. Both of us naked with Ann on top of my long, skinny teenage body, I became aroused with a new level of intensity. All the training that Nancy, the older woman, had imparted to me kicked in. Ann was having intercourse. After a smashing orgasm, she told me, "never do that again!" Later, Ann told me what happened after I departed. She said her mother found her crying, and she told her mother, "I'm not a virgin anymore". Her mother seemed not to be angry with me or her. Ann got a lecture about getting pregnant. After that, when we were alone at the house on Escarpa Drive, we had intercourse again, now in the downstairs study, this time with me on top. Each time we met and alone, we continued our overt sexual relation. Over the months, I was prudent not to get Ann pregnant.

Ann introduced me to some musicians trying to start a garage band, so here was a chance to use my Fender Stratocaster guitar. We had a couple of tunes based on TV show themes. This was my original California garage band named the Immortals. We tried to play Rolling Stone songs, like my friend Animal's band, the Syndicate. We were not a good band, especially the drummer. As an interesting side note, we added an electronic piano player out of the Navy who took us to party in Watts after the localized revolt. I guess this was an artifact of tolerance.

My days as a surfer were ending. Ann and her family spent a week in Isla Vista, near Santa Barbara. Dave Carlson and his girlfriend, who also was a friend of Kayla's, made love and surfing, as did I, but not Ann, who did not surf. It was an interesting summer. While wandering around without the young girlfriends, we met some "bad girls" who had spent time in jail. This was of little consequence, since we weren't interested, but of note, in their apartment, was the first time I heard a Bob Dylan album.

Next, Animal became involved with Kayla Marsdan. Ann and Kayla became close friends, which continued for some time in the future. Animal gained access to cannabis and convinced me to try some. I was distrusting the national mythos that had molded me since the 1950s. That "police action" loomed larger in South East Asia, but I felt safe, since classified as "1-S" with the Selective Service. The more I analyzed, the more the national mythos disintegrated. The smoking of cannabis was symbolic. Something always depicted it as a horrendous addiction of the lower classes. I felt I was becoming a disenfranchised person forced to the back of the bus of life. "Sure, give me a toke off that joint".

REVOLUTION I

•••

It is difficult to delineate the Puberty II and Revolution I divide in my mind. Let's start with Kayla and Animal braking up. The reason of him being still infatuated with his original girlfriend in Lakewood, near Long Beach, whose mother was the "manager" of his former rock-and-roll band, The Syndicate. Kayla met Moe. In my mind, Moe, with his real-life story, starts the complete and utter disintegration of USA-sian 1950s mythology. As a mid-western volunteer into the US Marines, in 1964 they sent him to Vietnam. He completely broke down and ended up in a military hospital in Saigon. His recollections about Vietnam were sparse, but the ones told were horrendous. He would talk about killing the enemy in a fire-fight, and examining the bodies to find adolescents ranging from twelve to fifteen years old. He ended up in a Saigon mental hospital and given LSD at that hospital, evidently as an experiment, and then released. Moe was living in Westwood Village, staying in a room above a local sandal maker, listening to Bob Dylan albums, and now passing out LSD to anyone he met, especially young students like me, Kayla and Animal. We were lucky because Moe had pure Sandos Laboratory LSD he gained after returning from Vietnam. It was an unknown entity and completely legal. There were rumors about LSD in the news and in magazines. We knew it would drastically alter your perception of reality to the unreal. So Animal, Moe, Kayla, and I climbed to the top of the hills above the amphitheater at Occidental College and each took an ample dose of a sugar cube laced with liquid LSD. As we "came on", Moe returned to Vietnam, and would not let us keep our heads above the grasslands while he made exploding noises and coached us.

The visual and acoustic perceptions of LSD are overwhelming. Skin peeled off all the surrounding objects in soft sparkling lights and off the sky in a rapid motion along with the sound of rings hitting a solid steel barrier in soft but consistent simultaneous ringing increasing and decreasing in key. The subconscious rational portions of the mind mixed with the experience, creating both exhilarating and frightening perceptions.

In the wee hours of the morning, we emerged at a parking lot probably several miles from the hill near the college. We bought a huge bottle of orange juice and drank it after being physically exhausted. After we consumed the bottle, Animal and Moe went to sleep in Animal's VW van and parked it near where my mother lived. Kayla and I returned to my mother's house, and I unlocked the front door.

A party was winding down at my mother's house in the wee hours of the morning. It was fascinating to talk to and witness inebriated adults with flakes falling off the walls and ceiling and bells striking a pavement from one thousand feet with slow motion sound effects.

* * *

In college, I was now a serious student. Unlike Animal, who eventually dropped out and pursued the life of a jazz musician. School and the pursuit of scholarly activities became my life anchor. I wanted to be the Renaissance man, touching all subjects. I played music, drew art, wrote, and studied mathematics.

The conflict in Vietnam was expanding in 1966. There were rumors that the "1-S" draft exemption was going to be removed, so all males of a certain age currently in college would be eligible, that included me as a potential participant. As a history major, I encountered several professors who taught the "lost" history of socialists in North America, like Eugene Debs and Daniel DeLeon. Besides these personalities, they taught searing anecdotes from USA-sian history, like the fate of Joe Hill and the subjugation of USA-sian socialist parties by having their leaders thrown in prison. Besides the submerged contours of USA-sian history, the professors would emphasize various passages from Karl Marx. Simultaneously, on the Long Beach State campus, the African-Americans organized the Black Student Union. The same organizing process also took place in all the urban centers across the country. The Black Panther Party was emerging in the Rockford area near Oakland. Simultaneously, love-ins became a spontaneous counter-culture gathering of mostly middle-class Anglo youths. The new music reflected all these changes in USA-sian culture. In the cities, the fist "underground" music stations came into being that would play songs you would never hear on "top forty" radio. The lectures of the "left" professors matched what I perceived as going on in the world and in North American society. I now had a philosophical basis for my rejection of 1950s mass culture.

The civil rights movement transformed into Black Power, the spreading resistance to the United States government resulting from the encroaching conflict in Southeast Asia and acceptable birth control for women setting the stage for women's liberation, became the trinity of the mid-1960s and of this chapter, Revolution I.

For the time being, I remained at the boarding house in Belmont Shores, but I now knew several students who were the nucleus of a growing collegiate counter culture. Russell Sheen had moved to Seal Beach into the first of a set of three houses on 12th Street. Through Animal, I also met David Schoen, Jonny Matson, and Gill Johns. By the summer of my sophomore year, I moved out of the boarding house and shared the third of a set of three houses on 12th Street with Gill. I maintained my connection with Payam, who also moved out, then into his apartment. He landed a job in the Los Angeles Harbor at the Yankee Whaler Inn as a busboy. Through Payam, I could also land a busboy job at the same restaurant. Later when visiting Eagle Rock for the weekend, I purchased a '56 Ford Sedan from a person in Pasadena, so for the time being I had wheels because my mother's Austin Healey required a massive amount of maintenance to drive it on a Southern California freeway. While at the Yankee Whaler Inn, I could make minimum wage, with free dinners and some trickle-down tips from the servers. With a car of my own and a job and a place I enjoyed living in, I was at the top of my student world.

David Schoen was a chemistry major at Long Beach State College. Both he and Animal introduced me to Stony. Stony, whose real name was Steve Averal, studied sociology at State College, so he was closely akin to a history major like me. Stony loved to play records and smoke copious amounts of cannabis. Often to retreat from classes, the stress of rejecting the war and organizing against it, and to just "drop out" for a couple of hours, I continued to visit Stony. In the late sixties, electronic digitizing of music was a science project. It didn't exist in the populace until eight-track tapes in the 1970s. Stony had the best vinyl, mostly jazz, record collection I had ever encountered. He grew up in Pasadena during the Beat era, and had immense knowledge of jazz, a broad spectrum of blues, and other off-center music. He had a penchant for "New Thing" jazz, which described to the uninitiated as chaotic and random. Ornette Coleman is the primary example of this style of music. As I migrated into the student movement, Stony was sympathetic to my revolutionary impulses. His little one-room apartment with a restroom was a hideout for me to collect my thoughts or, frequently, to forget them.

When not in Eagle Rock with my main squeeze on the weekend, Ann, I would visit Stony, Russell, and Johnny Matson. Johnny was a student teacher who ended up joining the US Navy. Before entering the military, Johnny discovered a "hippy commune" near Sir Gorda in Big Sur. Myself, Johnny and Animal drove to Big Sir in Animal's VW bus. I met a few counter culture types, the most notable an African American jazz musician from San Francisco who could no longer play the saxophone because of bad teeth. After that, David joined the US Air Force. By now, I was very much afraid of what was unfolding in South East Asia. The stories from Moe, who had moved to San Francisco drove this home, and was an original participant in the Haight-Ashbury scene. Moe published his poetry and was a regular at a San Francisco underground radio station.

The dreams of an alternate society replaced the shattered myths of USA-sian culture of the 1950s in my mind. The counter-culture youths centered on campuses, but the counter-culture spread to every urban area, suburban area, and even to some rural areas. It reflected counter culture in the music, news, and what went on at school. The unified delusion of 1950s culture, with its white, Anglo center of gravity, melted in the new primarily urban culture of the 1960s. Gill, Stony, Russell, and I attended love-ins at Griffith Park in the Los Angeles area. Given my experience in Big Sir and what I witnessed at love-ins, I just was not your hard core "hippie". The change in the youth culture fascinated me, but was too much of an intellectual to internalize the "New Age" idioms, like eastern mysticism, astrology, chakras, Hinduism. On campuses, it became obvious counter-culture youth were transcending class and race confines, which defined North American society. And the first large Anti-Vietnam War demonstrations took place. By late 1965 and early 1966, I was not only disillusioned with established North American politics, but with my nation's world military presence as an empire.

Animal, the dedicated jazz musician, and introduced me to Chip Bradley, or just the "Colonel." Chip played saxophone and Animal played trumpet and flügelhorn. Chip lived in Hollywood and worked at a local newspaper. We would go to his apartment, smoke large quantities of cannabis, and listen to Charles Mingus, Eric Dolphy, Ornette Coleman, Thelonious Monk, electric Chicago Blues, and others. Chip had conservative parents in Riverside County, where Animal grew up. Animal had known Chip since high school days. In defiance of his parent's views, Chip would bring home Socialist Labor Party newspapers he would buy on the sidewalk outside his job at a major Los Angeles newspaper.

In 1966, towards the end of my sophomore year, Ann, along with her mother and brother, moved to Woodland Hills, a neighborhood in the San Fernando Valley. She would attend William Taft in the fall of 1966, and to be in the eleventh grade. The growth of counterculture also affected Ann, but did not have the growing distrust and projected anger I had with United States culture and government. I wanted to be an agent of change relating to the political climate of the time. Ann made several new friends, given the change in high schools. Wayne was attending Pierce College and had an easy-going personality. Wayne was one of Ann's new friends. He had long straight hair and was a serious student, though he presented the image of a "hippie". Wayne immediately and I immediately hit it off and drove to the Haight Ashbury in my 1956 Ford Sedan. Wayne would later take up residence in the "Haight" while attending San Francisco State College.

Kayla, now physically and emotionally involved with Moe, had temporarily settled in the Bay Area of Northern California. Kayla invited Ann to a retreat, focusing on Indian national culture and religion. I did not recognize it, but there was a shift in attitude that brought an end to my constant relationship with Ann, so we broke up. In the future, we would have relations with each other, but she would never again be my steady woman.

During the summer, I gained some extra units at Pasadena City College. Perchance, I ran into Carla Motto after class. When in Catholic girls' high school while necking, she would say to me "don't touch me there". We went on another "date" shortly after becoming reacquainted. My mother had separated from Greg, stepfather number one, and moved to a condo still in Eagle Rock, actually near the eagle rock. She rented the house on Escarpa Drive to a group of students attending Occidental College. My mother was not home in the condo, which I had access to, so Carla, now armed with her newly gained birth control pills, engaged in sex. Carla visited me in Seal Beach, but she was alien to "hip culture," and would much rather drink wine than smoke cannabis. Her musical taste had little to do with the emerging music of the counterculture, like the Jefferson Airplane or the Grateful Dead. She liked Motown and R&B. It didn't matter. She was more or less oblivious to the civil rights movement, soon to be Black Power, and the conflict in South East Asia. My short-lived relationship with her was a mix of the avant-garde and my teenage past. The relationship culminated with a trip to San Francisco, to the Haight-Ashbury district. We made a stop in Isla Vista, which is near Santa Barbara, California, to glimpse my mother, and then headed to San Francisco and to an address unknown. Unfortunately, I blew a leak in the oil pan of my '56 Ford, and had to put in oil about every hundred miles. There went all my extra money. Making it to the streets of San Francisco, and parked it on a street near Haight-Ashbury. We took a nap in the car, woke up, and I told her, "I have to find Wayne." We took off for Golden Gate Park. There, a small sixties miracle transpired. There was Wayne sunning himself, along with the rest of the hippies. I explained the situation, and he told me, "Hell ya! Come stay at my place."

Wayne's place wasn't one of those vintage Victorian houses so ubiquitous to San Francisco, but it worked. There was a kitchen full of dirty dishes, a living room in two sections, one of which was his bed area, and the other just for hanging out. There was a bedroom where various people crashed. And most important, there was a bathroom with a shower. Carla and I washed off the sweat and dirt, had sex, and fell asleep. We had made it to Haight-Ashbury.

Wayne's apartment was a sixties' symphony of "sex, drugs, and rock-and-roll." The radio played counter culture rock-and-roll, cannabis flowed freely, and sexual intercourse took place out in the open, by several couples at any time of day or night. Wayne was a business major at San Francisco State and by now I was turning against corporate power over not only the USA-sian government and culture, but was now associating corporate power with what was happening in South East Asia. Wayne spoke in favor of American business, and I was questioning the entire process in non-exact and nebulous terms. I wonder how Wayne fared when San Francisco State exploded in revolt a couple of years later.

Carla wanted to be a business secretary and get married, and I still associated her with the established culture. But she certainly liked the sex and the rock-and-roll sans cannabis. As women's freedom was injected into mainstream culture by the beginning of the 1970s, I wonder if she embraced it, adjusted to it, or rejected it.

To make money, Carla and I went to the local underground

press, and purchased a stack of Oracle newspapers at base price, then stood out on Haight Street, and sold them to tourists as they gawked at the "hippies". Carla ditched her long hair wig. I never could understand why the wig. And she ditched her mini-skirt in favor of a more hip, long dress. We made a reasonable pile of money. I went back to Wayne's, cleaned the kitchen, and made the whole "commune" with an enormous meal of pasta. Someone scored red wine, and it was another buzzed night filled with sex, drugs, and rock-and-roll in The Haight.

Carla wanted to get into a bar on Haight Street. Okay, we were in there a while and I was uncomfortable, so I suggested going to a rock-and-roll event plus a light show at the Fillmore Auditorium. We did. Carla was angry about something, and left with a stranger, but showed up at Wayne's apartment shortly after the concert was over. I guess I didn't understand the message she was sending me.

There was a sinister thread I didn't know about while crashing at Wayne's apartment. His girlfriend, married to one of his fraternity brothers at Pierce College, in the San Fernando Valley, Southern California. Her husband called the San Francisco Police Department and sent them to Wayne's apartment in the wee hours of the morning. Carla and I woke up to flashlight beams and strange voices. It so happened that I had us wrapped up naked in blankets on the floor after a night of communal partying. The next morning we took the money left in our pockets, depart The Haight, and baby the '56 Ford back to Southern California. We made it. Honestly, who knows how long we would have stayed at Wayne's if the police incident had not happened.

I sold the '56 Ford to Kayla's brother. I could gain my mother's 1957

Austin Healey, which I had driven before. It was not a reliable car. Driving down the Long Beach freeway, oil would spray out of the engine. It was a typical Brit car that has trouble with oil and water. Later I sold it. I saw Carla one more time after our memorable trip to Haight-Ashbury. It was the usual night of copulation, but without either of us sure how much we had in common. In retrospect, she had excellent taste in R&B music.

I continued to share a beach bungalow, the first of three houses on a 12th street in Seal Beach, with Russell. Gil lived in the third one and Johnny Matson lived in the second, with all three little bungalows on a 12th street in Seal Beach. David Schoen lived in an apartment two blocks away. Russell and I returned to another Griffith Park love-in. There was a huge drum circle, which later became a fixture in the new-hippie/new-age culture. A protest theme permeated the crowd. A costumed character appeared in the uniform of an air-force general. He had a label—"General Waste More Land." This was a pun on what was becoming one of the arch-evil characters in the Lyndon Johnson administration. Another character was "General Hersheybar" who parodied the head of the Selective Service. At love-ins, many icons of "new-age" culture were popularized. I, myself, ignored them and simply enjoyed the merry-go-round in the park.

David Schoen had an affair with Sharon Sparling, an ex-wife of a music major at Cal State Long Beach. She worked at a hamburger stand near the corner of Ximeno Avenue and Anaheim Street in Long Beach. I even helped Dave write a love poem for her. They had an unstable relationship that broke up shortly after that. Then one night in Russell's bungalow, Sharon and I literally had sex on the grass carpet of his front room. Sharon had beautiful blond hair and an erotic-looking body with a seductive mid-section. I did not know it, but this was a life-changing event. She lived for a short time in Hollywood. Here Sharon, myself and Zeke from Long Beach State College while took a low dose of psychedelics, and wandered around one park above the Hollywood Mountains. After that, Sharon and I started going together. Next, Sharon moved into a residence in Burbank.

Sharon's best friend in high school was Barbara Perkins, who first had a relationship with Animal, who having dropped out of California State University Long Beach, and besides, jazz music was rapidly transforming into a mystical guru of some generic flavor. Barbara's relationship with Animal faded rapidly, and Barbara ended up in a relationship with David Schoen. The five of us sat around Sharon's house in Burbank and had conversations that would fuel and satisfy any sitcom. From Burbank, Sharon moved into the same Hollywood apartment that Animal's high school friend, Chip Bradley, and me with her. Barbara moved into the same apartment building on the first floor.

By now, what was happening in South East Asia terrified me. My old surfer buddy, Dave Carlson, had a Canadian family, and I had him visit the apartment on Franklin Avenue where Sharon and I lived. He felt I was unpatriotic and scolded me for my wanting to take asylum in Canada. I never saw Dave Carlson again after that. The living quarters for me, Barbara and Sharon on Franklin Avenue didn't last long. Before my junior year at Cal State Long Beach, Sharon, her toddler child and I moved back to Seal Beach. We moved to at least four houses, but ended up in an old-but-charming set of "boxcar" apartments. A fellow radical student, Paul Glass, who was moving out of his place, offered me a beautiful old railroad apartment within Seal Beach. It had vines of purple flowers draping the front that created a small jungle environment with chairs where the other students in the building would hold events. This was a calming juxtaposition against the energy of the student movements, black and white. Sharon and I, along with her infant son, moved into this apartment. She had the car and a welfare check, and I was, among other roles, a dead-beat student now trying to scrounge money anywhere I could. I even could get a small amount of money from my father, typically on my birthday and more often from my mother, but not consistently, during my first two semesters at college.

During this time, I could get a job as a teacher's assistant at the Huntington Beach High School.

When I started, I wasn't even twenty-one years old while attempting to work with youths that were almost as old as I was. My incompatibility with the discipline of teaching. I attempted to take courses on the teaching path at Long Beach State. After signing up for two classes and loathing them, I dropped them. I continued to focus on the social and political issues of the day.

At the end of my sophomore year and starting with my junior year, I had become active in the Student Action Committee at school. It rapidly transformed me into a student activist. It started this transformation when several of us would "sit-in" in front of on-campus military recruiters. Several other personal transformations took place. I took a class in American Social History. The teacher was a radical assistant professor. This class had a tremendous influence on me. Instead of a memorization of historical facts with no interpretation, the emphasis was on studying history, so it could be useful and to transform society by understanding historical processes. The teacher did not reflect any specific organization's view of North American social history. And he didn't specifically subscribe to any group's ideology. He presented North American social history as a series of ideological conflicts whose antagonists and arguments took place in religious organizations. This meshed with what I now saw as a civil rights movement transformed into an African American militant minority attempting to defend their communities. The course content detailed the creation of the Empire of the United States as it existed in the 1960s, with Manifest Destiny transforming into a colossus, the USA-sian Empire, whose economy rested on the raw materials taken by a whisper from, as what were to be called later, developing Third World countries.

What I was witnessing was a national mythology breaking down before my eyes. I was in a counterculture that now actively opposed the war in South East Asia. I picked up Mao's Little Red Book. At first reading, it impressed me. It was about revolution, and there was now revolution brewing all around me. But the extracts rapidly grew thin. They didn't supply the guidance of students originating from "the middle class." In addition, I learned that most of the North American social radicals, aka "socialists", now almost a meaningless word unless you launch into a detailed explanation by what you mean, had tried to import their radical theory from a European experience. For example, the Socialists centered in Minnesota and Chicago in the nineteenth century tried to import German Social Democracy without original theory. Given there were a few exceptions, Daniel DeLeon actually was the first to come up with a "Soviet" organization, but to no avail in the USA. The original Communist Party USA was even worse, including its later Stalinist and Trotskyist factions. It imported all their revolutionary theories from Lenin and the rest of the Bolsheviks. Before he turned against all left-leaning world views, Jay Lovestone's assertion was correct in that capitalism was much stronger in North America and therefore needed a different revolutionary theory than that as presented by the Bolsheviks.

In the middle of the great energy of the radical movement forming in the later sixties, I looked to radicals that were steeped in Western, what we would call "first-world," culture and material reality. Two immediately captured my interest.

The first was Antonio Gramsci, the Italian Communist who understood the modern forms of industrial production. He wrote several essays that are directed at what he calls "Fordism," and in the twenty-first century we think of it as "optimized waterfall production." They used the same mode of optimized waterfall production in the Apollo project at the end of the nineteen sixties. Next instead of "special bodies of armed men" that are the primary means of control defined by Lenin in State and Revolution, Gramsci understood that in the advanced capitalist societies of North America and Europe, the primary mean of control was not armed men, but what was spoken on the radio, and in the future many more advanced forms of media and even in the back alleys and side streets. The creation of social myth was and still is the primary means by which those who control society maintain continuity, conforming to their advantage. In his essays, he defined this process as the cultural hegemony of the oligarchy, the elite or the ruling class... take your pick. What is more important is Gramsci proposed the basis of a long-term revolutionary program, mostly non-violent, to dismantle the ruling hegemony.

The second was C. Wright Mills. He was an independent sociologist with an independent radical viewpoint. He wrote several essays, but the most important was White Collar: The American Middle Classes. When he wrote this book, blue-collar workers still had most of the predominance that they had in the nineteen thirties and the nineteen forties. Mills carefully described how "pink-collar" workers were an emerging working class. He did not know he was describing the dominant paradigm for workers in the late twentieth century and beginning of the twenty-first century.

Myself and the rest of radical students at Long Beach State transformed the Peace Action Council into a new chapter of Students for a Democratic Society. The person who made the motion in the

Student Action Committee meeting, Pat, was a transfer from Long Beach City College. Later, after he had dropped out-of-state college, I ran into him, and he claimed he was now an anarchist. Our organizational move had occurred. I, personally, doubt that only a fraction of the radical students read the Port Huron Statement. The statement was basically a set of goals, but no actual program to implement them.

At Long Beach State College, this collection of radical students comprised many, and often inconsistent, views of the world. If there was an ideology that ran as a common thread, it was Chairman Mao's writings. But there were many other views of the world, especially among the influencing professors. Professor Tom was an actual member of the Communist Party USA. He was an excellent and very patient teacher of modern European history. As far as I could tell, he had a lukewarm appreciation of the sayings of Chairman Mao. Other professors originated from the old left, often with Trotskyist or independent socialist tendencies, and viewed the Soviet Union, China, Cuba and other similar revolutions as various corrupted "workers' dictatorships". The same spectrum of views existed in the minds of radical students, but not as clearly defined. The lack of organizational unity existed from the beginning.

Two students, in particular, influenced me when interacting with them. Beth was a dazzling woman, who had at one time been a member of the Socialist Workers's Party. She was a tireless organizer against the Vietnam Conflict. Al was a lifeguard, and, like me, a history major. He had studied philosophy at El Camino Junior College with a professor, Jack Forrest, who had once been a member of the Communist Party USA. Al was a master at inescapable facts of physics and reality, poverty and hunger, revolution and violence. But the focus of his study was often on South America. This was a common thread that ran through the worldview of several radical students. They were excellent studying the conditions of peasants and workers in developing blocs, maybe countries or groups of countries, but in hindsight, offered little on how to lead USA-sian radical students to be effective, to go beyond protest and affect USA-sian society with a more permanent action that would outlast the era of protest against the conflict in South East Asia.

Though not a student, Sharon became involved in the student movement as a non-student. My immediate student activity all transpired in Seal Beach, a community with a long "Bohemian" history. My friend Rick Anthony rented a house a few blocks from where Sharon and I lived. The streets and houses of Seal Beach buzzed with counter-culture. Rick's house became something of a meeting place. Rick, and Jerry Harris, another radical student, and I would discuss events and concepts often into the wee hours of the night.

At state college, we started publishing a radical student amateur magazine called Apathy Axe. The first issue was incendiary. On the cover, we had a caricature of Eldridge Cleaver holding Mickey Mouse and Donald Duck in the palm of his hand. The headlining article had the title, "The Student as Nigger." This put the radical students on the map at Long Beach State College. The headline did not alienate the Black Student Union, but bonded the radical Students for a Democratic Society with the Black Student Union. Yes, by now the organized Black Student Union a natural, but often uneasy, ally of the radical students.

During the middle of all of this activity, they asked me to report to the US Selective Service Office in Los Angeles. I showed up deliberately late, and it was the last formal request I received. After my "failure to report on time," I was now officially AWOL from military service. I may not have planned it this way, but until 1973, I only lived at one residence for any length of time, making it difficult for the Selective Service to locate me.

While living in Seal Beach, I met several non-college students through activities at the Peace Center on Anaheim Street. This office front was the focus of the meetings, teach-ins, and community action. The Peace Center had a different orientation than the radical Students for a Democratic Society at Long Beach State. Near the Peace Center was a bar, the first bar I entered legally in 1967. Professor Ron took me there for a beer. The bar, Joe Josts, it a traditional bar in Long Beach. I met several off-campus oriented people, of which one of the more interesting was Davey Crockett (yes, that was his real name), who was very much a local, and came from a traditional blue-collar background. The Peace and Freedom Party affiliates were often organizing at the Peace Center. For a time, the Peace and Freedom Party was a political force, especially in California. A local chapter of the Black Panther Party was organized during this period, and had connections to the Black Student Union at state college. I enjoyed working with contacts at the Peace Center, which were grounded in the community of Long Beach that was lacking in the college student movement. As often has transpired in USA-sian history, the community organizations in Long Beach broke into various sects, each with their agenda.

Sharon and I attended several sessions at the Peace Center, some learning sessions headed by professor Tom in the Cal State Long Beach history department, who was cautious and patient in explaining his Communist Party world-view. But by now, I viewed the Soviet Union as another empire on the planet. The Soviet Union officially promoted a social democracy, and aligned itself with the cause of workers and peasants in developing countries. Stalin institutionalized the fabric of Russian culture, and viewed as a Czar in Russia who was not a Czar. As the Soviet Union modernized, it effectively became a competitor to the USA-sian empire, and it was a social democracy only in name. Even though I rejected the ties to Soviet Empire, my learning, driven by the disgust and rejection of USA-sian mainstream culture and its approach to foreign wars, racial discrimination, and mass deception of both blue-collar and white-collar main stream workers. Other than ignoring any allegiance to the Soviet Union, I found the group educational.

Rick Anthony's upstairs apartment was another focal point of our student culture in Seal Beach. Rick had, and still has, social skills lacking in my personality since I was quiet and serious. When visiting Rick, they consumed quantities of cannabis. Almost all the students in both the student radical movement and the counterculture indulged in cannabis in some form. Possibly, in retrospect, we might not have been as "romantic" as we expanded our movement if we used fewer hallucinogens, but the drugs came with the rejection of mainstream culture. As our student movement expanded, so did the circle of people with whom I came into contact. Several people would show up at the apartment that Sharon and I lived. Dudley, who became a photographer for the Liberation News Service, was one of the few males who didn't have a girlfriend. When he caught on to the open sexual culture of the late sixties, he was the leader of exhibitionism. Members of the Long Beach State Student Council would show up at our apartment, mostly because of the association with a woman across the hall. The girlfriend of Dana Rohrabacher showed up for who knows what. Dana, who knew me personally, would be a congressional representative from Orange County, California, in the United States Congress.

Another interesting interlude took place about this time. Steve Watson, another activist in the student movement, whose father was a Methodist minister, invited Sharon and me to a two-day, non-stop event known as the Urban Plunge. In retrospect, it was like sessions that later compared to "EST" but did not use authoritarian methods in the exercises. The sessions went nonstop for 48 hours, with little sleep. Participants visited gay bars, Black Liberationists in the inner city, and similar centers of non-mainstream cultural concentration. Leader-directed discussions continued after each experience. The entire experience solidified the subconscious of the urban counter-culture in my mind.

The protest at Long Beach State culminated not with an Anti-Vietnam protest, but over a series of sculptures created in the art department as a master's degree project by Bill Spater. I don't remember exactly how many sculptures were in the exhibit. Two that seriously flew in the face of existing culture depicted a male receiving oral sex by a female with her head emerging from a television set, in the street vernacular, a guy getting a blow job from a TV. A second sculpture had a nude female masturbating while straddling an ironing board. The art was a criticism of core current USA-sian culture but was perceived as pornography by those who rejected the radical visual critique. The sculptures were confiscated and Bill was denied his Masters of Art degree.

A mass of over a thousand students marched on the administration building, several of them occupying it. Originally, I didn't enter the administration building, but I decided I bound my fate with the most active of the protesters. We were all arrested and corralled in a room.

Russell Sheen has this tendency to go berserk around the police. He was the only student in handcuffs. He wiggles up next to me, and whispers, "John, John, I have some uppers in my back pocket, you gotta' get them out and eat them, about five bennies."

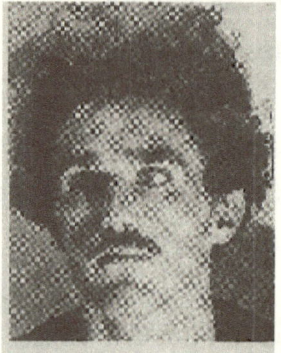 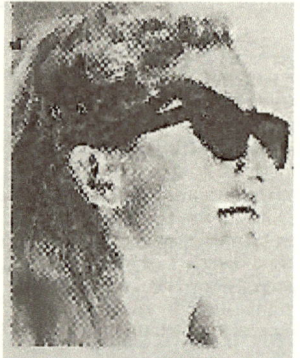

Sharon's and John's mug shot

The police arrested us, including Sharon, and transported us to the Long Beach jail where we were booked for trespassing and disturbing the peace. Each of us had a mug shot taken, and we ended up listed in the local paper, the Long Beach Press Telegram. Being wired on the uppers, and looking like a Russian anarchist. My parents were notified and by the end of the night, we were all out on bail. I don't remember who did this or how it worked. We had a lawyer for the entire group. When we went to trial, all of us pleaded "no lo contendere". The verdict resulted in a period of probation for each of us.

Another notable event took place after this. Professor Ron held what was a fund-raiser for social action. It included a barbecue and even liberal parents, which included my mother attended. We invited the Long Beach Black Panther Party to the gathering, and later in the afternoon, they showed up. Lined up in a semi-military formation on the professor's lawn, this completely freaked out the moderately wealthy, mostly Anglo, white neighborhood. Then the radical students, myself included, formed a line kneeling in front of the Black Panthers, forming a barrier. I felt a great deal of adrenaline, but not really fear. It was what I had to do. Several years later, friends questioned all this, asking if it shocked the neighborhood meaningfully? One thing for sure, the neighborhood sensed that it was not business as usual.

The radical students at California State College at Long Beach had a tenuous alliance with the Black Student Union. The Black Student Union produced a protest-related play. Both Sharon and I took part in the play. She was a white social worker in the ghetto. I was a white police officer in the ghetto. I don't remember all the details, but at the end of the play, I end up killing one mother on welfare. What an ominous portent of the future. Me, as an actor in the role of a police officer, killing an unarmed Afro-American. The prop I used in the play was a 45 gauge revolver from a member of the Long Beach Black Panthers. The man's nickname was Squeaky. Squeaky would empty the real bullets out and replace them with blanks. We did several shows, including the last one together, in Santa Barbara at UCSB, Isla Vista. Sharon practiced free sex, now common in the late 1960s, and had sexual intercourse with one of the cast members. This angered some or at least one woman in the

Black Student Union, and that was the end of both Sharon's and my amateur acting career.

How did activist activities go over with my family? My mother, a strong social democrat, left-Democrat, and socialist, supported my activities, and she opposed to the conflict in South East Asia. My father, a former Marine Airman, removed all financial support once I departed the "controlled" environment of the boarding house I lived in before moving to Seal Beach. The few times I visited him and my stepmother in Brentwood, it was intense and emotionally loaded with excessive drinking of alcohol. It seethed with conflict over differing views of the world, and when returning to Sharon, I was depressed and emotionally drained. I was an outsider to my father's second family, and I knew it.

With the organizing of a formal chapter of Students for a Democratic Society at CSULB, the chairperson, Andor Skotnes, came from South Africa and was a very effective leader. While Andor was the chairperson, the organization was effective. Unfortunately, he departed the university for UC Berkeley, and after that, the organization was dominated by egotistic males, the possibility of which I was one. In retrospect, it would have been better if the women had equal or even majority control. I think we would have been more effective.

While remaining a talented student, and kept up with my studies along with the student activities. I intensified my studies of history, sociology, psychology, and economics. I loved to listen to classical, jazz, blues and some of the popular music of the 1960s. Unlike other radical students, I didn't focus on the malfeasance of the USA-sian empire in Asia, Africa, and South America, although I knew the basics of raw materials extracted from client areas of the USA-sian economic empire and the resultant production of local commodities. While searching how the middle class and supported in the "permanent war economy", I would spend hours reading books in our "boxcar" apartment on 11th Street in Seal Beach. The romantic disease that infected most of the young radical students bit me. I would stare out the window, looking at the beautiful ivy in the front yard in my calmer moods.

Those of us that were broadly defined as part of the counterculture rebelled against just about every existing convention. One of the radical students, Carol Merrill, would visit me and Sharon in the apartment. She would show up in a mini-skirt and no underpants. Dudley, already mentioned, was another radical student, and he would show up about 6:00 PM each day to watch the news to see what had transpired that day around the country and world. I admit, watching the news was addictive. The news was never boring. Dudley had a difficult time attracting the opposite sex when he started school. Why? I didn't know. But that changed. Jen Rollins also lived in Seal Beach. She had excellent looks and an open and gregarious personality. I also felt attracted to her. She ended up having sex with Dudley on the floor of our apartment. This must have been some kind of key therapy for Dudley. After that, Dudley now turned into the unleashed exhibitionist.

In the late sixties, shortly after the beginning of the era of sexual freedom, feminism became a central issue, and that movement continues to affect modern society all the way into the post-modern era. This affected the leadership of the student activist movement, which included Students for a Democratic Society and several other organizations. Personally, I behaved poorly in private with women while publicly encouraging the emerging feminism.

After the assassination of Martin Luther King Jr., there was a huge rally at CSULB on the lawn of a large, grassy mound. Speakers spoke. Sharon was at home in Seal Beach with her son. I saw a young woman, though stout but not in the slightest bit obese, that was very attractive to me. Like Sharon, she had blond hair and blue eyes. I was infatuated. Then I sat down and talked to her. I found out she came from Los Alamitos and was a freshman at CSULB. Her name was Jan Johnson.

A short time later, Sharon and I attended a party in Lakewood, California, hosted by "Blackie" Tomas Blackburn and his wife, Mary Blackburn. Jan knew about the party and also attended. I spent most of the evening talking to her and took her back to the apartment where Sharon and I lived. We talked for several hours, and a lot of passionate kissing and petting took place. I found out she was totally inexperienced with sexual relations. Then Jan went home without having sexual relations with me.

Meanwhile, Sharon spent the night with one of the radical English professors, and showed up in the morning a little ruffled, but ready to carry on. My relationship with Sharon was unstable. From time-to-time, we would have a one-off fling with someone else, and then either forget it or not say anything until sometime later.

Rick Anthony's apartment was a nest of radicalism and epic counter-culture rites. Rick himself, was now going with Steve Averal's sister, and had at least six people living in his apartment. Some rooms were even partitioned with Indian print tapestries. One student who lived there, Terry McGuire, was probably one of the most forward and vocal students in our milieu. So he was impulsive. He would talk first and think later. Then I did something that he would be "on me" as long as a knew him. I had several meetings with Jan, expressed my love and told her I wanted out of the relationship with Sharon. This was a genuine statement, but I waffled back and forth in my mind. Maybe after the second or third meeting with Jan, she had me as her first sexual partner in Terry McGuire's bed at Rick's house. Next, I met her at her mother's house in Los Alamitos when her mother wasn't home.

For some time after this, I believe I made one bad personal decision after another. Jan's family was interesting and when I met her mother, Pat Johnson, we had an immediate affinity for each other. She seemed to ignore all my behavior and focused on my radical world-view. She was a sociology lecturer at Los Angeles State College. We launched into long discussions and arguments on history, society, everything going on around us. I must admit, even though she was at least twenty years my senior, I was attracted to Pat. She was married at the time to Cliff, a very nice, soft-spoken person. He built dulcimers and was a teacher. Jan had a brother, John, a great young blues guitar player, not molded so much by the Chicago electric blues, but by the English blues revolution of the middle- and late-1960s. I believe he had every album that John Mayall released. The entire family fascinated me.

After long discussions with Pat, I came to realize she was old left. She was a friend of Jack Forrest, who taught at El Camino College, and several friends were former members and even current members of the Communist Party of the USA. In reality, Pat's politics, at least with local and national issues, were very much like a left-liberal in the Democratic Party. The difference between her and, let's say, my mother, who knew the Hollywood Ten while involved with the film industry and supported a form of socialism, Pat was insistent on the support of the Soviet Union and a planned economy in the USA. She genuinely supported most of what the radical students were doing at CSULB and in the Long Beach Community. Pat also had a shade of paranoia. For example, she was sure "Blackie" was a government agent. She depicted some popular musicians as government agents, Phil Ochs for example. This bothered me. I believed that living through the anti-communist hysteria of the 1950s had corrupted her perception.

I needed to fish or cut bait. I decided twice in 1968 and 1969 to leave Sharon and have a steady relationship with Jan. But where? I had some friends who had little to do with my radical politics, but were interested solely in either music or art. Murray Bernstein and Zeke both lived in Long Beach, in inexpensive housing on the cusp of the ghetto. Both of them knew people in Seal Beach, including Steve Averal and Johnny Matson. Steve influenced both Murray and Zeke with his vast knowledge and collection of music. Murray, who was struggling with his sexuality, and having a great deal of difficulty with relations with the opposite sex, focused on Jonhny who often presented himself as heterosexual even to the point he was engaged to a student at CSULB named Janet, but was, in fact, bisexual, and later openly gay.

I searched for a place to land in Long Beach with them or near them. Of course, Murray didn't want to discuss the government, the black student union, the Black Panthers, or anything of that ilk. He wanted to discuss sexual relationships and Freudian psychology.

He couldn't understand why I didn't have a psychoanalyst. So, for a short while, I lived at Zeke's and Murray's apartment while I tried to plot my next move. Amid all this, Sharon attempted a half-hearted suicide. In retrospect, Murray and Zeke were good supporters. I high-tailed it back to Seal Beach and continued my tenuous relationship with both Jan and Sharon. At one point, I even proposed a dual relationship between two men and two women. Such an idea appealed to me, since I was in total rebellion against main-stream culture.

Meanwhile, Russell Sheen had now become involved with a married woman in Seal Beach who he had lured away from her husband. Both he and the woman, Joyce Brontson, short in statue but all curves, left for a trip across the country. Russell kept a diary, writing a journal, and ended up in Chicago in 1968 at the Democratic National Convention. He wrote everything he witnessed in Chicago, and was eventually arrested by the Chicago police. There were several passages in his diary detailing the brutality and police murder on the streets. Russell had a history of loathing police. The Chicago police confiscated his diary and threatened to send him to a mental institution.

I continued with my studies, my activism, and my relationship with two women. I was also seeking employment. Pat Jensen moved to an apartment in the San Fernando Valley. She contacted a local alternative private school in the San Fernando Valley. Pat and I visited the school, and it seemed like a decent gig, but where would I finish my schooling? Then the relationship with Jan and Pat transformed into the bizarre. Jan joined me and Pat in her new apartment, and that worked for a short while, but Jan was a student at Long Beach State. Pat wanted me to move in with her to her new apartment. We had never been intimate, though I would be the first one to admit I was very much physically attracted to her. Jan and Pat ended up arguing. In the future, they were not to have a good relationship, and this was the beginning of a repeating behavior pattern. Perhaps Pat was a little tilted, since she took quite a few diet pills. Next, Jan accused her mother of trying to steal "her boyfriend." I freaked and returned to Seal Beach, attempting to reestablish my former relationship with Sharon. As usual, Sharon had been a free agent while I was in the San Fernando Valley. Jan departed the whole affair with seriously hurt feelings and a sense of betrayal. In hindsight, I don't blame her.

I reconciled with Sharon, and continued with that rocky relationship, moving back to Seal Beach on 13th Street. The student revolution continued around us, as we witnessed what was happening at other colleges. I finished an expansive term paper that was overdue, almost 100 pages of typing, called "A Theory of Social History." There was very little original thought in it. It was a re-hash of what I had found in many books. Ideological effect in various Christian churches during different historical periods, like the Social Gospel Movement, was the focus of the paper. I had my revolution on my mind most of the time. I was convinced that the United States society around me would fall like a house of cards in the next few years.

I pressed Sharon, intending to a long-term relationship. We had a verbal agreement that we were to be married. We had her second child. Sharon stopped taking her birth control pills. And Sharon ended up pregnant.

Dudley invited most of the CSULB student council to Rick's house for what turned out to be an all-out orgy. It surprised me that the responsible student council would have an orgy with the radical students in Seal Beach. Dudley started the entire sexual free-for-all by having intercourse with his current girlfriend in the middle of the living room, with us wide-eyed youths watching. Sharon immediately bed Galen, someone with whom she had slept with before. We all followed suit, me included. I copulated with one student council female and sometime later a second council female who was a beautiful oriental and had already consumed an unknown number of males. One homosexual student council male sat naked in the corner of a room and watched the entire thing unfold. No male had gay sex with him. Sharon departed with a local Seal Beach denizen, Ken Angeletti, who was not a student, but knew several radical students, including Galen, with whom he went to high school. Sharon was totally infatuated with him. She was not happy to depart Seal Beach in May 1969 to visit friends in Berkeley and to witness the aftermath of People's Park. A short while later, Sharon headed off to the San Bernardino Mountains, unexpected, with Ken, leaving me alone to take care of her toddler son. Obviously, this really pissed me off and when she returned, and we split up. I departed Seal Beach with my books, and moved to Long Beach, once again living temporarily with Murray and Zeke. I returned to Seal Beach from time to time in the next year to visit friends, but Long Beach was home base mostly, from late 1969 until 1975. By the end of the summer, Sharon gave birth to a baby girl, and put it up for adoption. She had me sign paternal papers before the birth of my child.

Ken was a bad influence. He was a downer freak and a drug dealer that came from a West Coast mafia family. He had a supply of money through family and non-family connections, but often ended up in the Orange County jail for petty crimes. Ken also had a certain charm about him that worked with the opposite sex. My behavior dis-shelved Sharon, but later, Ken was her complete undoing.

REVOLUTION II

• • •

Living in Long Beach redirected my focus. I became less a student and more a member of the community. I moved from a beach community with many students to a lower-middle-class and working-class neighborhood just outside the Afro-American Long Beach ghetto. Now living with Murray and Zeke, I landed a job as a dishwasher at the Kona Hotel along the beachfront. I had a little pocket money and could rent the apartment next door to Murray and Zeke. Borrowing a bike, I could get to work by six in the morning. It disadvantaged me with no car.

During this time, I kept up my correspondence with Gil in the US Army stationed in Vietnam. He wrote several letters, which I published in the Long Beach Free Press, an underground newspaper, under the pen name of "Sarge." I also discovered the Phinius, a local head shop on Anaheim Street. Ran by Mike Sweeny, who allowed no drugs in his shop, and had strong ties to the Afro-American community, because he was married to an African American woman. Bruce Kunkle, once a musician in the Nitty Gritty Dirt Band, ran a music shop next door in the same building.

Davy Crockett and Rick "the sign painter" lived within walking distance of my apartment. I had a new community to which I needed to adjust. Instead of the Seal Beach charm, I now looked over the cityscape of apartment buildings, palm trees, yellow-orange sunsets colored by city smog, and single-engine planes vanishing into the sunset of pollution augmented colors.

Not having many activities when living in this city apartment on Gaviota Street. I continued my activities at the Peace Center on Anaheim Street near Joe Josts's. I would come home from work, no longer smoking a cannabis but drinking a quart of cheap Eastside beer, reading the New York Review of Books, underground comics, and a few remnant textbooks. It was obvious if I didn't get a job in education or with the government, which was just about impossible given my radical background, I would wash dishes or working in some kind of civil service role that would hire me if I could count to ten and breathing. This issue of no genuine job would torture me in one form or another for three years.

It was even more apparent when the dishwasher job at the hotel ended. I should have seen that coming. The whole coast along the City of Long Beach went into an economic tail-spin as the US Navy departed and all the "old money" dissipated. I could get work as an extra with the Teamsters or Longshoreman's Union a few times, but this was a standby move. I also did not want to be yet-another clerical worker in a large business bureaucracy. Being felt trapped and somewhat hopeless. These feelings would increase in intensity as time passed. It was 1969, and I was close to finishing my degree from Long Beach State. I kept up with my studies, and was determined to complete it.

Hanging around the Phinius, I discovered that the owner, Mike, now fostered a collective comprising some fellow radicals from San Diego. Jan Johnson, now returned from a trip to the eastern part of the US, had joined the collective, and lived with a new boyfriend associated with the same collective. I never met the young man, and I don't know who he was.

I ran into Jan at the Phinius, told her where I lived, and she joined me at my apartment. Jan was not a small young woman. Someone once told me Jan reminded them of a "R. Crumb female" in his underground comics. Alternatively, Jan was a "big country girl", "le femme de provence" with all the curves in the right place. She had such a pleasant smile with her blue eyes and true blond hair. Like Sharon, Jan had no trouble attracting males. We had a lengthy conversation. Jan spoke to me straightforwardly. "When I was back east, I met a psychologist, who asked me 'who fucked you over so bad?'" Gulp, of course it was me. Jan continued, "I spent a week with him. We had sex in every room in the house. He likes to do it doggy style. You know, the guy I am living with told me, regarding our previous relationship, that he was glad that John blew it" After this conversation, we once again ended up in a sexual relationship. After the conversations and tryst, Jan returned to the work commune at the Phinius and her current boyfriend. Jan returned the next afternoon, and it was a repeat performance like the day before. Jan returned the day after that, abandoning her current boyfriend, and moved in with me at my Gaviota Street apartment.

* * *

To involve myself with politics in the Long Beach community, I assisted the Black Panthers with their children's breakfast program. It took place in a city park in the ghetto area. There was hot food on the portable burners, with the most of the food going to children. Initially, some of them probably thought, "what is the white dude doing at a Black Panther breakfast program?". It was easy to fit in since I already had several contacts in the African American community. While in the park, I would help serve and cook and clean up.

Jan and I now were two radical students working in the community for what we thought to be a new revolution in the USA. Several People visited us in the Gaviota Street apartment. They sent Larry Teeter as an organizer from the Communist Party USA. He didn't have the subtlety or talent of Tom Foley and did not jell well with the radicals in the Long Beach Community. He was a nervous little fellow that played a mean game of chess and giggled a lot. I remember him mockingly singing the Beatles Revolution, "... free your mind instead". Shortly after Jan and I established our residence, Bruce Kunkle broke up with his wife and needed a place to stay. Bruce built a little bed area in the front room out of scrap wood. Soon after Bruce moved in, John Johnsen spent a lot of time at our apartment. John was an excellent electric blues guitar player, and Bruce was a semi-professional musician who still played a gig here and there in Long Beach. I carefully observed how John Johnson would play his bluesy arpeggios on his guitar. This is where I got my knowledge of blues guitar playing.

During my initial period of stay in Long Beach, the FBI visited my father's house in Brentwood. Later, he told me the FBI had a long rap sheet on me. I don't know what was in that file, but by now, they certainly didn't want me in the military. To his day, I have never had to apply for a government job. It would be interesting to know what they could dig up. Maybe some of this had to do with me and Jan taking part in a Weather Underground demonstration at McArthur Park, downtown Los Angeles, led by none other than Mark Rudd, the once famous radical. Instead of making obscene gestures at the Feds, I just stuck my tongue out at them and wiggled my fingers. Jan thought this was hilarious.

Daily life was smooth at the apartment on Gaviota Street, but we soon got word of a group of students renting a large two-story house on Mahanna Street, perpendicular to Anaheim Street, about three blocks to the west of where we lived.

I became close friends with Ginny Miles and Jean Lander. I had met Ginny several months before at community meetings at the Peace Center on Anaheim Street. She was a student at Long Beach State, but was pregnant and unwed. Gene, also a student at Long Beach State, a psychology major, supported her emotionally and physically. In particular, he also thought her newly born child, Maia, needed a father figure. Jean and Ginny involved with the International Socialists, IS, a group formed in Europe and the United States. Inspired by Hal Draper, and what was as "Third Camp" socialism, with the emphasis on workers' control from "below" instead of top down. It intrigued both Jan and me with the fresh theories that were not formulas of the Communist Party USA or emerging groups based on the theories of Chairman Mao. In the

Long Beach Community, "the movement" was dividing into various sects and factions.

The radical students at Long Beach State mounted a unified campaign to nominate Jerry Harris, an SDS leader, as student body president. In a close election, and with a monumental turn-out in numbers, Jerry came very close to winning. This is another piece of college history that has vanished in an obscure tray of micro-fiche.

Jan and I gave up the apartment on Gaviota Street and moved into what amounted to a student commune on Mahanna Street. Pat Johnson, Jan's mother, the same woman who attempted to get me to move to the San Fernando Valley with her, visited the Mahana Street student commune. In her serious manner she told us "you two should really get married". She pressured Jan and me into marriage. This was yet another poor decision on my part. I had no job, only a few units to complete, gaining a bachelor's degree that would lead to no job I could stand or qualify for. Against our better judgment, we made plans to get married at the end of the year, 1970.

The student commune worked as well as expected for about nine months. It was a huge two-story house with six bedrooms. Ginny and Jean moved in and had a bedroom on the first floor with her infant daughter, Maia. Russell Sheen and Joyce Bronson also moved into a second bedroom on the first floor. Jan and I took the west-most room on the second floor. A very nice, obese young woman named Hannah took one room down the hall. Also down the hall a young woman, an elementary school teacher, who stayed with the commune for a few months. All the way down the hall were some interesting science fiction fans, but they departed shortly after Jan and I moved in.

In some ways, this student commune was the high point in my senior year. Phil Watson, another student turned community organizer, showed up regularly. We had shared meals and spread expenses among all the participants. Many of the meals I would consider unhealthy and even gross these days, but they fed the crowd. I cooked pasta and then burritos with re-fried beans cooked in bacon grease. Davy Crockett showed up regularly. Many other students and community members would appear from time to time. For those few months, it was a beehive of combined student and community activity. And the participants, myself included, enjoyed it.

Jan and I planned to marry around the end of the year. As expected, Pat Johnson would show up from time to time and suggested that we marry in the First Unitarian Church in central Los Angeles. Pat remarked, "I can invite all my friends." I got it. Looking back on Liberal Unitarian Youth, the church was the choice of left-leaning intellectuals. Several of Jan's frustrations and resentments fermented below the surface. She was not that happy with what she was doing and where she was going. Jan would pick up her beautiful handcrafted guitar that her father made from scratch and sing "Can't Find My Way Home", by Blind Faith, to me. "Come down off your throne and leave our body alone, somebody must change". We continued an attempt at a working relationship.

Before married, I finished my bachelor's degree in history. I continued to get work as an extra through the Teamsters Union. I realized that in the real world; It was at a dead end. Russell Sheen would often join me in the lineup at the Teamsters Hall. Once we both got a job unloading freight from a vessel. We had to hitchhike home, and the police pulled our ride over. We helped the driver consume all his illegal drugs, mostly downers. By the time we returned to the Mahanna House, we were so stoned that we could hardly walk. I went upstairs and attempted to sleep it off. While sleeping, a large community meeting was underway. Eventually, I joined the meeting, very groggy, but had little to say. Jan asked me, "what happened at the docks?" "We hitchhiked home and our ride got pulled over by the police, and we helped him eat his downers, so he wouldn't get busted."

There were a series of incidents that I didn't know about until months later. John Jensen, though a great blues guitar player, had started on heroin. Of course, this quickly caught up with him, and he ended up in rehabilitation. He swore he had come clean and was not using. In retrospect, I believe this was an accurate statement. What no one knew at the time was that Russell Sheen was taking heroin. I didn't discover his secret vice until months after the fact. Sadly, John Johnson was blamed for something he didn't do by his peers. One night, Russel and I were walking to a liquor store close to Mahanna Street on Anaheim Boulevard. The police pulled us over and quickly started frisking Russell. They claimed he had swallowed a balloon of an unknown substance. Once again, Russell fought arrest and handcuffed, then taken away in the patrol car. I considered it pure harassment. The Mahanna House went into a panic, including his pregnant girlfriend, Joyce. We got Russell out on bail. In hindsight, he probably had a balloon full of smack. Here was a basic lesson I was to learn in the next few years. When I first moved to the core City of Long Beach, I considered it a core blue-collar community. In reality, it was a collection of the most repressed groups in the society riddled with drug use, crime, and a lack of community values. The Black Panthers and associates were the best leaders of this community. Maybe it was the youth that would attract the most degenerate elements in this disintegrating naval town.

Jan became particularly frustrated with the remaining radical student leaders at Long Beach State. She was rapidly turning into a feminist, and considered the college student movement dominated by self-serving males. To make matters worse, Rick and my associate Terry, when they got wind of me forging a marriage with Jan, the two were in total opposition. Years later, Rick admitted and apologized for helping torpedo my marriage. Before the wedding, not Rick, but Terry visited Jan's mother, Pat, in Los Cerritos. Words were spoken and Terry told Pat to "buzz off, bitch." Cliff, Pat's husband, threw Terry out of the house after Pat and Terry almost came to physical blows. Hmmm... what a solid ground on which to build a marriage.

That winter, Jan and I were married in the First Unitarian Church of Los Angeles, as Pat had desired. It was a windy and cold day when I took that ride to the church. Russell was my best man. All of Jan's friends from Cerritos High School were attending, including her best friend in high school, Toby. Now Toby had a sister, Nina, who also turned up from time to time at the Mahanna house. Both she and Toby were Jewish in tradition and culture. Nina was a beautiful, dark-haired woman, but spoke with a slight speech impediment.

We had a wedding reception at Pat's house. It was about an eclectic, a collection of people that you could imagine in the 1969 time frame. My stepmother and father were there at the reception, along with many of my friends, sans those that had issues with me getting married to Jan, along with a mix of Black community organizers and students from Long Beach State. Despite the clash of cultures and inevitable disagreements, it was a good reception. John Jensen put a blues band together that rocked everyone's socks off, particularly those who liked electric blues. I consumed a large quantity of wine and fell asleep. The next morning I woke up, shook off the cobwebs with a slight hangover, and could use Cliff's Volkswagen Bus to drive myself and Jan to Idyllwild, a resort area in the San Jacinto Mountains, where friends of Pat's and Cliff's family owned a cabin. We mostly talked for a day about our families, and how Scientology converted the owner of the cabin's daughter. I asked Jan, "how did her mother, an old left red, deal with her Scientologist daughter?" "Oh, she never questioned or talk to her about it, you know." In retrospect, I was completely adrift. I had no job, was about to get this youthful woman pregnant. The pregnancy ended up as a miscarriage, which, although devastating, was a blessing disguised. We were not prepared to be a parent.

We returned to the Mahanna house with all our presents. The most important was a car presented to me by my father as a wedding/graduation present. It was a low-mileage Volkswagen Bug that would be my transportation until 1976. Rick and Terry sent the stain on Terrie's bed, where Jan and I first slept together. Another torpedo in my marriage. It really pissed Jan off, and she would have nothing to do with the two student activists or anyone who ran in that circle of friends.

After the science fiction fans moved out, a divorced mother who worked at a bank in Long Beach moved in. Her name was Jill. She tolerated our student ways, showing up for work each day and then returning to our student commune. She was very hip, but easily corrupted by the underclass culture that existed in the Long Beach ghetto. Barry Goldstein was another regular visitor to the Mahanna house. He had already graduated from college, and was working for the County of Los Angeles doing data processing. This seemed very far away to me, but indirectly, his influence on myself and Ginny as a software worker would be a life-changing event. Barry was another organizer of our Third Camp socialist group.

Bruce Kunkle had given up his music shop business, and that part of the Phinius was now empty. Gene Lander and Ginny Miles made a proposition to use the space now vacated to house a book store. Gene contacted the book distributors and could raise the money to get the store off the ground. Many of us in the Mahanna house helped build the bookstore. We painted the floors, put together the shelves, sorted and cataloged the inventory, and put together working shifts. The name of the bookstore was the "New American Bookstore." The transactions were brisk, and the bookstore was a success.

The owner of the Phinius who had leased the entire building complex made a bold move. He decided that the decisions be handled democratically by those who worked in the collective. The decision was on the direction of what was to become of the community center. This collective would decide the direction of the community center. It turned out that two individuals whose name I don't remember decided that New American Bookstore was run by "Trotskyite counterrevolutionaries." In some senses, they were not lying. Third Camp socialism, as a body of theory, referenced several works by Trotsky, starting with Hal Draper, but were also critical of Trotsky. The genuine conflict originated with the rejection of Stalin as a revolutionary leader. Hard line followers of Mao Tse Tung considered this reactionary, therefore racist, therefore fascist.

The New American Bookstore had to move into a less expensive, hard-core area on Anaheim Street. Those of us at the Mahanna house running the store tried to make it work, but without the draw of the Phinius, we had a doomed bookstore. These events mirrored what was happening nationally. The student movement was shattering into sects and factions. The most consistent opinions came from the Afro-American community. They were well justified in not trusting non-Afro campus- and community-based radicals. Now what did the old-Left that was associated with the traditional Communist Party of the US do when confronted with a fragmenting student movement? Their answer was to work and organize in the Democratic Party as a "left tendency." From my viewpoint, this might not have been such a bad idea, as long as that was not the only activity your activists were undertaking. I could not stomach the uncritical support of the Soviet Union from the Communist Party USA.

While we tried to make the bookstore work in the new location, just a few doors down was a bar that was a front for an upstairs brothel. It was a micro-melting pot. The bar, populated by middle class white students, workers from a shrinking blue-color segment, and the truly under-classed, whom I would designate as the lumpen-proletariat. Hookers that worked in the bar made friends with Mahanna house residents. Specifically, an artist and his girlfriend befriended Jill. They were both junkies, and ended up being the people in the house involved in one of the most addictive drugs on the planet, "smack" or heroin. While several of us thought we were associating with the genuine community of Long Beach, we were actually getting a potent dose of lumpen culture that was "lost humanity".

While in my senior year, another incident took place at Long Beach State. Two sociology professors, Robertson and Steele, ran a class that addressed current culture. They co-authored a book entitled the Halls of Yearning. In their class, they addressed one forbidden topic after another. What took the campus by storm was a display of pornographic films as part of the curriculum. They introduced other unusual approaches. They would both show up for the lecture with Afro hairdos. Jan was more impressed with their class than I was. But in hindsight, I could see a transition from the 1960s into the 1970s. What was once iconoclastic was now becoming the norm in many social subcultures. I had a difficult time establishing a rapport with the students who originated after this transition. I had the feeling of being tied to a previous era.

The emergent feminist movement of the late sixties continued to gain momentum in most facets of urban society, except for those dominated by hard-core cultural conservatives. Women assumed social and economic roles that were traditionally thought of as male jobs. This caused confusion in several progressive males. I became confused how to support the burgeoning feminist movement. I didn't really understand what a "feminist male" was. "What is a feminist male?" I asked Jan. "It is a male that supports our movement." "Yes, but..." Was this new role necessary? Can't we just be equal, considering what both males and females are capable of? "Jan told me that questioning the feminist movement puts us on the defensive".

Jan, Gene, Ginny, Barry, Dave Crockett, and others continued to hold meetings of Third Camp socialists at the Mahanna house along with fellow activists. In a single apartment behind the house, lived John Germanicus. He was an intense fellow that had a child with a woman who I never really got to know, but he had married her on his psychotherapist's advice and had a baby. He was also a radical student at Long Beach State and had not "come out." His wife would complain that he would go for a walk and vanish for hours. He later came out and established that he was gay. What was the shrink who convinced to him to marry and have a baby thinking?

There were others that flowed through the Mahanna house that were not students, but young people trying to stand on their own in a transforming world. They were certainly part of the counter-culture, but not students. Gordon, a stout fellow with broad-rimmed glasses and a cheerful personality, and Wayne who would end accompanying me to Fresno, was a self-confident person in his own way, tall, about my height, always seemed to know what to do next. During these activities, I met a Vietnam vet, Van, who lived across the street from the Mahanna house. Actually, Gordon introduced me to Van. Even though this was a sleazy neighborhood, Van drove this fancy SAAB sports-car, and in his apartment he had the very latest stereo sound system. He also had copious amounts of cannabis. I hung out with Van from time to time. Jan thought little of him. Perhaps she considered him a charlatan, much too full of himself. In Vietnam, he was an officer, a lieutenant in the US Army, and portrayed the role. While in Vietnam, he made a pile of money running contraband. I never asked what the contraband was, but he told me he was headed to Fresno to buy a house in the burbs and study art. And later on, that is exactly what he did. He seemed amused by the radicals across the street. He tolerated us, but didn't really take us seriously.

One night, the people who were home at the time had an orgy. Hannah, who was obese but an amiable person, had become friends with Jan. They were close. When all this unfolded, Jan told me that Hanna had never had intercourse, and asked if I would be her first sex partner. I agreed and had intercourse with Hannah. It was not the most pleasant experience, and afterward I had some mixed feelings mixed with a bottle of Southern Comfort. Jan tried to have a same-sex experience with a woman named Suzanne, also very nice and who, later, who would find a steady boyfriend. Jan and Suzanne ended up sitting at the end of the hall talking. Gene and Ginny Miles were not at home, as well as Joyce, who by now was several months pregnant. But Russell Sheen, and Jill ended up having sex on the floor next to the bed where Hannah and I were copulating. Later, when Joyce discovered this tryst that had taken place while she was away, she was totally pissed and then some. The first thing she did was a sexual hook-up with Bruce Kunkle. It was Russell's turn to become incensed. He caught Bruce on the balcony of the second story of someone's house in the Anaheim Street area and tried to push him off. This all became history as both Russell and Joyce moved out. Joyce spent her time with Bruce and John Johnsen. Years later, I read a story about a New York Met baseball pitcher who married a strip club performer. Her quote was, "If I ever find out that he, the pitcher, cheated on me, I'm going to do the entire team, starting with the ball-boy." This was Joyce's attitude and did she ever follow through.

The Mahanna house was losing its focus. Ginny Miles and Gene were talking about moving to Berkeley, which they did. I heard from John Johnson that Jan was not happy with her marriage; this must have been true because at one point she told me she wanted to spend the night with one leader of the Third Camp movement as a new boyfriend. I did not take it well. I argued with her, and she told me, "You have shared me before with my previous boyfriend." Then I misbehaved. I gave her several swats across the ass. Jan moved to an annex of one of her mother's friends. I tried to make amends with her, but to no avail. I moved out of the Mahanna house into a bachelor apartment that was previously occupied by Phil Watson, a brother of one of the Long Beach State student leaders that ended up helping to establish Peace Press, in Venice, California, Steve Watson.

Jan and I partook in one more activity together. We took a trip to visit another Cal State Long Beach student, Galen Parker, who was living in the Laguna Hills. I don't remember exactly how the connection occurred, possibly at my suggestion, but Russell contacted my former steady girlfriend from when I was a freshman, Ann. Russel brought her to Galen's house in the Laguna Hills. It was a tense gathering, with Jan in the kitchen delivering her homily on feminism and feminist politics.

I slept with Jan, but we did not touch each other. Russell slept with Ann. The next day, Ann told me, "Your wife is angry." This was a correct statement. It was an amorphous collection of people in Galen's rented house in the rural Laguna Hills. We all returned to the Mahanna house with mixed emotions. I now slept on a bed in the rear screened in storage room. I took any job I could, delivering papers, selling subscriptions to the Los Angeles Times over the phone for minimum wage. That was a real shit job. I realized that given the skills I had, it was going to be very difficult to find a job that wasn't minimum wage. As a result, I ended up in a general state of depression, along with everything else I was dealing with. My family on both sides didn't understand why my marriage was disintegrating. I was an outlaw because of my uncompromising opposition to the Vietnam conflict and what I now viewed USA-sian Empire battling various forces around the planet, those revolutionaries, or as a competing empire like the Soviet Union, which seemed to have some institutions in place to assist their populace under a dictatorship.

For a brief time, Jan and I both moved back into the Mahanna house. She slept under the stairs until she could find an apartment. I continued to sleep in the storage room. We rarely slept together. I withdrew and turned silent. Deciding to read a copy of The Lord of the Rings that I borrowed from Rick Anthony, attempted to recover. I was close to just wandering in my mental wilderness. Not knowing how to put any of the life's pieces together. I loaned Jan and her new boyfriend my car to travel to Detroit to attend a national conference of the Third Camp socialists. At that point, I gave up on the relationship, and try to be her ally and friend. While the two were in Detroit, I wandered from friend's house to friend's house, basically homeless but with a roof over my head, thanks to Gil, Rick, and others.

For the immediate time, I struck up a relationship with Nina, the sister of Jan's best friend in high-school. She loved female-oriented movies and had a sophistication about her. She liked to talk about her previous relationships, like people in Seal Beach, including her high school boyfriend or an Afro-American jazz musician in Chicago. We had long conversations about human relationships. This was a pure juxtaposition against my concerns about political economy. I didn't have money to take her to the movies or to buy her dinner, so it didn't take her long to figure out that I was a draft fugitive and so poor I didn't have a pot to pee in. The relationship didn't last long. "I'm moving to Berkeley," was the last thing she said to me.

Gordon found an inexpensive apartment near Anaheim Street. I moved into the closet. By now, I stored all my 33 RPM records and books at my mother's house. I was a man who could live anywhere. A homeless person with a temporary home. Sometimes Wayne would come over and we would drink really shitty wine, try a short dog of Pagan Pink. We had conversations about the war and about how there was now work and some of the more popular aspects of Third Wave Socialism. It was fun because, from these guys, it was from the gut. Ideological baggage didn't exist.

Joyce made her rounds, including a visit to Gordon's apartment. Joyce told me about Bruce and John Johnson. She told me Bruce was studying the same sequence of British Blues artists that John had emulated. She also told me that Bruce, John, and the health food store on Tenth Street, The Umbilical Cord, were moving to Fresno. Curiously, the former neighbor across the street at the Mahanna House, Van, was also moving to Fresno. Jan returned from a Third Camp Socialist convention in Detroit with her current boyfriend. All I wanted was my car. Jan made a few off-center comments about my affair with Nina, which I ignored. I was happy I had wheels again.

Everyone was moving. I helped Gene and Ginny move to Oakland. It was at the center of activity for the Third Camp Socialists on the West Coast, which is no surprise. I stayed with Gene and Ginny for a couple of days, visited Berkeley, attended a meeting of the Third Camp Socialists, and then I returned to Gordon's apartment. After that, Gordon, Wayne, and I drove to Fresno, with an interesting stop at Ann's, my girlfriend who you met in Puberty II, at her rented house in Topanga Canyon. Ann wasn't home, but we had an interesting conversation with her roommates. Loading a rocking chair, clothes, and the few books that I had with me, and headed north on highway 99. I intended to meet Gene and Ginny in Oakland. I never made it to Oakland. It would be over a year before I would see Ginny again.

I stopped at the Ohmbilical Cord health food store. For what took place that summer, there must have been some kind of conjunction of stars. Gordon, Wayne, Bruce Kunkle, John Jensen, and Joyce, now obviously pregnant, were living there. There also were several people there I didn't know. The Ohmbilical Cord was a commune of Long Beach refugees, a few students from Fresno State College and Fresno locals. I felt it was my duty to work for the Ohmbilical Cord commune. After all, I was eating their food. My other source of income came from a Shell credit card. I believe the card was a gift sent to me after I graduated from Long Beach State. I would use the card and offer it to anyone else that would give me cash to buy petrol. Later, my father was really pissed when he paid off the bill. I'm not sure how the company made that connection. Maybe it was on the original application.

The weather in Fresno during the summer of 1969 was brutal. The two months I was in that vicinity, it was often over one hundred degrees Fahrenheit for two weeks in a row. I worked early mornings and late evenings on the Ohmbilical Cord's small farm. The tasks comprised drying peaches, apricots, and figs in the blistering heat, producing great dried fruit without preservatives. I did not know it, but I was witnessing the initiation of organic food production in central California.

Mark Gold lived for a short time with Animal in Seal Beach when LSD appeared initially at Long Beach State. He lived in Seal Beach for years. Four of us—him, me, a sociology major, and Russell—used to stay up to the wee hours of the morning rapping. Mark would argue "you explain human behavior by the interaction of symbols" and I would argue "the physics of the real world we live in limit human behavior". In retrospect, we were both correct. He also was a good friend of Stonys. I must admit, both Mark and Stony could always hustle up work, something I would almost always fail doing. Mark showed up at the Ohmbilical Cord and we reconnected. We went to some waterfalls near the road to Yosemite, highway 41. Myself, Mark and a girlfriend frolicked in the blazing sun and water. Mark had a special talent for attracting the opposite sex. We went to his girlfriend's house and drank wine, smoked some cannabis, and listened to Goodbye Cream, a high-energy rock blues album. Even at 10:00 PM that evening, the heat was sweltering.

I found a spot in the barn area to keep my rocking chair. It was one of the few rooms with a few pieces of other furniture. During the noon hours, I would rock and read Frank Herbert's science fiction classic, Dune, in one-hundred-degree-Fahrenheit-plus weather. Perfect. The work impressed me. Subsequent novels by Frank Herbert did not. Van showed up at the Ohmbilical Cord and he took me, Gordon, and Wayne over to his new house he had just purchased in the 'burbs north of Fresno. He introduced us to his current female companion, a hot divorcee from New Port Beach. We returned to Van's house a few times, once for a party where we were drinking homemade sangria in a hollowed-out watermelon. Not an unpleasant drink in one hundred degree weather. He told us about his admittance to Fresno State College and his plans to study art. Van was a vet who had really set himself up. Of course, some of it had to do with all the money he had from his time in Vietnam.

Joyce, who floated between me, Bruce Kunkle, and John Johnson, completely outdid herself one day about ten in the morning. She walked outside where several of us were working and announced, "I'm horny." This now very-pregnant woman copulated with any available male that was willing interrupting their work for the Ohmbilical Cord farm. This display put Gordon off. I must admit, I thought the behavior was over the top. After that, she was much more subdued. Surprisingly, my old high school girlfriend, who I hadn't seen since she spent the night with Russell at Galen's house in the Laguna Beach hills near Trebuco Canyon, arrived at the Ohmbilical Cord. Ann was driving up the coast with her girlfriend, who had a babe in arms. Her car, also a VW Bug, had broken down in Fresno. I have forgotten how Ann found the Ohmbilical Cord, but she found it, and there she was. So we reconnected once again. It was too hot to sleep inside, so we found an empty portion of the garden to lie out sleeping bags as ground cover and stayed until morning and the heat and light drove us indoors. I explained to Bruce, Joyce and Ann what I thought was going on regarding society, the planet, the government. Burce told me "John, you should really teach this to people." I didn't know how to react, but I kept it in mind. Ann and I, along with Wayne and a local Fresno young woman, Alice, spent an afternoon basking in the sun and enjoying the Kings River and the temporary coolness it provided. Alice was another sexually active young woman, not to the extent that Joyce was, but I was not sure whether she was available or engaged with a boyfriend. At one point Alice invited me down to the river, but at the time I'd had enough experiential overload. Ann kept on humming a Neil Young song, "Down by the river, I shot my baby." After the VW was fixed and Ann drove off, not before I knew how to get in contact with her where she was living in Topanga Canyon. Ann met Bruce Kunckle and John Johnson and listened to some of their music. She did not seem as impressed as I was. But maybe she was saturated with guitar players by this point. I wasn't. I remember a beautiful jam that I copied later when playing with the Fabulous Baxters. "Heatwave" was the jam song. This jam took place when Bruce and John drove to a house in the middle of different farm to jam with local some musicians.

Evan was another participant in the Ohmbilical Cord commune. He also was a student at Fresno State College. He had a creative idea ahead of its time. This idea was a greenhouse that you could build on the top of any structure, including urban apartments that would feed a family of four year-round, vegetarian of course. Evan explained his ideas to all of us living and working at the Ohmbilical Cord. They did not receive his ideas as they should have. It may have been his style in presenting his plan. People didn't deem it practical, or they just dismissed it outright. I must admit that I thought this was a very interesting idea, but was skeptical of it ever being implemented on a mass scale. Bruce Kunkle had nothing to do with Evan's plan. Bruce was very much into the worldview of Wilhelm Reich, so for him, there was a disconnect with farming. Everything people did, Bruce would interpret their actions using a phrase he had read in one of Reich's books.

Gordon disappeared for a few days, saying he didn't like what was unfolding at the Ohmbilical Cord. "What is bothering you, Gordon?" "I don't like the way Joyce is behaving and given what is going on. I don't feel comfortable at the commune. I like Evan's ideas for food production. People should pay attention to them." "But Gordon, he comes off like a preacher and it turns people off." Some of the original founders of the Ohmbilical Cord, when they returned to the farm, cited several issues that bothered them. Maybe some of those living at the commune didn't pull their weight. I was happy to work on a small farm in Fresno that was part of a new commodity production, organic food. When Gordon returned, he told me he had found a new commune in the Sierra foothills where we could both stay. Next, we traveled up Highway 91 and then took Highway 200 into North Fork. It was hot, but not as hot as the valley.

We arrived at a single cabin that was populated by several what I could only describe as classic 1960s hippies. The leader, if there really was one, was a young guy about my age named David. His girlfriend, a woman much older than him, also seemed to hold this commune together. After talking to her, it turns out that she met and knew Woodie Guthrie, or that is what she said. This rural commune interested me, so instead of worrying about being hunted by the government, or looking for work, I hung out with these folks who all had issues just like I did.

One woman attracted me, a full-bodied woman named Nadie. She had divorced her husband and was here with the rest of the "Bozos on the bus". In hindsight, she resembled my former and future wife, a nice full-bodied country girl that had smarts. I never established a relationship with her, but we discussed several personal items. She told me about her former marriage. I told her about mine. I explained I had graduated from Long Beach State and was now dealing with perdition. "John, I have friends at Fresno State College. College isn't for me. I want to be here in the country where I won't have to deal with city life." It was excellent therapy.

All of us slept in a single, large wooden cabin with a kitchen next to the sole wooden room. The kitchen had a wood-burning stove, so this was primitive living. Daddy-Long-Legs insects would come out at night. You could see them on the ceiling. No one bothered them since they devoured other insects. The people that drifted in and out during the day, all had different stories. One young woman who always showed up with a dress but no underpants had hepatitis. I never learned the outcome of her condition. There was almost no sexuality in this hippie commune.

I met David number two, who had gotten into trouble in the San Francisco Bay Area for stealing bicycles. Like with Nadie, we had long conversations, mostly about abstract good and evil. "David, what do you think is going on in the Soviet Union, Vietnam,... the United States?" "What exists in the Soviet Union isn't communism. What we have here on our mountain is communism. The cities are evil. They will suck you in." Ironically, the only book I had with me at the time was Luis Mumford's The City in History. What a juxtaposition to a hippie commune. It took me a while to catch on, but several sixties refugees were under the potent influence of a Seventh Day Adventist woman who I never met. Some of them talked about the "mark of the beast," and several perceptions that would resemble what I would observe as "New-Age" folk. The mystical movement of the cows in the pasture, the signs seen in the sunrise, and so forth. The one theme that bound them was the aversion to the evil city and the importance of remaining in the countryside living a primitive existence. Well, I found this amusing, tolerated these odd perceptions as I continued to read my book or play music on a funky guitar with the bass string missing. I attempted to emulate some of the great blues licks that Bruce Kunkle and John Johnson played while listening to them at the Ohmbilical Cord commune. All the while, I was trying to figure out what the bleep to do next in life's mystery.

Towards the end of summer, David, number two, and I returned to Seal Beach to help Rick Anthony paint Stony's house. Rick had a way to get people to do things. He convinced David to pass out New Left leaflets on campus. Both David and I ended up sleeping on the roof of Sharon's and Kenny's railroad car apartment, the very apartment that I used to live in. I didn't care. I had no home, only temporary places to land. The result of the visit was I introduced Sharon and Kenny to the hippie commune in the Sierra foothills.

It was a beautiful mid-summer in Seal Beach. David and I would walk the boardwalk, and from time-to-time talk to the sunbathing young women. Back in the Sierra foothills commune, it was common for the young women to be butt-naked, but on the boardwalk they

131

wore tiny bikinis. David complained that the young women on the boardwalk excited him since they were clothed. Hm, it seemed about the same to me. The view across Seal Beach Bay into Long Beach harbor mirrored the cover of the science fiction novel, with the orange-red of light smog extruding buildings through the sunset.

Rick Anthony connected with an old friend of his, Bill Bevins, who was graduating from the University of Southern California with a degree in pharmacology. His project centered on the properties of cocaine. Bill, David, Rick, and I hiked into the Kings River Valley in the Sierra foothills. We drove from Seal Beach to Fresno and into the Kings River area where we hiked from the last road and camp parking near the north fork of the Kings River Valley. Because of a supply of one hundred percent-pure cocaine Bill had on his person originating from his pharmacology thesis, our journey time was super compressed. The coke affected us like an upper. During the journey, which I will never forget, we passed high mountain meadows, streams, and climbed above the timberline. Our supply of food was sparse. En route to the timberline, we encountered a Boy Scout troop that had exited from the valley of the north fork of the Kings River. Their story of killing 30 rattle snakes was a warning that we had to take a great deal of care in the valley when we reached our destination. Arriving at the ridge overlooking the valley was a sight to behold. We could see the waterfalls. David, who had once been there during the spring thaw, described the rush of water from the Kings River.

After another dose of Bill's pharm cocaine, we descended the switchbacks into the valley, descending five thousand feet in one afternoon. My shoes wore out and had a hole in the bottom. I completed this long excursion with a degenerate pair of shoes. We set camp near the clear, flowing river. On the way through the meadows, there were many streams of wild watercress. I collected it and ate it. We had little food, so not only was this one beautiful excursion, it was a study in basic survival. Once setting camp, we needed food. The obvious catch was trout, but how to catch the trout without dealing with the rattlesnakes? We would literally walk upstream, in the stream, look for a small waterfall, and try our luck at dry and wet fly trout fishing. While in the valley those few days, we could catch enough trout to eat. Along with native legumes and watercress, we had enough food to survive. Towards the end of the stay in the valley, we encountered rattlesnakes in the river and killed one. After skinning into the pot, it went dead and skinned. When the water came to a boil, it tried to wiggle out of pure muscle reflexes. So that is my one experience with rattlesnake stew.

To ascend, Bill gave us each a dose of cocaine and we continued up five thousand feet in one morning. By noon, we were back in the high meadows where wild watercress grew, but we were all starving. As a side note, I still love watercress to this day. On the way back to the car, we found what looked like a ranger's cabin. We actually broke into it and stole only food. We were starving. It might have been something like processed cheese in a can and some other protein. We re-locked the cabin and continued on to the car. Bill drove us to his parents' house, where I believe with clean clothes, or at least clothes that went through the wash, and a thorough shower cleaning, I was presentable but not new shoes. I purchased new shoes, departed Fresno after the Ohmbilical Cord, more or less folded, but as far as I could find out, the founders were doing fine with several new organic farming ventures. Organic farming was in its nascent stages, later to be a huge basic agriculture enterprise.

* * *

Being in a state of anomie, I retreated into what I knew as opposed to what I didn't know, even though it made little economic sense. I decided to re-enroll as a graduate student in the history department. Rick connected with me to find a place to live in Long Beach with his friend, Don DeLew. Don was an artist and had just opened an art gallery called the Volt Gallery, located just west of Long Beach Boulevard. The gallery contained the art of local Long Beach artists, mostly from Long Beach State.

So I moved into a small front bedroom and lasted about a month in graduate school. But, I could not re-connect myself to serious intellectual endeavor. I spent most of my time playing a cheap guitar with an amplifier that I borrowed from Stony. I attended a few classes as a graduate history major, often drunk on wine. Disappearing, I never returned to class. From time to time I visited Rick in Seal Beach, and talked to a sun-bathing blond who lived in Huntington Beach on the Seal Beach boardwalk, Gracie. I saw her a few times on the boardwalk and discovered she was a student at Long Beach State. I had one date with Gracie.

One day while bending the blues in my bedroom in the front of Don DeLew's classic Long Beach domicile on fourth street, a neighbor walked in, none other than Bill Spater, the artist whose "pornographic" art caused the demonstrations at Long Beach State, the same demonstration where I was arrested for disturbing the

The poster reads: May Day
Brotherhood Stomp and Sliced Bananas; Turnquist Remedy,
Of the People and Bill Spater and the Fabulous Baxters, Phinius,
sponsored by your local heroes of SDS

peace. I knew about his band, the Fabulous Baxters, which had played at one benefit put on by the radical students. He asked me to join the band as a second guitar player.

I walked over to Bill's house, and we talked mostly blues and old rock-and-roll. I met his longtime girlfriend, an amiable lady. Bill has been through a lot and has abandoned art after they confiscated his master thesis. His interest was now in music, specifically electric blues. Bill picked me up, and we drove to an upstairs flat near the corner of Santa Monica Boulevard and Western Avenue in Hollywood. It was an artist's flat and the drummer of the Fabulous Baxters was the resident. He was an excellent drummer who played the traps. His claim to fame was he was the drummer on "Do You Love Me?" in the band, the Contours on Gordy Records. So we had three electric guitar players in the band, a singer that did not sing loud enough, and a bass player that struggled to keep up with the drummer.

Right around the corner from the drummer's flat was one of the last really true Italian pizza parlors, Dominicos. Dominicos made the best New York style thin crust pizza I ever tasted on the west coast. After being re-acquainted at the Ohmbilical Cord, I reconnected with Ann. I went to her house in Topanga Canyon, on Tiger Trail Road. We exchanged stories. She told me she had become estranged from our friend, Kayla Marsden. She had lived with her for a time in Topanga Canyon and had withdrawn into herself. Ann told me Kayla did not get along with any of her roommates. I made a return to her mother's house in Woodland Hills. Her mother, still a successful child psychologist, had a poster on the wall of her dining room. It had two words on it, "Peace, Power." The experience was bittersweet and tense from my point of view. I knew that this was a temporary relationship, but with Ann it worked for short time. I no longer had anything to offer this young woman, except a past teenage love and a failed romantic image.

The art work in Don DeLew's house amused Ann. Likewise, the strange sequencing of the rooms with removed walls and ceilings. Ann persisted in her avant-garde behavior with her unshaven legs and a long dress with no underwear. She would often make jokes about herself, "as a floozy." I can't deny this. By now, we had both had a long history of short-term and long-term lovers. Ann asked me about literature on the Vietnam War. I gave her two books written from a radical viewpoint and two books published by the Vietnamese government projecting their view of the war. Ann was indifferent to my radical world-view, so I didn't focus on it. I introduced her to Rick Anthony, then Ann and Rick had a friendly conversation about the environment. In a moment of protest, Ann told Rick," I see what is happening to the land in Topanga Canyon and the San Fernando Valley. It makes me angry. I don't know what to do about it". Rick responded, "organize!". By now, I think Rick was tiring of me towing my latest girlfriend to his flat. The last time I saw Ann was at Don DeLew's house, though our paths would cross one more time in the nineteen seventies. She had visited me in Long Beach, and spent the night together twice.

Don had completely opened up the attic of this older house and turned it into a loft. To gain entrance to the loft, it required you to enter the master bathroom, which was painted black and red. A ladder led to the loft. There were several paintings up there. A very large one had a golden calf in the background and a large Moses-

like figure offering popcorn to the masses assembled below him.
There was also a water bed in this loft.

At one practice of the Fabulous Baxters, an ex-girlfriend of one of
the band members showed up. I played a version of Sleepwalk, and
she really liked it and accompanied me back to my bedroom. This
young woman had a feisty New York–Manhattan attitude, which
was the city she was living in. She talked little about her former
boyfriend, the bass player. She looked at the books on the floor of
my room, several which I had brought from my mother's house in
Eagle Rock after my travels in the San Joaquin Valley. "You are a
student radical, aren't you?" I answered in the affirmative. She told
me stories about Manhattan, about how foreign sailors had fallen
in love with her. She was a very good-looking brunette and an
excellent lover. I spent a couple nights with her in my front-of-the-
house bedroom. She went back to Manhattan, and I never saw her
again.

That I could ever be a serious student when I moved into the old
house that Don had remodeled was an illusion. The walls leading
through the front room were now a set of random panels, almost
a maze. One night while Don was painting, presumably influenced
by psychedelics-de-jour, he put a Rolling Stones 33 rpm record
with a skip on the turntable. The skip in the record had Mick Jagger
singing "Come on now" again and again. This went on for about
an hour and a half at about 2:00 AM, while Don was painting. A
cast of characters would come through Don's house. Don's best
friend at the time was a guy named Frank, also an artist, even more
egotistical and arrogant than other house visitors. One time, while
Frank's girlfriend was with him at Don's house, he said, "You know

why her hands are so soft? From rubbing my cock." Another one was Paris LaTour, a very feminine-acting gay male with a posse of sassy young women. He had the total gay walk. Sometimes the two females that accompanied Paris would show up without him. Another pass through personality was Bradly Unruh, the son of a powerful California state politician of the 1970s. There was a parade of very distinct personalities that came through this old house on Fourth Street in Long Beach.

A culmination of this parade reached its climax with "The Party at the Volt Gallery." The Volt Gallery was in the funky part of Long Beach on Anaheim Street, on the west side of Long Beach, past Long Beach Boulevard. The building had two distinct rooms painted stark white. Paintings from some of the best of Long Beach State artists lined the walls. The Fabulous Baxters were the band for opening night. We practiced and could get several songs down pat. These included "Hold On I'm Coming," "Knock on Wood," and "Jail House Rock." The drummer, the only former professional musician in the group, would let none of the guitar players play any solos. I was more-or-less the lead guitar player. Other than Bill Spater, Daniel Freeman was the third guitar player. I played a guitar with a name "Dan Electro." Bill used to joke about it, "Your guitar is Freeman on whites."

Don DeLew was the leader of the show at the gallery. Many people were there. I've always had a tendency to want to juxtapose people together who really came from different walks of life. The Volt Gallery party was following suit. I invited Gracie to the party at the Volt Gallery after convincing her while flirting with her on the Seal Beach boardwalk. Gracie most likely came from a conservative family in Huntington Harbor in Orange County, California. I don't believe she knew anything about my involvement in radical politics. I drove to her house and transported her to the party. Don prepared for the party by standing in the bathtub and painting himself blue from top to bottom, given a few places for his skin to breathe. He was the original blue man.

The party was a mass of people spilling out on the sidewalk. I arrived with my date and warned her, "Don't drink the Kool-Aid," since Don had spiked it with the psychedelic of the week. She didn't. The Fabulous Baxters set up and when the party was in full swing, we did our set. It was almost note perfect because of the drummers near didactic discipline when managing the band. After the Fabulous Baxters finished their set, my mind at the party was totally into music. A guy as tall as me walked up and pleaded to jam. Someone said, "This guy can really play the blues on a slide guitar." I had seen him before, mostly under negative circumstances, when the whole student radical counsel had been busted for cannabis and I had seen him sauntering out of jail. The big guy, Casey Kent, became a close friend for many years. I drank some of the Kool-Aid and other intoxicating drinks at the party. Casey and I jammed and people told us later that we had put together a tremendous impromptu session. As the party broke up in the wee-legal hours, people were entering from the street. I was out of it and I forced my date to drive my car back to Huntington Beach. Before the end of the party, a street white-Caucasian guy and street African American engaged in an argument about color. I do not know if the two drank the Kool-Aid. I have this image of Don DeLew mediating the argument saying, "I don't understand what the problem is. You are black. You are white and I am blue..."

Somewhere in my subconscious, I realized I could no longer operate my vehicle while driving back to Long Beach from Huntington Harbor, the VW Bug, also known as the "Wax-Mobile." The license plate had the letters WAX on it. I pulled over on Seventh Street in Long Beach and parked and headed for the sidewalk. I didn't make it. It turned out that my friend Rick Anthony drove by as I "just fell in the gutter." I woke up in his Seal Beach upstairs apartment on Eleventh Street. It was about eleven in the morning and I was still disoriented, but basically sober. After a breakfast of eggs and pancakes, I felt well enough to drive, so Rick took me in his Plymouth to the parked Wax-Mobile. I drove back to Don DeLew's house, and probably slept another few hours.

A couple of days later, Casey and I reconnected and became good buds for many years. We talked about blues guitar and blues music. He constantly referred to Robert Johnson as being the primary influence on his style. In after-sight, I would say that Muddy Waters had an equal influence. Casey played several Muddy Waters' songs, almost lick-for-lick, using his bottleneck on his white Gibson electric guitar. Casey was an outstanding bottle-neck guitar player.

Because of our "success" at the Volt Gallery, Casey and I projected delusions of grandeur and formed a blues band. Actually, completed, sort of, years later. We needed a singer. I still smoked cigarettes, and if I tried to sing more than a few bars, I always ended up coughing. Casey told me, "I have this friend, Lewis, who can sing, but he lives in Marin Country, north of San Francisco." That didn't work so well. We also need a drummer, so we visited Larry in Seal Beach, who used to be the drummer for Turnquist Remedy, something of a Grateful Dead-inspired band that also performed some blues and basic rock-and-roll. Larry said, "No thanks."

Casey grew up in the suburbs of Long Beach, and came from a prototypical middle-class family from Lakewood, California. Before I met him, he had established himself as the quintessential street hippie after dropping out of Schimer College and going to work for an advertising agency in Manhattan, New York. Something infatuated me with his stories about Manhattan. We both had a similar life issue. We were two reasonably intelligent young males who were both so economically poor we barely had a pot to pee in.

So when Casey became my best new friend, we went to bars like the Cafe Bistro, which was a hip bar with a decent jukebox, or rock-and-roll clubs on South Street and listened to bands covering songs from the late 1960s. Casey drank whiskey, bourbon, that is. By that time, I had severe dental problems and no money to repair them. I quickly learned that bourbon was a legal and inexpensive pain killer. Casey taught me the beauty of Robert Johnson's blues, covered by several bands ranging from Cream to the Rolling Stones. We tried to play a couple of other student-sponsored events, but they were all a disaster. Casey played an electric folk blue style, and I played arpeggio styles of hard electric blues. It didn't always work.

I don't remember where we found the "soap job." It was probably through the California Department of Employment. We signed up and met at a warehouse west of Long Beach Boulevard. From the beginning, it was a beggar's banquet, and one of the truly memorable and outrageous jobs I landed before I landed a "real job" in 1973. Zeke got in on the action, along with Casey and a young kid from Lakewood, Ron. We gathered at this warehouse and were organized into teams. Our team leader was a welder from Oklahoma named Leonard Charles Honeycutt, or just LC. So it was me, Ron, Casey, Zeke, and LC as the driver.

The first few days were more or less legit. I would meet LC at the warehouse and we would pick up boxes of liquid soap to be distributed around Lakewood and Long Beach as samples. The bottles had a plain to see label "not for sale." Then we would pick up Zeke and Casey and, finally, Ron in Lakewood, just off Lakewood Boulevard. I don't remember exactly how long the soap job lasted. It was probably three or four weeks. They assigned each team member a particular area to put Ajax soap samples on the doors of suburban houses. Supposedly, we were audited by the advertising agency in New York that was promoting the campaign. After a few days, LC realized the auditors weren't conducting a meticulous audit. So we stopped hanging Ajax soap samples after lunch and retired for the afternoon to Joe Jost's drinking beer and shooting pool.

Now, the manager of the entire operation, whom LC was in tight with, ignored what was going on. For example, one time when we opened the back of the van, we almost fell on the asphalt because we had consumed so much beer. The question was how to dispose of the soap so we could party most of the day. Casey and I built a throne of soap boxes in my bedroom at Don DeLew's. But LC had the soap market covered. He would go into various restaurants and bars and sell cases of Ajax well under market value. So the routine now became to hang a few selected samples on the doors of the area we were to cover that day, deliver our black market goods, and then go to Joe Jost's and shoot pool. Of course, this somewhat sleazy routine, fun though it was, had to end. Finally, I could accompany

LC to the boss's apartment to finish some last transactions. The boss had boxes of Ajax stacked from ceiling to floor that he was peddling on the black market. Such was the soap job.

I remained in contact with LC for several years. Casey and I would go over to his house for barbecues. If he became impatient while starting the fire, he would go out to his welding truck and draw some inflammable liquid, put it on the charcoal, and ignite it. It would look like a miniature explosion with a small mushroom cloud. Another time when kids visiting, LC looked at a kid sucking the thumb. LC showed the kid his thumb that had the tip amputated. "I used to suck my thumb and look what happened." The look on the kid's face was both alarming and amusing. LC had music that both Casey and I enjoyed. He played an eight-track tape of Jimi Hendrix's Freedom and some electric blues by Howling Wolf.

Casey and I attempted to play some music at "culture night" at the Phinius. We were both very inebriated, me more than Casey. I tried to play my guitar and struck only dissonant chords, "blat ... blat." So it was another lost night. I was developing a reputation as a drunk guitar player. This was true. I was attracted to a tall, young, brown-haired woman, Veronica, who still attended Long Beach State. There was a mutual attraction, but it never panned out. By now I had lost confidence in the opposite sex because of several reasons. I was living the blues, which was a state of depression. I didn't know how bright the bright spots were. At one point, David #2, who lived at the now moved hippie commune in the Sierra foothills above Fresno, arrived. He assured me that the new location of all the hippies in the Fresno foothills was even better than before.

I convinced Veronica to accompany me to Fresno and then to the new hippie commune. We looked up Joyce, who was now with a former California Highway Patrol officer and a devotee of Maher Baba. I talked to the both of them for a time and then continued on using David's instructions to find the new commune. That was the last time I saw Joyce. After arriving at the commune, it was interesting. Some of them were living in an old railway car. I again had a conversation with Nadie, but since I was with Veronica, we both camped out in the forest along with David. It was a peaceful camp out in the Sierra Nevada foothills. Veronica seemed to enjoy it, even though we only camped out one night. I tried to hide it, but mentally, I was in total turmoil. And this mental turmoil would continue into the future. Veronica could sense my confusion and delusion. On the return trip to Long Beach, she looked at me and said, "You really are upset, aren't you?". I was.

One night, to my total surprise, Sharon Sparling showed up at Don DeLew's house. She was wearing a white uniform and was living somewhere in Long Beach working a job. Then she told me the story about her and Kenny's visit to the Sierra Foothills to the same commune I had recently visited with Veronica. With Sharon and Kenny came turmoil. David#1, was one of the camp leaders. David#1 became totally infatuated with Sharon. "Sharon told me David was in love with me. That he wanted to run away with me." Listening to Sharon relating this story in the front bedroom at Don's house, where she ended up in bed with me. "I thought to myself, can she ever reel in males". I ended up sleeping with the same woman I had been with for a couple of years, but hadn't seen for months. A short time later, there was a knock on the front door, which was right next to the bedroom. As irony would have it, in walked Rick

Anthony, who looked at us, and said, "It sure is good to see you two in bed again." Kenny was a petty criminal and was probably in jail. Sharon was attempting to dissolve the relationship and live in Long Beach. Too bad that didn't happen. As abruptly as she walked in at this period in my life, she disappeared into the night. I caught up with her again, though, a few months later.

A few weeks after the soap job, I convinced my mother that she owed me a certain amount of money. In retrospect, it was a sleazy request, but I pressured her, and could get three hundred dollars to travel to Europe as a "starving student." So I began with my plans. Casey had endless stories about New York City and his college that he dropped out of, Shimer College in Mt. Carroll, rural northern Illinois. So we began with this grand plan to drive across the country. I toyed to travel to Europe, but I did not know what I was doing. "A passport?" That would mean communicating with the USA government,

Bill Bevins rented an apartment towards the North End of Seal Beach, and we reconnected. He was also a friend of Don DeLew, so that was an easy lateral. While hanging around his place, I once again ran into Jen Rollins, a onetime Seal Beach local who had moved to Manhattan, New York, but from time-to-time returned to her old stomping grounds at Seal Beach. I told her about my plans to visit New York City en-route to Europe, so she sweetened the pot by offering her flat as a temporary safe port in Manhattan. I spent several nights with her. She was a top-drawer lover, a very sensuous woman.

Casey and I continued with our extended discussion on the current situation regarding political economy. He rejected my recent allegiance to Third Camp Socialism, and argued that the Socialist Workers Party with their single-issue approach was the best direction for the student and community movement. That meant protesting the war in Vietnam, still in its zenith, but not adding any other issues when trying to organize demonstrations. While still living at Don DeLew's, the killing of the students at Kent State hit the news wire. I drove to Rick Anthony's house in Seal Beach, ran up the stairs, and pounded on the door. "The revolution has started!" Long Beach State came to a screeching halt regarding all liberal arts departments. I suspect that nursing, criminology, engineering, and athletics continued with a few bumps in the road. There were no mass protests on the local campus. Students milled around and with attraction to impromptu events sponsored in an ad hoc manner. I borrowed Don's "Arab" headdress and wore it to campus. It seemed to be the thing to do. This amused Casey. "You are returning to Long Beach State as an Arab!" I felt that the country was on the verge of civil war. We, as students, actually believed that President Nixon would send troops into the colleges. This was not a class uprising, though from the view that way in the Black community. It was a base conflict that would be a fundamental contour of USA-sian national politics for a long time, the traditional, mid-USA culture steeped in myths of the 1950s in conflict with a new urban-centric culture of youth and minorities. Both cultures included a range of economic classes, with the so-called middle class dissected in half, between the old and the new culture. Those few with true power over the political economy wanted the whole social disturbance put to sleep like a rotten tooth at the dentist's office. And when we reached the age of disco, general excess, and self-adoration, they achieved much of what they wanted, or at least a semi-pacified new culture that had lost its historical roots.

When Jen returned to New York City, I connected with her friend Kathy Lewis. Kathy was married to a well-known counter-culture type in Seal Beach named John Lewis. I had met both of them briefly years before when married. When John was arrested and sentenced for selling contraband, most likely LSD, the relationship fell apart. Kathy had a string of boyfriends, and I established a short-term relationship during one of the interim phases. She was one of Jen's best friends, so it seemed strange. This was a vacation for me. We would lie around Kathy's bed, watch grade-b science fiction on a local channel presented by "Seymore," and have sex. I bid farewell to Kathy, though I glimpsed her later that year. She was a very sweet woman. I heard a few years later that she married a rich medical doctor who lived in the Philippines.

I moved my books and important documents to my mother's house in Eagle Rock and departed from Don DeLew's in my VW, aka the Wax-Mobile. I had my money and both I and Casey had a pocket full of uppers. We departed about 8:00 PM on an April night. The original plan was to parallel Route 66 on US Interstate 40, but we got into a heated political discussion about something and stayed on US Interstate 15 headed to Salt Lake City instead of heading towards Santa Fe. The plan was one of us would sleep and the other would pop an upper and continue driving. This way we could travel non-stop to Mount Carrol, Illinois, to Poffey's Bar, which Casey insisted we visit. Casey took the first upper, and I awoke groggy about 7:00 AM local time in the fold-down seat of a VW bug. Casey dozed off, and I drove through Utah past a town I visited as a kid—

Fillmore, "The Cleanest Little Town in America." Before Salt Lake City, I turned onto US Interstate 70 towards Denver, Colorado. As we climbed the interstate into the Rocky Mountains, the VW Bug, now a graduation present paying off its worth, sputtered up into the altitude. Casey woke up and shortly thereafter we saw a Ford sedan literally encased in ice where it had stalled out. Luckily, we made it over the peak, descending into the city of Denver.

When we both were awake we discussed many things, such as the state of the student movement, lost girlfriends, Trotsky and the Russian Revolution, Mao Tse-Tung and the Chinese revolution, Cal State University at Long Beach, Shimer College, drugs, including uppers, downers, hallucinogens, psychedelics and narcotics, Joseph Stalin, Richard Nixon, friends at school, fellow radical students and I should say, former students, blues guitar players and singers, Russian poets, Black Panthers, family members, types of beer and types of whiskey, jazz compared to blues, Eric Dolphy, Charlie "Yardbird" Parker, Robert Johnson, how much fun the soap job was, would ever get laid again, how to find work in Manhattan, Casey's friend Bob Hill, and also his friend Luis Mannick, McSorleys Old Ale House, Manhattan subways, Junior Parker, the White Horse Tavern, "A," "B," "C," and "D" avenue on the lower east side of Manhattan, the "two-fold" path to nirvana: whiskey and Darvon, "TreeSloth" aka James Whiteker a Long Beach local, shot dead by the liquor-store owner, B.B. King, the mad Long Beach bomber who bombed the Peace Center on Anaheim Street and the Long Beach Police Station, Casey's cousin Mark, Chris Hope, a bass player in an mid-sixties Long Beach blues band the "Howlin Blues", Zen Buddhism, John Coltrane, Liberal Unitarian Youth, Gurus from

India, yatta da yatta...

This is what you do when you are both wired on uppers in a VW Bug headed into Colorado.

It was the first time I had been to Colorado since my birth, being born in Denver, Colorado. We stopped for food at some nondescript, fast-food joint mid-morning, and continued on into the great plains of Midwest US. Denver reminded me of the San Fernando Valley in Southern California, but above 5000 feet sea level. Casey dozed off for a while and I continued on, playing the radio to keep me awake. We switched from US 70 to US 76 in Denver and continued on US 80. Traveling through Nebraska after sunset at the time was almost hallucinogenic. It was dark. Totally freaking dark. Looking down the highway, a light looked like a search light streaming into the night sky. You could swear there were tornadoes in the distance, but they were illusions caused by weary eyes with little sleep. Sleeping in a VW Bug is an art. It's especially an art when both drivers are over six feet tall.

When the Wax-Mobile arrived in Omaha, Nebraska, during sunrise, it was a relief. There was daylight. Casey and I took shorter shifts driving. We had to. The time behind the wheel now came in four- or five-hour increments. Driving in Iowa was amusing. We cruised at about seventy-five miles an hour over US 80. The constant up and down of VW moving over the rolling hills not only kept us alert, but it created a unique sensation that I have not felt since. There just weren't a few rolling hills, there were hours of them. By late afternoon we were in Illinois, headed to Shimer College and Poffey's Bar. It was early April, so the trees were mostly barren and gray in the dull gray sky. Poffey's was a classic mid-western tavern with old wood trimmings from a time past. Casey and I had a nondescript mid-western beer before heading southeast to Chicago. By the time we arrived in the Loop, it was dark. I believe we actually grabbed something to eat and plotted our next move. We tried to take the Interstate from Chicago to New York, but soon realized we would spend a lot of money on tolls, something foreign to me. So we took a set of highways to parallel Interstate 80. It was a tough drive in the middle of the night, but by daylight of the second day on the road, we were approaching Sharon, Pennsylvania. The paralleling highway we took had many trucks and when we would pass each other at high speed, the VW would list as each truck passed in the opposite lane.

During that night, while I slept, Casey did most of the driving, but by the time we reached Sharon, I took over. Dead tired, but the drive was nice as we rejoined US 80. There was some green appearing in the hills of Pennsylvania. Stopping briefly, I watched guys in tee-shirts playing ball in 45-degree Fahrenheit weather. Spring meant a lot to them. California kids were not used to this perspective. By the time we reached New Jersey, Casey had woken from a superficial sleep, and insisted that he drive into Manhattan. With an increase in the population density increased as we neared the metropolis, but surprising how close we really came to the center of the empire before it became dense. An immediate difference between the West Coast and the East Coast was apparent. The West Coast was spread out across a converted desert, defining the essence of suburbia. The East Coast was compact, even when suburban, it was compressed. So when we entered the city, we entered the City.

Casey now was literally in the driver's seat. I believe this is the only time we stopped during the drive when we bought a bottle of bottom-drawer bourbon and consumed it, since we were so jacked up. We entered Manhattan. We had traversed from Los Angeles to Manhattan via Chicago in forty-seven hours.

Jen Rollins lived in a bachelorette flat in on West 68th street. It had one room that was both the living room and a loft in that living room that was her bed area. The other "room" with a sliding door was both the kitchen and the bathroom. I had never seen such a tiny living space. But this was Manhattan. We were not in California anymore. Jen, Casey, and I ventured into the Manhattan night, us dead tired, but quite hungry. It impressed Jen how well Casey knew the subways. Casey knew exactly where to get to Nathan's hot-dogs. We probably picked up a little more liquor to bring us down and went back to her flat. Casey crashed on her couch, but told her he would look up his friends in Brooklyn from Shimer College with and whom he had worked with at the advertising agency. Jen and I had sex in her loft. She told me this was the last time for a romp in the loft, since she didn't fully trust the wooden framework. That was the last time we were intimate.

In retrospect, Jen was an excellent host. She had her own life in Manhattan and here I was on the doorstep like a stray cat. She worked for an office as an office manager. Evidently she learned the skill when first moving to Manhattan when she went to work for one of the socialist parties. She showed me the excellent delicatessens. We went to some great movies, including Seven Samurai, which I had never seen before. I had two rotten teeth, and she sent me to a free-dental clinic. The extracted teeth would cost me many dollars later in life for the bridgework, but I was no longer in pain. I departed the clinic, took a good dose of bourbon, and got a room at the YMCA. I couldn't stay at her flat. She hosted several other people, so I knew I had to do something. The initial plan of traveling to Europe did not occur. I didn't trust my mother to bankroll me. The three hundred dollars that I had when entering the city evaporated quickly. The fifty-cent cokes, in 1970, really drove that home. Jen connected me with an employment agency. I walked in with a bachelor's degree in history and ended up with a job in the Brooklyn garment industry. It hit me again. All the intelligence that got me through college didn't count. I had no actual income. It was difficult to have relationships when you teeter on the dregs of society. I was descending into the wilderness.

Spooling zippers eight hours a day at minimum wage in Brooklyn doesn't really work. I departed the YMCA. Towards the end of this stint in Brooklyn, I was sleeping in my car parked on a Brooklyn road. I lasted at the job about six weeks. Casey's friends who lived in Brooklyn felt sorry for me, and let me crash on the floor of the room that he was staying in. I kept taking the wrong subway trains to the factory and after being late too many times. They fired me, being non-union worker.

My best memories of the both Brooklyn and Manhattan were the book and record shops in Manhattan, along with McSorleys Old Ale House, the very first place where I tasted an India Pale Ale brewed by Ballantine, and not available on the West Coast playing in a blues club with Casey in Brooklyn, the gardens on the grounds of the Brooklyn Museum within walking distance of the apartment where I had a crash space. I think it was in those gardens that I realized I was crushed, and in the wilderness of my perceptions, being isolated from all aspects of society. There was enough money to make it back to the West Coast. I thanked Casey's friends for putting up with me. Leaving Casey with them, I headed out through Jersey. I don't really remember where I stayed, except in St. Louis. I believe I stayed in my car for several stops. It takes some creativity for a man over six feet tall to curl up and go to sleep in a VW Bug. In St. Louis, I checked into a flea-bag hotel with an actual bed, and went to a bar and had conversations with the locals about New York City while listening to an original recording of Stardust on the jukebox. The room had a fan that mediated the 95-degree, mid-western heat.

I arrived at my mother's house in Eagle Rock, broke, no job, twenty-three years old, running from the government who wanted to draft me. I enjoy playing the blues on the guitar, but right then I didn't own one. After a couple of days mooching off of mom, I returned to Seal Beach, and look up anyone I could find in my state of wilderness.

WILDERNESS

•••

The cool breeze of the Pacific Ocean welcomed me as I entered Seal Beach. At Stony's house, I temporarily occupied the back room, a converted garage on the first floor. After a brief rest, I went for a walk in my old beach town. The first person I ran into was Sharon Sparling. She then accompanied me to the apartment back room. Sharon explained her current situation. "Kenny and I got back together, but he is in jail. After he was in jail, I met a gay sailor. I seduced him and converted him into a bi-sexual. Later, Kenny found out and threatened to kill him". I told Sharon about my trip to New York with Casey and meeting up with Jen Rollins, who Sharon knew. Sharon continued, "I'm staying at Mark and Debbie's house on Seventeenth Street. You should come visit." After all this catching up conversation, we had sex and short time later, Sharon departed.

For a while I wandered between Seal Beach and Eagle Rock. I spent some time at my friend Jerry Harris' beach-front apartment.

A tall woman, Sue Andreas, also lived in the same beach front house that Jerry had rented as a co-renter. Sue worked at the phone company in Long Beach. Sue became a friend I was in touch with for several years. She told me stories about how she had attended school to become a model. "Walk like this", while demonstrating a model walk. Sue definitely had the look of a model. Perhaps she was put off since I never insinuated I wanted to be intimate with her. But at this point in my life I needed friendship more that I need activity between the sheets. During the visits, I met Sea Hope, a gifted blues guitar player who played with the Howlin' Blues band in the mid-nineteen-sixties, and about the same time, since he knew Sea, I met my future roommate, Jim Gaspar. Jim and I immediately became friends. He had graduated from UC Berkeley with a degree in physics, and was now working on a master's degree in physics at Long Beach State. Sadly, a Vietnam vet addicted to heroin showed up at the same beach front apartment with his supply of "China White." I tried this drug one time, sniffing it like cocaine. It was so strong that I ended up on the floor, with my eyes open, but in a complete opiated dream state. About a month later, we learned the vet committed suicide on the Seal Beach pier with a self-inflicted gunshot.

I spent time with Jim Gaspar in his bedroom at the back of his mother's house in Belmont Shores, Long Beach. He had guitars, amplifiers, and recording equipment. We would jam, talk about various things, including science fiction, physics, space, politics, colleges, and, of course, music. Jim loaned me one of his guitars, and I ended up crashing at the house on Seventeenth Street where Sharon was staying. Once again, her flame Kenny was in the Orange

County jail, so she obligingly jumped into my bed. The scenario at Debbie's house at the east end of Seal Beach was chaos. Kenny got out of jail and picked up another young woman who would become a well-known pop star. Her name was Rickie Lee Jones. Jim and I hit it off with Rickie. I played a couple of games of chess with her, and later we went to Jim's bedroom flat in Belmont Shores. There, Jim and I backed her with our guitars while she screamed the blues. Jim had a reel-to-reel tape recorder and recorded a portion of the jam. Years later, he was so proud he still had this tape. I wish I had a copy. Rickie Lee Jones gave me the "stink eye" after the jam at Jim's mother's house. I believe it was because I didn't make a pass at her.

Debbie, whose house I was using as a crash space, had her steady squeeze, Mark, but she had also had flings with Mark Gold and Stony. She was a feisty but fun young woman. Debbie was also friends with an art history major at Long Beach State, Kay, whom I would meet later. Debbie's Mark, who appeared and vanished from time-to-time, said he had gained a discount on the rent by having sex with the owner of the house. I figured "bullshit", but Kenny said, "Yea, it's true". Kenny took me to the owner's house where she had a whole stable full of males, many older than me and quite drunk. I talked to the owner for a while and she quickly psyched me. She was this very intelligent middle-aged woman who liked to keep a stable of males, mostly through guile and through the power of her property. How much the owner knew about current politics surprised me. I had heard rumors that in the late 1940s and 1950s Seal Beach was a hot-bed of vice. Perhaps she came from that era.

Sleeping at the Seventeenth Street house was an adventure. Sometimes with Debbie, when she was not occupied with someone else. Sometimes with Sharon when Kenny had vanished and sometimes by myself where I could find space. One afternoon, Kenny and Sharon wanted me to join in for a threesome. With agreement, "Okay, but let me get a beer first". I walked down to the liquor store at the corner of Seal Beach Boulevard and Pacific Coast Highway and bought a "long dog" of Ranier Ale. After that, I returned to the house on Seventeenth Street to join this mini-orgy. There were all these guys out front looking like none-of-my-friends. One of them, in beach shorts and looking directly at me, said, "What are you doing an' why are you here?" "I came to visit". "We are narcotics officers, and this is a drug raid. We suggest you leave". I think it was the bottle of Ranier Ale that saved me. Realizing that I could not return to Mark and Debbie's. I don't remember those destined for arrest, probably Debbie's Mark and Kenny. I looked up Jim and tried to plot my next move with little money and only the belongings I had in the VW Bug.

Sue Andreas and another woman I had met briefly, named Marlene, had moved to the vicinity of East Second Street in Long Beach. I visited them and made friends with several people I had not met before. A rock-and-roll band lived in the house next door. This band had some success playing at a concert in Arcata in northern California. Terry, the drummer, was in a relationship with Marlene, but when he went to New York to visit his friends in the rock-and-roll-revival band Sha-Na-Na, Marlene ended up in a relationship with another person in the house, someone who was one of Terry's friends. These were two old houses in the front facing Second Street and a separate upstairs guest house in the back of the first old house. It had a bathroom and a bedroom. It thrilled me to be there. Since Kenny was in jail, Sharon showed up, and stayed for a couple of days, then ran off with a friend of Jim Gaspar, "Old Joe" and his friend named Reeb. Then she returned for one more fling, took a shower, and went to get Kenny out of jail. I would see her one more time. That is one more very sad final time.

I don't know if it was luck or the just right mix of chemicals in my system, but I auditioned as the guitar player for the band in the next house, "Darling Randy and the Rock-in' Pneumonia." Darling Randy sang the songs and played a rhythm electrified acoustical guitar. And in the same house, lived Terry, the drummer. The band members lived in this neighboring house on Second Street next to the house where I first landed. It was a grand old Long Beach house with two stories. There was a room that was lined with egg cartons to mute the sound. This former dining room was the music practice room. There was only one downstairs bedroom on the west side of the house. This is where a young woman named Kay had her bedroom. Kay had just graduated from Long Beach State with a degree in art history. Physically, she was sort of busty cute. She had a gregarious personality, and I was attracted to her.

By this time, I was even more emotionally unstable than before. I had won the job as the lead guitar player for the Rock-in Pneumonia and Darling Randy gave me a room upstairs in this old house. I had a mattress and a few clothes. The only book I had at the time was "My Life", written by Leon Trotsky. The downstairs had a beautiful old rock fireplace and the patterns on the wood and the glass front door reflected beautiful sunsets as they poured in.

Next to my bedroom, Darling Randy, whose real name was Steve, had his. Terry also had his bedroom on the second floor next to mine. Both Darling Randy and Terry had stereo systems that played vinyl records. We would listen to what inspired either of them at the moment. Right across from me, Dennis had his bedroom. He was not a member of the band, but was a close friend of Randy's and Terry's. Like Terry, Dennis grew up in a rough desert country in the city of Fontana. Fontana ended up a depressed blue-collar town just west of San Bernardino. Most of the time, we referred to Dennis as "Thumbs." He like to take lots of uppers, and was constantly working on automobiles with inferior tool sets. Thumbs had plans for an engine that was similar in concept to a Wankel rotary engine.

So my life had turned into a non-job as a rock-and-roll musician. Darling, the leader, funded my crash space, but I needed money. I even tried general relief at the welfare office. They told me to go away. "We don't support aspiring musicians." So I tried my luck at a job of driving an ice cream truck in what the hiring manager and the dispatcher identified as a "good route." It wandered through Carson and parts of Torrance. Of course, the band was not pleased, because I would arrive from work burnt out and tired. I would often play "The Song" I heard all day. They counted the truck inventory at the end of the route and if I ate any, they charged me the face amount. I did this for about a month and then checked out.

Darling Randy and the Rocking Pneumonia still needed a bass player. Besides Randy playing the electrified acoustical guitar, Terry on drums, and myself, we needed that bottom end. We found Clyde. He was a competent bass player, and we got a gig at the "Post and Paddock" in Belmont Shores. Casey had returned from Brooklyn, and had reunited with a former flame, Kim. So Casey and Kim would visit the second street band house from time-to-time. We hired Casey as the roadie for the gig. He took an immediate dislike of Darling. The gig did not go well. I had hit my mother up for the last of the money "promised" me and bought an amplifier. It was way too heavy, but the guitar was a gem, a Gibson ES335 in vintage bright red. The band had trouble with the sound balance in the club. Clyde, the bass player, introduced the band to a saxophone player I had seen around town. He was crippled in one leg, but played a mean sax that fit in with the style of music we played. Darling and Terry, as I mentioned, were very much friends of Sha-Na-Na, a revival rock-and-roll band from this period. The type of songs Sha-Na-Na reflected our song selection.

Kay Stellar, whom I mentioned earlier, had rented the only downstairs bedroom. She had an Australian sheep dog with those white eyes that lived with us in a decent but uncultivated and uncultured backyard. I became quite enamored with her, but we never quite hit it off. I was playing music, but I was deteriorating emotionally. By now I was incapable of any stable relationship, and Kay sensed it. I also sensed that I was going over the edge. We would go to the beach at Long Beach harbor to listen to the silent waves and talk in the dim light. Another time I took her to my father's house in Brentwood and after my brothers went to bed, he put me and Kay up in a guest bed. She stripped naked from the waist down, and I did nothing. That must have disappointed her. My final escapade with Kay took place at the Long Beach Pike, the local sleazy amusement park on a pier. We went slumming and walking around this vintage sailor-shore-leave hangout. I looked at a tattoo parlor, and said to Kay, "I bet you won't go into that parlor and get a tattoo." I woke up the next morning with a bandage on each arm and a headache. One arm had a star and the other a crescent moon. I lost that bet. And often I would just sit there in my bare room reading, and then return to band practice. Sometimes I would exit my room and talk with Thumbs for comic relief.

One night, Casey came over, and we went into the rehearsal room. Darling came down from his bedroom and objected. They exchanged words between Darling and Casey. Darling resented Casey possibly because I told Darling that Casey was a good blues guitar player or that Darling thought Casey had invaded his private space, and impinged his domain. Casey hit Darling and left. Casey never returned to the Second Street house. Later, he confessed he was sorry. That didn't affect me. By now I had realized that Darling was an egotistical asshole. That's actually a quality you need to be successful in the popular music industry.

I have to admit, Darling really hustled to gain his objectives. The Rocking Pneumonia auditioned for a gig in an old air hangar used for concerts in Seal Beach. It landed us a paying gig at a high school somewhere in Orange County. Darling kept on trying to find us work. His next connection was with a soul band called the "New Days." This singing group, three Afro-Americans, needed a backup band, so they connected with Darling Randy and the Rocking Pneumonia. I don't remember how Darling fit in, maybe singing backup or strumming on his acoustical guitar or possibly both. I had fun playing with the New Days, with the exception that the leader wanted me to play with a wah-wah peddle. Now my feet have never been that well connected to my brain, so that was a bit of a struggle. I learned songs like "Cloud Nine" and "Do You See Me?" I thought we had a great sound. We went for an audition for a USO tour, and were declined. Those running the audition liked the Rocking Pneumonia, but not the Afro-American soul group.

One night late in 1970, the saxophone player and I went to Cafe Bistro on Seventh Street in Long Beach. He stayed at the club and. Probably because of some uncomfortable news, visited Sharon Sparling in Seal Beach. I had heard she was staying at a court apartment on Tenth Street, close to the beach. I had the address, drove there, and walked in. Sharon seemed visibly upset. Asking her where Kenny was, then she told me, "In jail". I thought to myself, "Again". I tried to convince her to come with me to Cafe Bistro, where I had left the crippled saxophone player. She begged me to stay with her. Oh, I wish I would have. I told her I had to return and pick up a band member. She told me she couldn't because the "Checkered Daemon", or Gary, was dropping by. The Checkered Daemon moniker has its origin in Zap underground comics. I had met this kid Gary, a good, local surfer punk, a few years prior to this. His family, consisting only of his mother, was a severe "non-family." I had tried to mentor him a few times with homework help, and he seemed to soak it up.

But Gary had connections to underclass peoples from Lakewood, Bellflower and beyond. He arrived and sold Sharon a bag full of downers. It wasn't until Kenny showed up a couple of days later at the band's house that I learned Sharon had committed suicide by taking the overdose of downers.

HARROWING

•••

On the news of Sharon's death, I couldn't suppress the thought that I was the second person to see her alive that fateful night. The scenario played out repeatedly in my mind. What if I did return and stay with her as she requested after I took the saxophone player home? What if I called up one of the band members and asked them to pick up the saxophone player at Cafe Bistro? What if I would have recognized the terrible mental state Sharon was in? What if... what if, ad infinitum. I went straight to Gehenna. It devastated me.

I stopped eating regular meals. Watercress and cream cheese sandwiches and bourbon whiskey (Jim Beam, Jack Daniels, Hill and Hill... or "Heaven and Hell") was a typical breakfast, usually consuming the sandwich first and then the liquor later and after that, who knows what. I had access to uppers, downers, and hard drugs that came from different sources. Darling and friends could get nasty drugs from their connections in Manhattan, New York. Jim had his connection with "Old Joe," a street-wise Latino who could cruise Main Street in downtown Los Angeles, and score anything he wanted. Some pills, like Percodan, a narcotic, made it into my hands.

Casey took me to Bob Hill's mother's house with my amplifier. They planned a party with some friends. I met Bob's sister Pam and his brother Gary, never having met them before. After that I attempted to jam. After the incident between Darling and Casey, the only place I jammed blues music with Casey was away from the band, so at this party we could play without conflict. Within an hour after arriving, I felt sick. While trying to make it back to the band house on Second Street, I passed out in Casey's car. The next morning, I woke up ill, nearly fatally ill. I could barely walk. The whites of my eyes had a yellow tinge and yellow tinge in the pigment of my skin. I was severely disoriented. Darling looked at me, and said, "You are sick. We just lost our lead guitar player." They took me to Harbor General Hospital, where I was diagnosed with Hepatitis-B. I was transferred to a hospital in West Long Beach, west of Long Beach Boulevard. Among other maladies, being diagnosed by the staff with a case of malnutrition. The first week I was there, I was in a private room. The hospital dietitian came to visit and asked me what foods I wanted to eat. I was skinny as a rail and probably weighed about sixty percent of my normal weight. I knew I was one ugly looking soul. While in the private room, the rule was no visitors. Perhaps the staff wanted to see if I was hooked on some drug. What I was hooked on was the drug "depression". After a week, my skin and eye color were close to normal. I spent weeks in the hospital slowly recovering. For reading material, I continued Leon Trotsky's History of the Russian Revolution. With me was my Gibson ES335 flaming red guitar, brought to me by the drummer of the rock band I was in. I put the guitar under the bed after they moved me to a shared area. I was in the "cuckoo's nest". My best guess is that I was in a rehabilitation hospital with several people with severe psychological issues, myself included. I was angry, lost, and depressed. Even suicidal. I wrote a few letters, as if they were my last that I would ever write. The deaths of my former lover, loss of my daughter through adoption, and the death of other friends were dragging me further into the depths of Gehenna.

After I was in the hospital for several weeks, I spent time with social psychiatric workers. They asked me several questions. I told them about the suicide of the young woman I planned to marry, the suicide of a Vietnam Vet I met and befriended in Seal Beach when I returned from Brooklyn, the suicide of an artist friend, that graduated from CSULB when I did. Then I would run down all that was wrong, including a litany of injustices in my mind at the time to the social psychiatrist. The social psychiatrist told me I was too angry and emotionally unstable to be released from the hospital. She may have been correct. Perhaps it was the angry faces I drew in the art class for what my benefactors considered a paramount anti-social icon. So I switched from art to making an intricate balsa-wood model airplane. That didn't impress my social worker benefactors. I could walk out the door, so it wasn't a prison. I kept asking for a formal release, but was told, "You aren't ready for the general social milieu". Some freedom was possible. I parked my Volkswagen Bug near the hospital and, up to that point, depart periodically. I didn't understand the rules for other patients, but they didn't depart the hospital temporarily like I did.

One day, it might have been in the late spring, I flew over the "cuckoo's nest". I had departed twice to see how Darling and the Rocking Pneumonia were getting on. This time I took my guitar and what few possessions I had, and drove to my mother's house in Eagle Rock. She was not happy I was there, and I know my father wasn't because, by just ditching the hospital, I left a legal and economic mess. I did not check out of the hospital. I simply vanished. As a result, I left several thousands of dollars in unpaid medical bills. Of course, my father's lawyer challenged some of them. From my viewpoint, they would not release me, even after being in the hospital for almost three months. I would do better somewhere else. The staff at the hospital thought otherwise. My father ended up paying the bills after some legal negotiation and possibly he had some pull since he was also a medical doctor.

While at my mother's house, I alternated between pouting, self-pity, and depression. I listened to records on the stereo, and looked at the few pictures I had of people I knew, including one of my estranged wife Jan, who was living with her girlfriend in San Francisco, smiling and looking with a relaxed smile. Estoy perdido. Being lost, I had a college degree and no job. I was an enemy of the US government because of their insane war in Southeast Asia. The one important asset I had was my car.

What happened next was the worst and the best of my harrowing of Gehenna. After a phone call, I drove to Long Beach to visit visited Ginny Miles. Ginny lived in an upstairs apartment off of Anaheim Street in the middle of the Long Beach ghetto. Ginny was also a radical student at Long Beach State. I had known her for several years. She dropped out when she became pregnant with her daughter Maia. The biological father immediately vanished from her life, offering no support, physically or mentally. I explained to her what had happened to me the last few months. She seemed sympathetic. I have always had a soft spot for single mothers and still do. She told me what her daughter was doing and where her former boyfriend was, not the father of her daughter, but a person we both knew well, who had given her physical and psychological support, thus creating an easement of being a single mother. We talked about old friends while watching television; we began kissing each other. My friend now became a lover.

A mutual friend who worked for the County of Los Angeles doing data processing told Ginny to "learn software at the junior college, then take the county examination and you have a job". She had studied information science for a year and then landed a job at Transamerica Corporation, a financial powerhouse on the west coast. She continued to work for Transamerica for several years.

Ginny and I had a live together relationship. Unfortunately, she was just about as unstable as I was, but differently. I was severely depressed and even suicidal. She was under psychiatric care and deeply confused. Her flavor of depression and confusion centered on attempting to be a mother and maintaining a place to live. I could tell how disoriented she was. She did not put away things. Trash piled up on a screened-in porch. But, she always had work clothes and drove to work. If this seems like the basis for an unstable relationship, it certainly was. I didn't remain in cohabitation with Ginny for a short time at this apartment. While I was there, I got another dose of ghetto life. It wasn't bad. Most of the neighborhood folk just wanted to work and live. But my relationship with Ginny was unstable. And she had an unstable relationship with me. Over a period of a couple of years, she would want to be a lover and then, for an unknown reason, reject me as a lover and want me as a friend. Then, for many years in the future, she was simply a friend, but I'm getting ahead of myself.

The Peanut Gallery on Broadway Avenue in Long Beach, California, was a favorite hangout for hippies, artists, musicians, students, counter culture types and fellow travelers in the unhomogeneous hipster community. Everyone I knew simply called it the "nut bar". The hipsters that frequented the dive were mostly a little "off" was one reason for its nickname. Being a simple play on words was the other reason for the name. Ginny enjoyed visiting the "nut bar". This is where she would see people she knew from school or where she used to live in the Long Beach community. For me, the "nut bar" always had something of a negative connotation. When going there, the surroundings often amplified my depression and anger.

After Ginny and I parted ways the first time, I occasionally returned to the "nut bar". Making out and getting affectionate with an African American woman is one of the few excellent memories I have of the place. But one night while playing pool, for some lost reason, I became angry and deliberately smashed an empty beer glass while speaking nonsense to the clients near me. Depositing the glass and fragments in the trash, and immediately I departed. Trouble did not occur because "Jungle George", the bartender, I had known me for some time. I didn't return to the "nut bar" for almost a year. I was embarrassed because of my poor behavior. By the time a new owner ran the bar, none of the typical clientele could recognize me.

Now find a job. I found one doing inventory for a company called Associated Inventory Management. I made what amounted to a minimum wage when I worked, but not enough to collect unemployment when I was not working. The job was depressing, since I worked with a few laid off aerospace workers and whose lives had fallen apart. But it brought in some money. I knew I had to do something else. I was still friends with Ginny, even though we didn't live together. She convinced me to study information science like she did so that I could also get a job with computers and data-processing. I did just that. I went back to school. This time it wasn't for scholarly pursuits, it was to pick up a trade so I could gain something other than a shit job. For all the negative aspects of my current and future relationship with Ginny, this here was her best gift. She pointed me in the right direction when I was in a state of total and desperate despair.

I informed the managers at Associated Inventory Management that I was off their payroll and was learning a new skill. Next, I was attempting to make peace with my dad, and at least convinced him I was seriously trying to find work. In reality, I think it was some really abrasive phone calls from my grandmother in Santa Barbara with my dad that did the trick. He told me what my grandmother said, punctuated with, "What are you going to do to help John and get him back in school?" I went to work at the Beverly Hills Medical Clinic in their emergency facility. I showed up to work at the emergency clinic each day on time and had an amiable interaction with the employees. When I was not hand sorting paper records, I was on the front line with the nurses. We treated attempted suicides, a worker falling into the pizza oven, high-class prostitutes coming in for their weekly checkup and generic ambulance cases because of a vehicle incident. I worked with my dad and his partner, owning and operating the emergency room. Of course, sometimes my dad wasn't there since he had an orthopedic practice on a different floor. The ER was on the first floor for quick ambulance access. When my dad and I were working together, the relationship formally friendly. It remained thus from here on out. However, there was always an unspoken barrier. I believe he wanted me to renounce my political beliefs. Having changed these worldviews, but I never renounced them like he would have preferred. I don't believe he ever fully pardoned me for when the FBI came to his house looking for me a few years back. For about four months, I worked for the emergency clinic, besides attending information science classes at the local junior college. I gained outstanding grades in information science courses. The problems were like fun puzzles to me. In one particularly tough course teaching "low-level machine language", the typical grade on the final exam was between 50 and 60 percent correct. The instructor returned my final exam and told me "you should frame this and put it on your wall." There were no wrong answers. Having scored 100 percent. I now knew I would work in computer technology. I was not always perfect in these classes. In another class where a higher level more abstract language was being taught (Fortran), I authored a program on a deck of punched cards. The program ran without error, given the logic was complete. There was one issue. I forgot to print out the answer. The people in the information science classes almost all had a previous work history that they wanted to leave behind and enter the world of computer technology. Not all the students could actually grasp the concept of writing computer software. However, in 1971, there were several work roles available. Many of these were associated with computer operations, which did not involve authoring code. I did not become a close friend of anyone in the classes, though for a certain amount of time I maintain contact with one classmate. The atmosphere of the classes was strictly business like, so there wasn't much socializing, though after class we met up at a bar near the school twice.

I contacted my friend Jim Gaspar, who had rented an old multistory house on Daisy Avenue in West Long Beach. This was to be my home from 1972 to 1975. It became known as the "Daisy House." Jim lived upstairs and I forget who lived in the room across from him. It might have been Dave and his wife. Yeah, I don't believe anybody lived in the bedroom downstairs. Dave was addicted to Seconal. He stumbled around the house as his wife helped him walk. He was the original "Dave's Not Here." (A reference to a skit by Cheech and Chong.) Evidently he had some legal, medical connection for the stuff.

The backyard was large. There was a fireplace we could fire up in the winter. Something warped the floor because of multiple earthquakes. The house was built in the early twentieth century and in its heyday was a palace.

For minimal rent, Jim let me occupy a "fishbowl" entrance room offset from the front door. Here is where I studied computer technology at the junior college level. Through this restart of my life, and, yes, I was still an emotional mess, but there was a glimmer of hope.

While going to school, the city college which I paid for myself, I still had a love of rock and blues music. Jim and I got together with the drummer from the Rockin' Pneumonia and played for a large family gathering at Jim's parents' house. This motivated me and Jim to play more music. While studying and with work in Beverly hills, I ran into another drummer, Dave Emgee. The three of us formed a new group, "The Mean Jeanies". As far as bands go, we were okay, but not great. Then we met Dave McKesson who had a recording studio down the street. Dave loved the Eagles, so we learned a couple of their songs after he joined the band. As before, we were okay as a band. Practice continued, but it did not interfere with my primary goal, to learn of enough information science to land a decent job. Jim had his own distractions. He was working on a master's degree in physics at Long Beach State and also had a job as a teacher's assistant.

Having finished enough information technology at the junior college level and with a nominal bachelor's degree in an unrelated subject, I landed a job at United Computing, what in later years might labeled a "startup," but to me it was a real data-processing shop that specialized in numerically controlled machinery, id est, robots and the initial stages of computer graphics. I was getting a wage of seven hundred dollars a month. I could actually put some money in a savings account. And I could eat. I could purchase things and actually have fun. Oh! I came to appreciate importance of a steady income. I would go down to the corner of Daisy and Tenth Street, and actually buy cuts of beef when I could afford it. But I continued to buy bottles of Eastside beer out of habit, a low-quality beer that would cost a pittance a quart.

REINCARNATION

•••

The exit from Gehenna took a couple of years. As I passed through harrowing, I focused on definite goals. Ginny Miles contacted me, and she wanted to get together with me again. Maia and Ginny wanted to move into the Daisy House with me. How could I say no, even though I had two minds about the entire relationship? So Ginny and Maia made the Daisy House their home for the next two years. Dave, as in "Dave's not here," had moved out. Where he ended up, I do not know. There was an empty bedroom on the first floor. There was a small separate bedroom for Maia, now about four years old. Ginny did not like the idea of me working at a new job and also being in a rock band. We argued, and I quit the band, though I was angry for a bit. On the plus side, we easily paid rent, since she was working at Transamerica Corporation and I was working at United Computing. Conflict existed between myself and Ginny, which was never resolved in the two years we were together. Ginny needed stimulation, and I did not provide it. I was a loaner, involved in my own ideas and goals. Despite this, mostly during that time, home life was flawed but functional.

We had an empty bedroom that needed to be filled. We met Mary Jo Mariam through our community connections. Some of the Afro-American community had started an inner-city preschool, which became known as the "Institute." They firmly based it in the black community. I recognized several African American community leaders when I was working with the Black Panther breakfast program. Mary Jo's daughter, Amy, about Maia's age, shared the common bedroom with Maia. Mary Jo worked in the Oil, Chemical, and Atomic Workers union, the OCAW in the Long Beach harbor. When I asked Mary Jo about her work, she simply told me "keeping the pipelines operational". Maia and Amy were happy playmates. Both of them attended the Institute. Mary Blackburn, who had long separated from her husband, was the primary organizer of the school. She and her boyfriend Bobby organized and handled school operations.

I sometimes I cooked food for Maia and Amy. I learned that when I fed them, to always put the dog outside. I learned this after cooking a meat dish and returning to the kitchen for the next task and then checking up on the two girls. The food was gone. "Did you two finish your lunch"? "Yes, we did John". There was the dog in the corner with a shit-eating grin. For a teasing meal, I purchased some green food dye and made the girls green eggs and ham. "Eeuu... what's that?", they exclaimed. "It's green eggs and ham", I responded with a smile. "We don't want green eggs and ham". Then the entire scenario played out. "Would you eat them in a box? Would you eat them with a fox?" I finally got them to taste the green eggs and ham, and the two girls consumed the meal.

* * *

It was an interesting juxtaposition as I led this transitional life. While working for a company, often supplying software for what was, for lack of a better word, robotic-controlled machinery. I once again became involved in community organizations. Casey had returned from where ever he had wandered off to, and was living with his parents in Lakewood. He was also a regular visitor to the Daisy House. Casey convinced me that the Socialist Workers Party, SWP, had the best answer to oppose the Vietnam War. Instead of stacking issues on top of the anti-war movement, demonstration organizing should stick to a single issue of that war in Vietnam. I agreed this populist bottom-up strategy was the best approach. You could stack issues, like the destruction of the Black Panthers, Farm Workers, destabilization of Chile, and the other actions of the USA-sian empire opposed by progressives, but I thought they should be discussed in a one-to-one conversation with sympathetic supporters, and not with a multi-issue slogan.

So after some discussions with myself and Casey, we invited the SWP into the Long Beach radical realm. The culmination of their influence occurred during one of the Culture Nights at the Phinius, which had now once again become a center for community organizations. It was a raucous affair, with objections from an opposing set of viewpoints of those sympathetic to the Cultural

Revolution in China, and associated with the world-view presented by Mao Tse-Tung. My work with the SWP didn't last long. A cadre visited the Daisy House while organizing at Cal State Long Beach. They discovered that my roommate, Jim, had cannabis, so that was that. It was against their rules, so they expelled me. My social life continued to center on the Phinius, which had a food co-op. It was short-lived, but for a year, vegetables and fruits were available at rock-bottom prices.

I realized I had to retool my education. I continued to take courses at Long Beach City College and then, with the permission of my employer, United Computing, I attended information science classes at California State College at Dominguez Hills. The school didn't have a bachelor's of science degree, only a proposed major, so I took all the classes in the proposal. Dominguez Hills had a minor in information science, but it was in the physics department, so I took several courses in electrical engineering focusing on computer hardware.

While a student at UC Berkeley, Jim, the initial renter of the Daisy House, had a summer job with Rodney Strong vineyards. He introduced me to Barossa Valley wines from Australia. He bought them for three dollars a bottle and they were excellent. Years later, I saw them in stores for between forty and fifty dollars a bottle. We had raucous and fun parties at the Daisy House. Jim and I started making homemade beer. The best batch, which we called the "Black Hole," comprised black patent malt and was like an Imperial Stout. We would serve home-brew and an enormous pot of chili, partying until the wee hours of the morning.

But there was a dark-side thread in the Daisy House. After

Mary Jo bought some land near Garberville in the mountains and moved to northern California. Jill, who was once working at the Farmers and Merchants Bank in Long Beach, moved in. Now, I didn't completely understand it, but Jill was now a bonafide junkie. To double the trouble, Old Joe, who was constantly on various strengths of narcotics, was also a long-term junkie. Old Joe also had connections into the Chicano mafia.

This environment was bad news for Jim. He eventually got hooked on "smack." I was lucky we all didn't end up in jail. Through Joe and his connections, Jim walked in one afternoon with about twenty thousand dollars' worth of street cocaine. Fortunately, it went somewhere else, and I never saw it again. Worse, this is when Feds started paying attention to activities originating in the west side Long Beach hood. I don't remember the exact amount, maybe between twenty thousand and thirty thousand dollars. Next, Jim showed up with a pile of counterfeit twenty-dollar bills. "Jim, what are you going to do with these bogus twenty-dollar bills?" "Just pass them off at bars and other places with dim lighting." I looked at the bills. The plates were good, but the paper was not. I am sure the Chicano mafia was the source of the contraband.

Jim ended up in rehab and lost his teaching position at Long Beach State. Through all the drama, I continued to study undergraduate computer science at California State University at Dominguez Hills. Dominguez Hills is an interesting real estate artifact. They nestled it between Compton, which now was a core Afro-American community, i.e., a "hood" and Carson, a core blue-collar community adjunct to the Los Angeles harbor.

The house next door was now vacant and my friend Casey rented it along with his girlfriend, Kim Bearson, who Casey had mentioned several times while in Manhattan and Brooklyn. Also, Casey and I could connect with our old "soap job" work partner, LC Honeycutt. LC also introduced us to Charlie Brown. Yes, that was his real name. He had a junkyard on Anaheim Street, Long Beach. You could just about find anything at Charlie Brown's. He ran your basic junkyard, complete with junk-yard dogs. Think of his business as Sanford and Son with no son. He would make runs to Mexico and sell stuff under market price. You would walk into his office and there was a picture of Martin Luther King Jr. and John F. Kennedy. Often there was an iron frying pan with ham-hocks grilling in a mass of grease. You could find just about anything you wanted from Charlie Brown. That would include tools, car parts, or the latest "import" from Tijuana to moonshine from Compton or African American whores. LC tried to get Casey and me in on some action with Charley's whores after haggling over the price. Casey and I chickened out. We got some of the moonshine, and it tasted awful.

Before things went south at the Daisy House, an amusing event transpired, from my point of view. Jim had a low-powered laser he borrowed from the physics department at Long Beach State. We climbed atop the second story, almost three stories above street level, and directed the laser in front of a traveling car. "Watch this", Jim exclaimed in whatever mental or physical state he was in. To the driver, it was a red light in front of them. The driver would stop, and we would hold the laser stationary. The car would start again, and we would move the laser in front of them as the car proceeded down the street. Of course, it was probably highly illegal even in 1974, but it was entertaining to watch people's reaction to a red light mimicking their movement.

United Computing organized a visit to a customer plant in Orange County, southern California. The plant used our low-level software that I had been working on for a year. I thought to myself, "how is the customer using the three, four and five dimensional numerical data?" Then the Atomic Baby goes into shock. "Nuclear warheads". The factory is using my software to build nuclear warheads. The warheads cost thousands of dollars that will either never be used or destroy humanity. "I'm in a living nightmare". At that point I decided that in the future, even though United Computing had advanced computer technology, I must depart the company. In late 1974, I moved to a different group in United Computing, and became part of the Unigraphics project instead of working on the transformation of numerical data for robotic machines. I ended up on a project where I was working twelve hours a day in February. I didn't see the light of day literally for two weeks. I received a letter from Mary Jo Mariam containing pictures of me surfing when I was a teenager. I was tired and confused. Why did Mary Jo take pictures from who-knows-where and send them to me? I was annoyed. Months later I discovered that when Mary Jo moved to the mountains outside of Garberville south of Arcata in northern California, my former teenage girlfriend, Ann, was working near Mary Jo at an alternate school, and had given Mary Jo my photos may be to "blow my mind". It deeply nonplussed me. It worked.

After Jim made it out of rehab, he returned periodically, though living at his parents' house. Jill stayed on and then Bob Hill, a friend of Casey's and whom I knew, moved into the Daisy house. Bob liked to hustle cars. He would buy cars, maybe do some work on them and turn them for a profit. Fine, but phone calls came in when he was out working or hustling. I became annoyed and started short-circuiting his transactions. It was an amusing conflict, but he remained a friend for years in the future.

Jill remained there for a time. One night, while Ginny and I were in our bed, Old Joe came in angry and pissed, asking who had stolen his stash of heroin. He had a thirty-eight special revolver, and was waving it at my face saying he was going to shoot someone for stealing his stash. Fortunately, Jill, a prime suspect, was not around. This was the first time I ended up looking down at the wrong end of a thirty-eight revolver. Eventually, Old Joe calmed down, and realized that we weren't the ones who took his stash.

Shortly after this incident, Ginny and I split up and Ginny departed the Daisy House. She would remain a friend several years into the future. After her departure, there was a void in my life. When not working again, I turned to music. For a short time, Dave, the drummer, and his interesting bass-playing associate and I formed a band. That didn't last long. Next, Jim and I reconnected with Cee Hope, and attempted to form the West Side Kings, an electric blues band. That also didn't last long. As a good part of this life thread, Jim had recovered and was now working for McDonnell Douglas on the space shuttle project. So Jim and I kept in close contact. Given my social void, next I became involved with Rachel. Somehow, she had a negative reputation in the larger Long Beach community. As a short, somewhat unattractive young woman, she had two strikes against her. Russell Sheen once told me she was one of the most intelligent woman he had met on campus. Her negative persona manifested itself as a constant complainer. Rachel was the last woman to hang with me at the Daisy House. I had been living by myself, so she managed articles I needed, like towels, blankets, and other essential stuff. Maybe this worked for a short while, since Rachel was recently divorced and Ginny and I had broken up. Though she was disliked in the Long Beach community, I had a soft spot for Rachel. She wasn't evil, just a constant complainer. At a smaller student protest outdoor meet at Long Beach State, a few years before, Rachel showed up at the protest. She arrived riding a camel to where the group had gathered in front of the bookstore, completely buck naked. That took some guts, so I didn't forget the incident.

Around 1975, I jettisoned myself from the Daisy House. We had one last party. "Send Me Dead Flowers" was the theme. It was an oblique pun on the Daisy House. We held it in the afternoon and quite several people attended, including at least one woman with whom I worked with at United Computing. After the party, I moved to an apartment on Broadway Avenue above a male gay bar. The Peanut Gallery, a.k.a. the Nut Bar, was within walking distance from the apartment, but I was ready for a new environment. I had had it with Long Beach and all the baggage that came with that city's environment. After a short period, I left the apartment after one tenant threw a tantrum when he couldn't get the front door open.

I moved once again from this Long Beach milieu to North Redondo Beach with two fellow workers from United Computing. The government was no longer hunting me. The Vietnam War was finished. I could disappear into a lower-middle-class North Redondo Beach neighborhood without repercussions.

ENGINEER I

•••

I exited the west side of Long Beach and all the good, bad, and ugly. I remained in touch with most of the people I had met while living in Seal Beach and Long Beach. Two of the people I worked with at United Computing needed a roommate, so I moved to North Redondo Beach. The house was in a neighborhood being converted into dense housing, a "short" way from the beach. TRW, the aerospace corporation, still existed to the east of the house, so there were several aerospace workers in the neighborhood. But also it had torn several houses torn down, so we had a quintessential party house, with no houses next to us. If there was an on-Earth equivalent of Animal House the movie, it was here. The place was on Ernest Avenue. Across the street from the house was a park where kids played baseball. We christened the house "Chez Ernest."

The parties were of a different ilk than that of the Daisy House. Mostly, it was folks from United Computing, their friends, and the friends and acquaintances of my two roommates, "Ski" and

"El-Starkero." I also had a nickname, "Catfish." There was a cheap painting on the front living room wall with four horses. We nicknamed one El-Starkero and the other Ski. They named the last two "Catfish coming" and "Catfish going." "We weren't sure if you were coming or going," exclaimed my roommates. There were a couple of amusing events that took place at our parties. One reveler drank too much, so we put him up on a couch in the living room. At four in the morning, he woke up and went back sleeping in the park across the street. "Ski" checked in on him at 4:00 AM. He had vanished, but his car was still there. We found him sleeping in the park, woke him up, and got him back on the couch. "Ski" checked in on him later in the morning and he was back in the park. The sprinklers came on at 7:00 AM in the park and the fellow's car was gone, so all ended strange but okay. At another party, someone passed out in the hallway leading out of the kitchen. "El-Starkero" started our vacuum cleaner with the big bright light to illuminate the cleaning path. Then he brought it slowly through the hall and whispered in the guy's ear. "Trains coming. Trains coming."

As mentioned before, at work, I switched groups. I had been working with the modification of basic robotic machinery so a specific machine could use effectively it. Now I was working in the Unigraphics groups. You can think of Unigraphics as the digital equivalent of a drafting board in three dimensions. It was an upgrade for my skills. I grasped most of the new tasks, and soon found myself on loan to Los Alamos Labs near Santa Fe, New Mexico.

The first trip was interesting. I took a flight on Trans-Texas airlines. Peers at work had nicknamed it "tree-top" airlines. When it landed, I needed to rent a car, but I didn't have a credit card. I paid cash or check for everything. The rental company had to make desperate calls to the home office in Carson, California. I don't remember exactly how they resolved the lack of a credit card issue, but I ended up in a '70s car headed from Albuquerque to Santa Fe. During trips to Los Alamos, I would pass Raphael's Silver Cloud Lounge, a notorious New Mexican Bar, mentioned in popular songs. On each trip I had with me in the car, I had a vast deck of 80-column punch cards in a tray that had the Unigraphics Software logo. Also in the car, I had an old-old school multi-platter hard drive, and wasn't sure it had survived the cargo hold of the plane. They required me to get Unigraphics operational on the complex minicomputer system at Los Alamos.

I spent the night in Santa Fe and showed up at Los Alamos the next morning. It was an armed camp with tanks, towers, and men with automatic weapons strapped into various positions, some relaxed, others nervously in hand. "Don't be afraid, you'll be okay," I told myself. Later, the client told me there was a revolutionary band in the mountains, therefore Los Alamos had become an armed camp. I was met at the gate by an armed guard and taken into a complex with the graphics system. They based their graphics system on a high-speed connection between two mini-computers. Jerry was the manager. Working at the same complex were several engineers and scientists from UC Berkeley. I knew that this was the birthplace of the atomic bomb. And I also knew that they had recently detonated some small nuclear devices in the New Mexico desert to the southwest of the complex. No escape for the Atomic Baby.

I made four trips to New Mexico and while there ate at Philomenas restaurant, a delightful place which served local, New Mexico-style stacked enchiladas. Unfortunately, the restaurant ceased to do business a few years later when the owner passed away and the kids ran the business into the ground. I also drove down through New Mexico, including Taos, Tres Ritos, and Santa Fe. I viewed New Mexico as a wonderful place imaging that I would move there and live one day. New Mexico won my heart. People from an Anglo background were a minority in the state's population. I loved the area and went back two more times in later years to visit places like Taos and Santa Fe.

Eventually, United Computing convinced Jerry that to get this dual processor vector graphics system working, he should ship the graphics processor and its minicomputer to Carson. He did this, and in a short time, I had the system working, though not as fast in terms of execution speed as it should have been. Los Alamos declassified several very intricate computer-aided design images generated by a digital plotter. I appreciated them, and was fascinated by their intricacy and put them up on my cubicle walls. At one point, Jerry, the manager of the group at Los Alamos, visited our installation in Carson and looked at the plots the Atomic Baby had attached to the cubicle walls. He turned white as a ghost. I did not know it, but I had the complete plans to build an atomic device from discarded nuclear waste. One group at Los Alamos had actually successfully tested such a device before they banned all nuke testing. After this incident, to uncover software errors, Los Alamos sent images of the "Star Ship Enterprise".

When I told some of my friends about it upon returning to Long Beach, they seemed anxious that a recent student radical had plans for a nuclear device. I told them it didn't matter. By now I realized that a revolution in what was then called a first-world country, where the underclass is a small plurality and the powerful dominate not through arms but through thought, that only consider a non-violent revolution, not just a choice, but a necessity.

The women employees at United Computing were a constant source of amusement. I'm not talking about the secretaries, but the female engineers. After being hired, one of the marketing employees asked one of the new female hires, "would you get me a cup of coffee?" The answer was, "get your own coffee. I'm an engineer". The last year I worked there, I had the opportunity to become involved with two divorcées. One, who had recently graduated from Long Beach State with a master's degree in mathematics, liked to visit a bar near United Computing to drink. She would tell me she was married to her husband, but didn't love him. She was attractive, but ten years older than me. The second women, an original member of a systems team, had recently divorced her husband, and asked me out on a date, mostly to dance, more than once. She was cute, but not stunning. I told her, "No", not because of her looks, but her somewhat arrogant personality. I guess she needed that to be successful in a software shop in the 1970s. Dorothy Cleary was probably the most sexually active female software engineer. She had no fear of going fishing for male partners off the "company pier." She had a degree in mathematics, came from Montana State University, and was a good software engineer. Another one, named Sharon Shirley, was an excellent engineer regarding automated part tooling and automated machinery, was older than myself, but would only involve herself with salespeople and managers.

Several important events transpired in the middle 1970s. They sold United Computing to McDonald Douglas Automation, an aerospace company. We all had to have photographs taken and given badges. Of course, the general attitude was, "We don't need no stinkin' badges..." The other significant event was I moved to Venice, California. I took Sherry, the half-dingo dog, with me. The apartment was in the heart of a rough neighborhood at the corner of Fourth Street and Vermont Avenue. The front door of the upstairs apartment was steel reinforced. I could hear gunshots at night. For a while I commuted from Venice to Carson, but I was in the market for a new job. The skills I had attained in the Unigraphics group increased my marketability.

In the 1960s, cannabis surrounded me. In the 1970s, cocaine surrounded me. The owner of the Phineas, in Long Beach, who had always been clean as a whistle regarding any drugs, fell into a habit of cocaine. Ultimately, it cost him the business. Though cocaine is not as physically addictive as a narcotic, it is extremely psychologically addictive. If you take cocaine, all you want is more cocaine. The popular culture at the time associated the drug with sexuality. There is a long history of the drug that anyone can read, starting with Sigmund Freud. I experienced it from time-to-time, but it felt like an "upper" and to counter the effect, you had to consume large amounts of alcohol. This guaranteed a terrible hangover the next day. As far as sexuality is concerned, yes, it made you want sex, but while high, it was difficult to perform. Possibly, women liked men to use it, since the male would become aroused, but would only have an orgasm with great difficulty. Thus, through drugs, a female lover could conjure a "sixty-minute man". At one point I told everyone, "never bring that drug into my house." I meant it.

Besides the dog, Sherry, I imported from Long Beach. While visiting my father at the Santa Monica Yacht Club, I spotted a little, starving, half-Siamese cat. I took her home, fed her, and Lilly almost instantly became the terror of the apartment. Trained by Sherry, the half dingo, they were inseparable. I lived upstairs, but would open the door from time-to-time and Lilly would go out and pick a fight with a neighborhood cat. Then she would yowl and call "her dingo". That was the end of the fight. Even though the apartment was in a nasty neighborhood, it was three blocks from the beach. I walked to the Venice boardwalk, and enjoyed it in its latter-day, hipster heyday. Of course, by the turn of the century, it had become a hangout for the rich-hip and a shadow of its Bohemian past. Back then, you could find an interesting array of people, instead of what exists there today, bands of homeless lumpen-proletariat along with the gentrified locals. Coffee houses were scarce in 1977, but they were accessible and inexpensive. There were street performers, one of the most popular of whom was "Sunset Swami." He would make jokes about everything under the sun, in a manner similar to Lenny Bruce. An African American looking amazingly like Jimi Hendrix would play his battery driven electric guitar while on roller skates. The Venice boardwalk was a classic freak show you enjoyed without fear or stress.

I met Randall and Deanna Wills, who lived on Fifth Street near Ocean Park Boulevard in Santa Monica. They were friends for several years until their relationship disintegrated. Randall worked construction, and for several years, he was successful while establishing a partnership with a licensed contractor. His psychological addiction to cocaine, among other drugs, and real addiction to hard liquor would be his undoing, downfall, and ultimate death. But for a period, he functioned and supported his family, as free-swinging as they were. Randall and Deanna introduced me to "Hook", another classical character well known in Venice. Hook lost his hand, and I've forgotten the story of the lost hand, but it was likely recited to me at some point. He also had a limp. His wife caught him "messing around" and shot him in the leg with a pistol. Hook sold me a nice acoustic Guild guitar a couple of years later that I still own. They well knew him all over Venice as a singer and a harmonica player in a local band known as the "Canaligators". A clamp took the place of Hook's lost hand, within which he held a harmonica. One of his favorite songs was "Flip, Flop and Fly" by Big Joe Turner. It is also one of my favorites.

I spent a few nights in a bar near where I lived called O'Mahoney's in Santa Monica. The band members were old contacts from Long Beach and Northern California. So often with Deanna and Randall, plus folks from United Computing, including my old roommates in North Redondo, could be found in the Santa Monica pub on certain nights when the band was playing. The name of the band was the Mike McCullum Band, named after its leader. The band played a broad range of music, including one of the leader's favorites, "Deep River Blues." Along with something like "folk rock," they played blues and a touch of swing in a song named "Swing Shift Suzie." Fun nights often ended up in someone's apartment where sub rosa behavior took place.

While living in Venice, I had some not-so-good job interviews, like one with the County of Los Angeles. At least where they were blunt with me. The answer was direct and truthful. "You are overqualified for this job and too talented. Look for a better job." So I did. Eventually I connected with TranTelecommunications Inc. Several contributors, especially network scientists from UCLA, influenced the company. These scientists were pioneers of computer networking. Tran was building controllers of a hybrid packet and circuit switching network. To the reader who doesn't understand such technical terms, think of this as an extensive set of telephones with deep integration of software and hardware. They sold these hybrid systems to the California state college system for remote communications. This technology can be considered a predecessor to the Internet, which exploded into world-wide proportions in 1995.

I walked in the door at Tran and was met by my manager, Doug. We made our way into a lab that was buzzing with complex computer machinery. The smell of electrical discharge filled the air. He introduced me to a large oriental man with a huge laugh and smile, Howard. Howard escorted me to a shared office. But on the way there, I noticed a hole in the wall the size of a fist. Someone had written on the wall with a black marker, "Howard did this". So, along with the new technology, there was also frustration at Tran. Howard was never afraid to speak his mind. I always found Howard interesting and challenging to work with, at this job and at a job soon, at a different company.

ENGINEER II

•••

I now stepped into the world of hard-core engineering. I had completed most of the undergraduate computer science courses at Cal State Dominguez Hills. The head of the information science department advised that I shouldn't pursue a second bachelor's degree in computer science, but gain entry into a master's computer science program. But the rub was I was a full-time worker and then some. I visited University of Southern California and they were not interested. The options in 1978 for State College were very limited, so I tried Loyola Marymount University with my transcripts from Cal State Dominguez Hills, and I was accepted. Even better, most of the courses were afternoon or night courses. The Jesuits had pulled me into their fold. Working full time and taking graduate level courses is not for the meek. By the end of the night during weekdays and even on weekends, I was mentally exhausted. I continued with this routine until 1980. The Masters Degree in computer science at Loyola Marymount was relatively easy to enter. They accepted any undergraduate degree as long as you had a background in science and math. The comprehensive exam to complete the degree is difficult. The exam was 5 hours long with a fifteen minute bathroom break. You had seventeen and one-half minutes to answer each question. They were all written questions. While taking the test, I could see the sweat pouring off test taker's head. I answered all the questions, passed the test and shortly after that gained a Masters Degree in Computer Science. I had two standout memories during the two years I spent in this program. The first was three Roman Catholic priests studying computer engineering. The second was a colloquium in computer law that was fascinating.

Tran, introduced in Engineer I, was in El Segundo in Southern California. It was much easier to drive to El Segundo when compared to Carson, California. The switching system in Trans product was complex, in that it had different hardware units of memory to achieve larger memory capacity. I activated these configurable units as the software executed. At this point in the computer industry, they still entered program source on 80 column punch cards. Upon entering my new office, there sat another software engineer with paper listings. "Hi, I'm your new office mate John". "Nice to meet you, my name is also John". Here was yet another name collision. Nicolai also started the same day I did and was a friend of the "existing John". Nicolai referred to "existing John" as "Q". Ah, we solved the name collision. We now had Nicolai, "Q" and John R. "Q" graduated from the University of California of Riverside. Nicolai graduated from UC Berkeley and was a mathematician. "Q" and I worked on the operating system to run the complex network controller. Nicolai ran the numbers of performance and latency.

"Q" and Nicolai were always discussing a game named Dungeons and Dragons. "A Lawful Neutral character will obey given laws whether good or evil". Or, "can't a neutral monster be Neutral Hungry?" Now I already knew something about this game after looking at my youngest brother's D&D books. I was fascinated by all the levels and numbers, and the game struck me as similar to baseball with all its statistics. Years later, I told people you can't be a true computer nerd unless you've played D&D. There was a "Creepy Crawly" drawn on the blackboard in colored chalk with all its statistics, like how lethal was it or how fast it could fly. Of a more lasting interest, "Q" and Nicolai introduced me to science fiction fandom. I had loved science fiction since my mother took me to see Forbidden Planet when I was a child, so I was interested in fandom. Q told me. "You must attend a con". That would be a science fiction convention. It is an interest of mine to this day.

I continued to commute to Tran via bus or car after Tran moved to the edge of Culver City next to Marina Del Rey. I could perceive that the intensity of the company was changing, likely in the wrong way. We went from private offices to a huge bullpen separated by partitions. It became much more difficult to work in. My consternation really didn't matter. The company was purchased by Amdahl a couple of years later and vanished into what was then a corporate giant. An IBM-inspired company in Fox Hills, another designated area in Culver City, recruited me. It was also very close to where we lived. The company was named Cybertek. I worked there for a couple months before realizing I had made a mistake. They gave the software developers no respect. I have a distinct memory of administrators and especially the salespeople when showing visitors the company and then looking down at the developers and saying, "Well, these are just the programmers". Realizing the administrators and salespeople, that "programmer" was a derogatory term. Departing Cybertek was now a goal. The company never more than a niche player in the insurance software business, while low-cost mini-computers were profitable when compared to a large main-frame. I got one last lick in before I departed. Having authored a reporting system written in a low level computer language, I specified the functionality, documented its usage and had it signed off. This is what I didn't tell them. I wrote the entire report system in self-referential logic called recursion. I wrote the security segment using self modifying code. That means the software was programming itself. Later, I heard about it from the remaining employee developers. "John, what kind of programming is this? We don't understand it."

I had contacts at a company specializing in office automation named Jacquard. The contacts included Howard from Tran and "El Starkero" from United Computing. Jacquard was early office automation company originally based in Santa Monica. They based office automation on mini-computers, a technology I understood. Personal computers were looming on the horizon, but the personal computer was not available as the platform for office automation. Before they hired me, Addressograph-Multigraph Corporation from Chicago, Illinois gained Jacquard. The company was told "to grow." They tried to do this, but it was chaotic and inconsistent. I will never forget my interview before they hired me with Pam, one of the high-level managers. Pam was busty and big, but not obese. I always got along with her. When Pam shut the door of her office, she had a male centerfold from Playgirl Magazine. She had a good sense of humor, so I looked at the poster and then at her and said "but he doesn't have an erection". Pam laughed. In late 1980, they hired me into the networking group, where two managers often gave me conflicting priorities. Matrix management doesn't work unless managers in the matrix coordinate their goals. The people at Jacquard were interesting and quirky. The documentation group consisted entirely of women, many of them with odd haircuts and dyed random colors. I eventually realized that most of the women in documentation were gay. It didn't matter. They used Jacquard's word processor to produce top quality manuals. It is a perfect case where a company was "eating its own dog food".

Six months later, AM International seemed to run short of finance capital and they lay one half of the company off. I could see the writing on the wall. I would take long lunches. Word processors appeared on laptops. We also knew that Intel was about to release an inexpensive processor. My fellow workers at AM Jacquard could sense the end was coming. We all knew it. Our group went to a restaurant in Redondo Beach and consumed far too much alcohol. I convinced my primary boss, Marilyn, an attractive woman about eight years older than myself, to smoke a cigar. Marilyn and I walked out to the beach to sober up. We then walked out on the breakwater. I held her hand as we went over the rocks. "Marilyn, are you okay? Yea, I'm okay." Then we all went back to the workplace, and Marilyn made it home okay. Soon we had a companywide meeting, The Company was closing down. Addressograph-Multigraph Corporation, the company that had bought Jacquard, what would be in the future a "startup," was bankrupt. Most of the company was being laid off. The hard capital and a few of the employees could work for new buyers, based in Orange County. A very few workers did this. They locked the doors of AM Jacquard and that was that. I had hoped to join with a startup in Pasadena being organized by Nicolai, the former worker at TranTelecommunications. That opportunity fell through. I contacted recruiters, and within three weeks, I interviewed at Honeywell's Los Angeles Development Center. They hired me into the database group.

* * *

In 1977, I was married in Las Vegas. I had initially suggested a standard church wedding, but we decided against it. When the Justice of the Peace that performed the vows arrived at the bride's part of the oath, the answer was "I will not say those words." Something of an argument ensued with the Justice of the Peace. I think he gave up after a while and completed the ceremony. He probably thought "this marriage won't last a month". Of course it continues and has lasted many years. We departed Las Vegas the next day and returned to one of our favorite out-of-the way places, Beatty, Nevada, a mining town. I visited a miner's bar just outside of town. It was loud with drunks, and not a place to hold a conversation. Evidently, an off-shore company was using some nasty chemicals to drive some gold out of the hills near Rhyolite, now a ghost town. The ghost town itself was interesting, but the real prize lies to the west of this ghost town. There is another tiny ghost town, Leadfield, that leads to the entrance of Titus Canyon, Nevada, which ends in Death Valley, California. As you go through the canyon, the walls constrict almost to the size of a vehicle.

About half-way through the canyon, all vehicles had stopped. I exited the Honda Civic I had bought three years earlier and saw a photographer capturing images of a large group of mountain sheep. Everyone just exited their vehicles, with nobody complaining. We stood there viewing the largest group of mountain sheep I have ever seen to this day. After the vehicles started moving through Titus Canyon, the walls seem to constrict as you moved through. After swerving through the canyon, it emptied into Death Valley proper. The visuals and sensations were that of an alien world.

One time while walking in a mall during lunch near where I worked, an Afro-American man decked out in construction equipment, starting yelling at me, saying, "Hey! Hey! Did you go to Long Beach State?" I recognized him as Squeeky, a former Black Panther whose gun I borrowed for college plays, ten years in the past. He told me how members of the Black Student Union now worked at TRW, the aerospace company as engineers. "Dwight too?" "Yes" Dwight was the leader of the Black Student Union. I was not surprised. The people in the Black Student Union had lots of energy and smarts.

Also in 1980, we took a long holiday for two weeks. Our journey path started in El Paso. The train station for the next leg of our journey was across the Mexican border, on the other side of El Paso, in Juarez. The train departed early in the morning. First, we, including Maia and Amy, went to the immigration office in Juarez and it was closed. Next, we made a brave move. We boarded the train without papers and departed for Juarez. I couldn't help but notice a huge hammer and sickle painted on the side of a building wall by some Mexican Communists of unknown orientation.

After a daylight ride through the desert of northern Mexico, we arrived at Chihuahua, then hired a taxicab to take us to our hotel where we ate dinner. The restaurant was at the top of the hotel, and there was a dance floor with no balcony or rail at the edge. ¡Pobrecito! Too much tequila and off you go. Han muerte ...

The next day, we boarded the train that would take us to Cobre Canyon. There was a machine gun turret on the engine and a small platoon of federal Mexican troops on the train. I believe they were preventing attacks on the train by armed revolutionaries or possibly banditos. In the middle of the trip, there was a mix-up on trains headed towards the coast like ours, and another train on the same track headed towards Chihuahua. The crews and engineers argued for about an hour and finally we were on our way to Cobre Canyon lodge in the Sierra Madre Mountains. I seriously doubt if this lodge now exists, as it did in 1980. The meals comprised machaca al pastor, goat meat. I doubt if I could eat it now, but at the time it didn't bother me. We were told not to eat the mushrooms the local natives were harvesting. Hmm, shades of Don Juan and magic mushrooms. There were several Europeans in the group that stayed at the lodge, including German and French tourists. They told us that this route was popular in their native countries. The local natives, who spoke an unfamiliar language rather than Spanish, told me I was a mountain man from California. We visited the local small Roman Catholic Church near the Lodge. There were neatly ordered skulls placed under the pews. We were told that these were remains of dead parishioners. The priest allowed the skulls given the attendees would sneak them in even if the priest told them not to.

We stayed there several days before continuing on to Divisidero. It was a less primitive lodge than Cobre Canyon, but there were only a few of us there. My wife became quite ill, most likely from the machaca. We stayed in little individual cabins. So I left her in discomfort and went to the front desk and told them, "Mi esposa estas inferma. ¿Hay medico en los quartos?" "Si como no". I returned to the cabin and after a bit, there was a knock on the door. Standing outside the door was the platoon from the train. An officer led four men in armed with automatic weapons. After the initial panic, the officer introduced himself in perfect English, and told us he was the only medically trained person in the area. He gave my wife some drugs and a few hours later, she was okay. By the time we finally made it to Las Moches by train, we had missed our boat ride to La Paz. There was another complication. With two minors, we hadn't been admitted to the country since the immigration office at Juarez had been closed when we took the train to Chihuahua. So, in Las Moches, I took the entire party to the local immigration office. It was interesting that I was reporting to the office with myself and three other "illegal aliens." The officer would only talk to me in Spanish, and I eventually convinced him we could not get our passports stamped because the office was closed. "Nosotros llegamos, pero la officina no hay abierto." I believe the officer was concerned about the two minor young girls.

We took a bus to Mazatlán and took an airplane back to Los Angeles. I left the Sierra Madre Mountains and the resultant trip thinking, "We don't need any stinkin' immigration papers."

* * *

This memoir would not be complete without more on the story of Ginny Miles. In 1977, Ginny moved into the apartment where I lived in Venice after I agreed to help take care of her daughter Maia while she was working a software contract in Cleveland. Maia was a bright little girl that had been in the Daisy House with me in Long Beach. For a while she had her young girlfriend, Amy, Mary Jo Mariam's daughter who would visit from time to tome. After they sold the apartment, the new owner wanted our apartment because of all four apartments, ours was the best kept up. The new owner evicted us. In 1978, we purchased a house with three bedrooms and two baths in Culver City about three miles from the beach. Maia and her mother moved in with me with Ginny, assisting with the mortgage. And for a short time, that worked out. I was tolerant of my ex-girlfriend and her ways. Ginny often could not judge character in people. Or maybe she could, but as a rebel with too many causes, she would pick the dangerous course out of spite. Here, it was a boyfriend with bad habits and a careless attitude. He was a biker that couldn't get it together to get a motorcycle. Some notable land marks near the newly purchased house on Sawtelle Boulevard were stereo gas stations and stereo liquor stores at each end of our block. Tito's Tacos, a well-known institution, was in walking distance around the corner. In 1980, I paid Ginny her part of the mortgage and she departed on not so friendly terms.

DISTANCES

...

The first Iraqi war occurred in 1989. During the war, I went to Paris with my family for the price it would have cost for a spring break in Las Vegas. It was an excellent occasion but also wrought with some fear. We stood out as an obvious USAsian family, but on the surface, it didn't matter. The flight that we took to Paris, TWA Flight 800 from New York, was the same flight that would explode in mid-air in 1996. Various theories exist on why that fatal flight exploded, but probably it was because of a fault near the fuel tank. I guess it's just a matter of time and place when your number is up. I knew Paris had a large Muslim population, and I even viewed several mosques at a distance. My son was both excited and demanding. But he really broadcast "I am a kid from the USA". The stay on the Left Bank was educational. Most Parisians are nasty, but if you notice, they are almost as nasty to each other as to an outsider. The best food consumed there, other than the wonderful baguettes and local farm produce, were crepes and Thai food. Hot dogs were available on the street, which were the size of sausages encased in small baguettes. These Parisian style hot dogs became a staple in my son's travel diet.

The Louvre was massive and overwhelming. My son was in the second grade, and very enamored with the Teenage Mutant Ninja Turtles. It impressed him that each Turtle—Donatello, Leonardo, Michelangelo and Raphael—had art work in the Louvre. But the museum that fascinated me was Musée D'Orsay because the content was more concise and each exhibit fascinating. I must admit I am partial to impressionist art. A zoo near the mosque was one of the oddest I have ever seen. It was a zoo of microbes, bacteria, other forms of microscopic life. Ben asked me, "Dad, are these real?", while he viewed each one under the microscope. "Yes, they are. Outside of the microscope you can see the name. It has a common name in French and English. Here is the scientific name in Latin." I think my son was a bit nonplussed by the entire experience.

We stayed in a two-star hotel on the Left Bank. There was a common bathroom, but we had a private shower. The room was on the second story and overlooked a small rue that would support mostly pedestrian or bicycle traffic. We would watch street performers in their gaudy and bright costumes from the window. "Dad, let's go see them on the street." Reluctantly, I would give in.

In Paris, the drunks were very upfront. While in the Metro, a drunk had a sign out with an empty bottle of wine and a second bottle half full. The sign said, "Je a besoin un bouteille du vin". "I need a bottle of wine". A couple of days later, while returning for the afternoon to freshen up and recharge, and going into the hotel entrance, I noticed a drunk at the end of the rue. He was walking up and down the rue and yelling, "Je suis la rue, je suis la rue!" "I am the street, I am the street!" We waited a bit and when he was at the other end of the alley, we tried to enter our hotel room. The drunk immediately spotted me. He started walking down the alley in slow, deliberate steps, pretending he was a cowboy, and had his hands on imaginary pistols on his belt. We high-tailed it into the hotel. Fortunately, he didn't follow us.

The wonderful baguettes were delivered to the hotel each morning, and we would enjoy a basic breakfast of bread, jam, and coffee before continuing to wander around Paris. We found a Mexican restaurant, which had the re-fried beans served in a total homogeneous pureed form. I asked the owner, who originated from California, why the re-fried beans were done that way and the person told me that "it's the only way the French will eat them." Departing Paris and going through customs in New York and speaking with the paranoid agent taught me that when you enter the USA from a foreign country, the agent has almost total control over you.

* * *

After the onerous task of laying off half my group because of a change in technology, I continued as a group manager at Citicorp TTI. A group manager is analogous to a low level vice president at Citibank. My group comprising six remaining employees, including myself, who supported and changed the Unix servers in the data center. If anything went wrong in the data center, I got the first call. More than once I received a call at 02:00 AM by a computer operator that could barely speak English. Citicorp TTI business culture centered on many meetings. Sometimes, if you were a senior employee of any shade, you would spend a good portion of your day in meetings. This was predictable, since the process for software development was inefficient because of many manual, non-automated steps. Each day, they would review the attempted goals in a meeting. It was common for an employee to say, "Now is the time for my two-o'clock". They required all managers to attend several classes. Some of these classes I enjoyed. The excellent classes in business English improved my writing capability. The classes for learning French were simply fun. Picking apart the movie "Twelve O'clock High" regarding management styles was interesting.

After returning from the trip to Paris, I switched groups, and now was manager of the Unix systems development group for the Unicom processor, the base and core hardware of Citibank's ATMs. I was still a group manager, but did a lot of the ground dirty-work myself. The group liked my democratic management style, but several employees were rather annoyed with me when I called them out on poor work hours, or spending large amounts of time on the phone with non-Citibank businesses. One in my group, a Russian who had been in the Red Army in the Soviet Union, had many tales to tell when living in the Soviet Union. He and other Russians from the Soviet Union were very well-educated that worked at CitiCorp TTI. They knew the difference between a Bolshevik and a Social Democrat. The Russian that was in my group and myself had an interesting trip to Washington, DC. We both were attending a technical conference with our admission funded by CitiCorp. After we arrived, it started snowing. After attending the convention, we took the underground to the Capitol. Everything was frozen as we walked around in the snow. For the time, it felt like something out of a spy or thriller movie. The next day after this excursion, again we attended the conference. The storm had transformed into a blizzard and the third rail froze, halting metro transit. We had to take a taxi back to the hotel at inflated prices. I ended up walking in deep snow, visiting nearby bars with great bands. I returned to Washington, DC years later on holiday, but this trip in the blizzard is the one I remember best.

As a group manager, I could have come close to being fired for my behavior at one particular meeting, although I didn't yell or act in an obnoxious manner. The discussion continued about a particular release, which was absurdly late because of turnaround times for fixes and saves. Given the name conventions, it was called Sys822. People looked at me because I wasn't saying anything. I had gone to a mall, and bought a mechanical version of the Energizer Bunny, put a Sys822 label on it, put it on the table, started it up, and sent it down on the table. My comment was "Still going."

I continued as a group manager for the Unix systems group and eventually attempted to engineer a full-development environment on their Motorola base system normally used for ATMs. The idea at the time being to use their target hardware for development, so discrepancies in hardware and software are reduced or eliminated. After a few months, I requested that someone else be the group manager, and returned to being a developer. I couldn't take the boring meetings anymore, especially watching a one-on-one show with the manager and the most vocal developer. To stay awake in meetings, I would draw cartoons. People thought I was taking notes. See the Geek Apocrypha I, years 1985-1991. I continued with my role as a developer until the massive layoff, because of a change in hardware and software. I had the chance to apply for jobs with other groups within the company, but I departed for my next corporate experience.

I interviewed at several companies and had an offer from Amdahl Corporation. I was ready to join Amdahl in the Silicon Valley when a former employee from Honeywell recognized my name on my curriculum vitae, and had me interview at International Computers Limited, formally Computer Consoles Incorporated, in the Unix systems development group. The interview at Amdahl was stressful and I'm surprised they wanted to make an offer. I had to commute from Los Angeles to San Jose in a single morning and was exhausted. In the afternoon, I accidentally walked into the women's bathroom. Fortunately, no one was in there. So I turned down Amdahl and went with ICL. The recruiter was unconditionally annoyed with me. Fujitsu bought ICL, where ICL was an old-school British computer firm that now had a development group in Lake Forest, almost in San Diego County, in the south of Orange County.

When hired, I told the human resources representative I used to ride a bicycle to work in Santa Monica. She told me, "If you ride your bike down to this place, I guarantee you'll be a lot thinner." Commuting from Culver City to Lake Forest was a genuine issue. My stepmother and my father owned a condo in North San Diego at La Costa. It was closer and an easier drive to Lake Forest. So I made a deal to stay with them in La Costa three days a week, and commute from North San Diego instead of from Culver City. It was much easier when I was there by myself. I could control my food and set my own hours. This was important since I had to be at work by 6:30 AM in order to communicate with the Brits via a satellite video link. This was before the days of Webex and other similar technologies that appeared in the next decade. I believe that this work schedule permanently scrambled my clock. I became a hard core early morning person. My job was cracking what were "Unix kernel" software bugs as they arrived from the field. There were two people in the group. Phil, a young software engineer, and Joe, a Christian Palestinian that grew up in Iraq. Joe was very paranoid about just about everything. Phil was a joker. On April First, he hacked the internal system to print out an error message on all developer's and manager's monitors that the systems were crashing. Phil was rather amused to see all management run out of the office in unison.

During this period, the second inner city revolt took place after the police beating of Rodney King. I observed from afar since I was in San Diego. When I finally returned to Culver City the Friday after the rebellion, there were armed National Guardsman at the local stores. My son's baseball game in the park was canceled. The event shook the foundations of the Southern California social climate. At a company picnic shortly after the Los Angeles rebellion, one manager in Lake Forest passed out t-shirts that had an ICL minicomputer on top of an earthquake fault graphic. The caption was Riots, Computers and Earthquakes with palm trees aside the minicomputer.

Soon after this, when I absorbed a thorough understanding of the current Unix system that ran on ICL minicomputers, they sent me to the United Kingdom. I flew from LAX, departing about 5:00 PM West Coast time, and arrived at Heathrow the next morning. The company provided a car, but I had never driven a right-hand drive vehicle. But I learned fast. I had a reserved hotel room a distance from the primary facility in Bracknell. My first mission involved finding breakfast and then driving to work. It was completely dark at 8:00 local time. I had to scrape the frost off my inexpensive Italian-made rent-a-car. Brit newscasters at the time announced not traffic jams, but "tail-backs." Not knowing the roads, I carefully followed the map to Bracknell and found the facility where I was to work. I was on time, went through the security station, and reported to where I would be stationed for the next few weeks. Though dead tired, I started my job of cracking bugs using memory dumps with the identical method I used in the facility at Lake

Forest. For lunch, the workers would visit a local pub, or an older woman would wander through the facility and yell, "Troll-ee! Troll-ee!" She pushed a cart loaded with sandwiches and drinks. A Brit sandwich always had butter, even a peanut butter sandwich, and slices of cucumber in it. This combination was constant for all Brit sandwiches.

Food became an issue in the UK. I loathed the local food of overcooked meat and vegetables in a typical eatery that was practically mush. This I rectified in several ways. When entering a pub, I ordered a "plowman's plate," which comprised pickle, cheeses, and fresh fruit and veggies. Next, I drove to the equivalent of a British supermarket, Sainsburys. Here I would purchase fresh fruits, breads, rolls, cheeses, and an assortment of snacks that would hold me over from time-to-time. Next to Bracknell, there was a historic little town called Wokingham. Here I discovered an Indian-national restaurant that became a mainstay during my visits to the UK.

This was my first working trip to the UK. The dark, cold, and conditions got to me. I caught a cold, which turned into bronchitis. I visited the front desk and informed them of my medical condition. The service person on duty told me that a doctor would visit my room. In three or four hours, there was a knock on the hotel door. A doctor with his medical bag appeared. I explained I was coughing yellow mucus. He examined me and told me I had bronchitis and that it would be to my advantage if it didn't turn into pneumonia. He prescribed me an antibiotic and gave me detailed instructions on how to find the "chemist" or a pharmacy. Then he asked me "Are you EC?", that is European Community. I answered, "No," and waited for the other shoe to drop. "I'm from the states." "I'm sorry, but you will have to pay cash. That will be twenty-five quid", the doctor replied. I almost fell off the bed. This was the equivalent price of an excellent dinner. In the states it would have cost hundreds of dollars. I escorted him to the front desk where the good doctor took a shot of brandy and exited into the five centigrade temperature. I will never forget this lesson. It taught me how seriously the USAsian medical system was, and still is, broken.

I made several trips from LAX to Heathrow. I got along with the Brits, even though sometimes I had trouble comprehending some of the local dialect. When one worker approached me after seeing me struggling with a mistake on a form, she asked me, "Can I tepex that out for you?" I believe she meant Tipp-Ex, another brand of White-Out. I could make friends with a couple of mates, Andy and Martin. Sadly, Martin passed away several years later, and I lost track of Andy when he went to work for Sun and later Oracle in the San Francisco Bay Area. They were wonderful mates. Martin introduced me to British steam fairs. Large steam-powered engines would parade the grounds, as well as standalone engines that would thrash, cull, or cut. It was a glimpse into the British past and their dominant age. Martin also took me to see some beautiful old engines in Swindon, a city which sported a nested set of roundabouts.

I returned to Britain two more times while working for ICL. The first was almost at a moment's notice. I had one day warning. I landed at Heathrow and this time they did not require me to drive at night with little or no rest. I was met at the airport with a ride and immediately taken to the facility at Bracknell. There was a brief introduction to the issue. An ICL mini-computer server with a database system had been sold to the township of Leeds, and there was a bug in the file system. They immediately drove me to Leeds to meet Andy and Martin and be on the job the next morning. The township of Leeds was losing almost a million pounds a day due to file system errors in their database. Andy and I were to diagnose the memory dumps and Martin was the "project" manager reporting a status to his management every three hours.

The driver, a mate named Tim Newport-Peace with his British sports car, a green Triumph, took me up the M1. After rolling down the windows, he was smoking one fag after another. He had a cassette tape player in the Triumph blaring Gilbert and Sullivan while cruising on the M1 between 85 and 90 miles per hour. "This was my night to die", so I thought. I arrived at the hotel in Leeds, within walking distance of the client, a waste processing plant, went to the bar, had a double scotch to calm my nerves, and set the alarm for 6:00 in the morning, local time.

I woke dead tired and met my two mates and then walked to the client site. It was late February, with a gray and gloomy weather. This day I drank an abundance of tea. This routine went on for several days, with Andy making changes and loading the system into a test machine that was a clone of the production machine and me using my tool-set to crack dumps. Martin would send status reports back to headquarters in Bracknell every three hours. At first we wandered to the nearest pub near the plant and decompressed with a few pints of Boddingtons Midland Bitters, and would hit a local Italian eatery, which wasn't bad. After a couple of nights, we realized that we all wanted Indian national food. "Let's go to a fantastic Indian restaurant just off Dragon's Gate." We did. This had to be one of the best Indian restaurants I have ever experienced. The chicken tikka was amazing. So was the saag. This was a good night. Andy and Martin talked about a great pub called the Duck and Drake in Leeds. We found our way to the pub where there were eleven brews on the blackboard with brew details described, including specific gravity and alcoholic content. The beers were brewed locally in the neighborhood and carefully transported to the pub. To this day, this was some of the best brew I have ever tasted.

We made it back to the plant the next day, and shortly thereafter while we went for lunch, I inadvertently committed a faux pas. We were walking through an area that had no buildings, completely empty, nothing but concrete slabs and a few small walls. I looked at my mates and asked, "Nothing's here. Why all the space?" I got this long silence. Finally, Martin said "Hitler's handwork." Leeds had never reconstructed after the bombing by the German Luftwaffe.

After approximately a week working at Leeds, we fixed the bug in ICL's Unix file system, having to do with spreading information across multiple hard drives. Andy and Martin became good friends, both of whom I would cross paths with more than once.

My last trip to the United Kingdom for ICL took me once again to Bracknell, where I took the M6 to Manchester. Dodging lorries, I arrived in Manchester, lodging at a decent hotel. I did not have my previous mates with me, but had to meet up with a group of hardware engineers from my home base in Lake Forest, Southern California. For several days I commuted from the hotel to a plant where ICL mini-computers were manufactured in Ashton-under Lyne. On arrival, I donned a white lab coat and proceeded into the plant. There were robotics in the walls and traveling on rails through the plant. That part was impressive. This was in 1994. I met up with the hardware engineers and it was my job to alter the Unix kernel so they could analyze the issues they were having with the implementation. One hardware engineer told me, "This one is going to be a real sweetheart to debug."

The plant was cool to cold, but often it would be necessary to enter "burn-in rooms" to collect memory dumps. They were over 100 degrees Fahrenheit. Then I would take the results to the hardware engineers. They would make jokes about software engineers, and how if you weren't a hardware engineer, you had turned to the "dark side". But that was humor. I spent a week commuting from Manchester to Ashton-under Lyne. I became accustomed to the robots. Brit radio channel five would blare over the PA system, often broadcasting Rugby. So I had to work in a great deal of noise.

I explored some of Manchester. Several Chinese restaurants were near the hotel, and I indulged in them. Some folks told me that these were the best Chinese restaurants in the UK. Walking from the hotel to a local pub that served midland bitters, the local ale, I saw a group of socialists of some orientation selling their newspaper to the public. This was a scene that would only occur at a demonstration in the United States. The socialists with their newspaper made me think about world politics and economics. This period of the 1990s was the aftermath of the Reagan-Thatcher synthesis, often referred to as NeoLiberalism. It would define the major thread of USA-sian politics transitioning into the twenty-first century. The Reagan synthesis was an amalgamation of core business power politics, small town and mid-American culture, and what I always thought of as the mythic projection of Norman Rockwell paintings into the nostalgic USA-sian populace to cure a nineteen sixties hangover. A projection of fundamentalist Christianity found itself easily married to the rural- and mid-American values. Added were a core of Libertarians cuddled by the anti-government rhetoric, along with Objectivists and others who saw the growth of a centralized government as their principal enemy. After the Vietnam War, progressives, radical social democrats, and former radical organizations virtually disappeared from the USA-sian political stream until the beginning of the twenty-first century.

After my stay in Manchester, I returned to Bracknell and in a hotel near the plant. I recollect looking at the dusk glow given 10:00 PM local time and wondered what was coming next for me to deal with. Upon my return to the United States, my commutes to my stepmother's condo in La Costa were about to come to a close. I had enjoyed them, often writing science fiction at night. The San Diego area was pleasant. But this scene occurred only two or three nights a week. In early 1994, ICL, probably in concert with Fujitsu, shut down the Lake Forest facility. They lay the entire plant off in one fell swoop. So it was once again time to search for a new job.

There was no problem getting interviews. ICL even gave me a paper parachute, something below a tin parachute. I was hired by a company in Orange County, at Irvine, named Continuus, that specialized in Unix build-and-control tools. But after interviewing for Retix, which once was a competitor with the Cisco corporation for the telecommunications router market, I signed on as a software engineer with some personal reservations.

•••

My son's elementary school met or exceeded my expectations. The Culver City school district was small compared to the Santa Monica or the gargantuan Los Angeles school system. My opinion changed when he proceeded to the sixth grade and entered the Culver City middle school. When you hear from your child that math was "too easy" and he "wasn't learning anything," we looked at an alternative. About this time, I allowed Ben to invite eight of his friends, some that he had known since preschool, for a "sleep over". They continued to party until the wee hours of the morning. I found a stain on the ceiling the next morning. I swore that stain to be spread as I found it, liquid must have defied gravity. At the time we had a cable service named "On Demand", that had one first-run movie, MTV, ESPN and the Playboy Channel, which was scrambled. Many activities took place, one of them allowing all the preteen males to watch the first-run movie using the cable. I checked in on them at one AM. Some were asleep, but one very intelligent kid and also a troublemaker, Rory, still had the remnants riled up. I checked them again at three AM and they were all asleep in including Rory, who was laid out on the couch with his mouth open. I looked at the show on the cable TV. It was the Playboy Channel in scrambled mode. Preteens.

I enrolled him in all the sport activities that he could handle. I ended up managing youth baseball. Now, managing a youth baseball team itself was a course in management. The kids were always great. It was to the parents that I wanted to assign time out. One kid I'll never forget, a little red-headed kid, was probably the smallest kid on the team. He had enormous glasses and an attitude. I asked him what his name was, and he only told me, "Rambo!" The parents that complained to me typically were those that would not help with the team. Yet some parents were great and understood how to be an asset to youth sports and have fun at the same time. One time, while in early youth baseball, my son displayed a gross lack of fair play, so I threw him out of the game. Ben was angry with me for a week.

When Ben was eight, I enrolled him in flag football. He took one look at the kids and hid behind the tree, crying. The sight of the nine- and ten-year-old kids on the field was intimidating, but Ben was big, and he made it through the try-outs. That was the beginning of his football activity, which ended when he graduated from high-school. Ben's first football coach was Coach Kenny. He graduated from Cal State Long Beach like me and was on their football team before the state university eliminated the program. An Afro-American, he worked for the Los Angeles Police Department. He was an excellent coach. Football equaled baseball as Ben's favorite sport. One year later, Ben was in the baseball minors playing hardball. In baseball, he was a pitcher and a first baseman. Now, as a parent, I made a huge mistake. His skills deteriorated over time in baseball. I thought it was because of his great growth spurts. I never thought to have his vision tested. I met folks in the neighborhood with kids. Two kids across the street were also baseball players, so I got to know their parents, and went to neighborhood parties.

Science fiction fandom was another activity in which we became involved. I would go to conventions, with topics off the ordinary, or as the "fen" would say, outside of the mundane. The first convention was in Anaheim, and the next in Atlanta. Science fiction conventions were an excellent intellectual stimulus for my young boy. He fell in love with anime, Japanese animation. Both of us enjoyed Castle in the Sky, a Japanese animation classic. It was interesting comparing our opinions on anime typically viewed at a science fiction convention. Ben would tell me, "dad, let's go to the comic book store." Then I would answer "only if you can beat me in a game of basketball". I had installed a regulation basketball hoop supported by the roof of the garage. Fortunately or unfortunately, both of us were not good shots. As I recollect, I let my son win several games. After each victory by my son, it was off to the comic book shop. I wanted him to "earn" a trip to the comic book shop.

When I was available, I could help coach my son's Little League team. I perceived my son was struggling. This frustrated him. In earlier youth baseball leagues, he was a star player. When hitting, he would hit the ball as far as any other big kid. His woes were partly my fault. He needed glasses, and we didn't recognize that. At one point, I suggested my son play the catcher's position. He rejected that idea. Because this Little League team was more demanding than previous teams, my son became easily frustrated. I tried to explain to him what a tough and humiliating sport baseball could be. The team was a mix of upper-middle-class kids from the Southern California Marina district and ascending-working class Latinos. That the Latino boys were the more capable players was not surprising. The team rode from the gathering stops to the practice field in Marina Del Rey, in the back of the coach's pickup truck. I would throw batting practice for the kids. I would change speeds and throw them a knuckle ball from time-to-time. They hated that. The head coach would tell them, "You must learn to hit many pitching." The mix of kids was an excellent lesson for me and for my son. But sadly, it was the end of his baseball days. He was eligible to play another year but declined to do so. That made me sad, but I accepted it. My son graduated from elementary school in the Culver City district. Overall, the elementary school and Little League baseball were a wonderful experience.

My son Ben, typical of most kids, loved going to the movies. One in particular, a fantasy movie, Dark Chrystal, was an early favorite. I purchased a copy of Dark Chrystal and he must have watched it at least a dozen times. As a father, you don't question why your child likes to repeat media. You just accept it, even though you've memorized the lines. Later on, it was the same repetition for Star Wars. Ben always did his homework and had good study habits, which was one aspect of my son's behavior that made parenting easier. His love of media never interfered with his schooling.

Because of being a parent, many of your former friends that were not parents transitioned into the background. Not having the time to be with old friends that were not parents and the social pressure to be with new friends can be socially disorienting. Life between work and being a parent had changed radically since living in Venice, or North Redondo Beach and Long Beach. Many times I took on the role of "Mr. Mom" when I was the only parent at home. Being "Mr. Mom", had to do with work schedules. I had to get Ben to school on time, which fortunately was five blocks away, so he had no trouble walking back and forth. Then meal issues became a challenge. Lunch was fairly easy since I knew what he liked. The lunch pale typically contained a peanut butter and jelly sandwich plus some fruit. Then there was the question of dinner. "Ben, what is your favorite food?" "Sushi, dad". So when I was the sole parent and in something of a lazy mood, I often took my son out for sushi. Ben had been eating sushi since he was five years old. The other stand by was Chris's Pizza in Culver City. Chris's made an excellent facsimile of a real New York pizza. The entire family loved their pizzas. The only time things got dicey for me was when Ben took ill. Being the only parent when your son has chicken pox is not fun.

Given that the launching pad of puberty was approaching, I decided that a good but tough agenda was in order. I investigated Roman Catholic parochial schools. I derived my thought from the success I had at Loyola Marymount and the reputation of Catholic education. We made the decision. We enrolled my son at Saint Monica's Elementary School in Santa Monica. The location of the school worked out nicely for the nonce, given my current job. My son made friendships that lasted until his adult life while attending St. Monica's. This parish had an interpretation of Christian doctrine that seemed progressive, given a peace-and-justice ministry and a gay/lesbian ministry. I attended some sessions the church sponsored. What I discovered was the parish was an excellent way to connect with everyday working people in the community. I attended one particular session, and what happened surprised me, not expecting it at a Roman Catholic Church. A group of about thirty people entered a room. The leader of the vigil instructed us in yoga breathing and after that we spent at least twenty minutes in total silence. The meditation effect was amazing. Attending the session were several ministers and a deacon.

The number of non-Catholics at Saint Monica's Parish also surprised me. Other than children from Roman Catholic families, the next most common religion at the school was children with an Islamic background. I was pleased with my son's progress through the sixth grade. As I became acquainted with the priests, several pre-Vatican-II stereotypes were shattered. Father Michael worked with the movie industry in Hollywood, specifically certifying certain wedding and burial scenes conformed to canon and were authentic. Another priest cracked all kinds of jokes in mass and emphasized the importance of humor in spirituality. And yet another would arrive on a Harley, looking for the world like as an honest-to-God biker. The "biker priest" did things like arrange tours with the mosque in Culver City so non-Muslims could see it. Of course, the imams of that mosque insisted on certain dress and behavior. After the Northridge quake, my son continued to attend elementary school at Saint Monica's in Santa Monica. The church itself was badly damaged, but most of the classrooms were intact. One attendee of the church, "Ahhhnoold," as in Schwarzenegger told Monsignor, the head cleric of the church, "Just let me know how much you need to repair it". That generous gift helped quickly repair the damage.

My son gained entry to Loyola High School in mid-city Los Angeles. Loyola High School accepted several friends that had graduated from St. Monica Elementary. By the ninth grade, the initial grade at Loyola High School, which was designated as the freshman grade, given Ben, was almost as big as me. The football team immediately recruited him. Loyola was, and probably is to this day, a tough, all male, Roman Catholic, private high-school run by Jesuit Priests who had and still have a great reputation as educators. So my son had a lot to deal with. The classes were tough, and the curriculum was complete. By now, I was becoming a ghost of my former self. The revolts and passage of culture of the sixties were a memory. Memories of playing in bands had passed. The activity in the geo-political USA bewildered me. I knew times were changing. My son was now a teenager with the swagger that all teenagers should have. Now he was distant from me. When in Los Angeles, I would check in on his football practices, since Loyola High School is in fair vicinity of downtown of the city so it was fairly easy for me make an appearance. I tried to continue to be an active father, but I was now an outsider. In terms of academics, Ben was doing fine in high school. By now, I realized my son was in his own teenage world. He seemed to adjust to a fairly strict Jesuit high-school, complete with a dress code, which made it easy to shop for clothes.

I could attend few events at Loyola High School with Ben. The father-and-son mass and the athletic awards banquets were some of them. Ben and myself attending a production of Fiddler on the Roof is the one that stands out in my mind. A group of Catholic students at an all boys high-school was something to behold. I can still see a young guy sticking both fingers in the air and shouting "Tradition!" Ben told me, "these guys don't have the background to do this play". I agreed without being critical.

During the time, I got to see my son play football when in Los Angeles. He was an all-league offensive lineman, recruited by some small colleges, and at the time, I didn't understand why he wasn't interested. I was thinking about a scholarship and saving money, but my son had different interests. In hindsight, he was correct and in this case, his father, me, was off base. In 2000, he graduated from high school, and being accepted at several schools, which were difficult to enter. He chooses UCLA over UC Santa Barbara and Cal Poly San Luis Obispo. After being accepted into the Engineering program at UCLA, that fall he attended a meeting with the department counselor. The counselor told Ben, "we require you to take the calculus course targeted for science and engineering majors your first semester". Ben responded, "You mean the one I took here this summer after I graduated from high school and got an A in?" Mr. Martin was a math teacher at Loyola High School. The students nicked named him "Mean Man Martin". He had done a superlative job of grounding my son in advanced mathematics.

The transition from an all boy's school to a crowded coed dorm, including coed bathrooms, was a culture shock for Ben. In his sophomore year, he could move in with two other engineering students at a comfortable student apartment. Ben liked punk rock, so one of the few activities we did together was watch two movies, all about punk rockers. The one I remember best was "The Decline of Western Civilization". Initially, Ben didn't have a girlfriend, but he talked about females. He had a particular dislike of sorority girls. I gave him the "don't get a female accidentally pregnant" lecture. "Use a prophylactic if you decide to have sex. If you are embarrassed, let me know, I'll buy them for you." Ben would return home, which was near UCLA often on weekends. During his senior year, I knew he was home but didn't hear a sound. In the later morning I knocked on the door of his room upstairs and opened the door. He was in bed with a dark-haired Latina female. It turned out she was attending one of my alma maters, Loyola Mary Mount University. She became his girlfriend for a long period. He continued at UCLA until graduating from the engineering department in 2004. Ben graduated from UCLA with a degree in material science. He wrote his own resume, and immediately landed a job in Dominguez Heights, also known as Compton, a prominent ghetto area, performing material analysis. It turned out that Ben was hired, not only because he had a UCLA engineering degree on his resume, but because he attended Loyola High School. While working, Ben and his steady girl would guest DJ at the KXLU radio station at Loyola Marymount. This sparked my curiosity. "Ben, what bands do you to play on the radio station?" "We like the Stooges and X". "Really? I'm not familiar with the Stooges, but X I am familiar with. They are a punk rock band. Did you know KXLU was one of the first radio stations in the Los Angeles area to play punk rock? I first heard about KXLU in 1982 when I was working at Honeywell. The guy in the office next door had that station on all the time." "Dad, you heard of Shellac?" "No" "They are a great post punk rock band."

When I would see Ben, he would talk about the radio station and the programming it supported. Once in a while, I could listen to Ben and his good buddy Kyle, a regular KXLU DJ, or listen to my son and his girlfriend's antics on the station. Between all the technical information related to material science and his work, like extra-terrestrial solar panel production and the latest addition to his CD collection, we had a common ground to maintain a good relationship.

GHOST I

•••

The Northridge earthquake of 1994 devastated the Retix office in Santa Monica. They deemed only part of the building safe for the employees after this quake. It particularly hit hard the Santa Monica area. Instead of using the traditional Richter scale, they also measured quakes in G-force. A force of Zero-G is significant. I have a vivid memory of this quake. It took place in the dark on January 17, 1994, at 4:30 AM. The shaking intensified, knocking the television in the bedroom on the floor. Books came out of the shelves in the living room. A group of plates, nicknamed the "earth quake detectors" on a ledge high above the kitchen, were unscathed, as were a row of potted plants on a high wooden ledge on a rear deck. After making sure the family was secure, and without power, we realized that a major disaster had taken place. The Northridge quake had waves in it, not unlike waves in a lake or a swimming pool. It is my observation that the "wavy" nature of California quakes produces the Zero-G effect. Years later, on the Big Island of Hawai`i, I experienced another strong quake. The physics were markedly different. Instead of a rolling wave action, it was a violent shaking back and forth, similar to a bad subway ride.

Being recognized by the director and the company founder is a reason I was a fast hire at Retix. The director was a former vice president at Tran Telecommunications, and the founder was once a visitor to my apartment in Venice. One day during work at Retix, I ran into my old manager, Gary, from United Computing, my first job as a software engineer. He was manager of quality control at Retix. He told me he knew who I was before he saw me because he recognized my voice. Before the earthquake, Retix had a great holiday party at one building in the old train station in downtown Los Angeles, so Gary and I could reconnect at the party. But the situation deteriorated at Retix. They were competing with Cisco in the router business. The Retix router was faster, but rife with errors.

About two days after the Northridge Quake, I returned to work, but could not return to my office area. The chief technical officer came to me as they crammed me into the office space deemed safe on the first floor, and asked, "Have you ever traveled to South Africa?" There was a known error in one module for the Retix router in use by Rennies Travel, the Retix client centered in Johannesburg. The next day, I was on a plane to the United Kingdom destined for Heathrow. The plan was to meet with another software engineer from Guildford, a small town south of the M3 dual carriage way. My mate and I caught the next flight to Johannesburg, South Africa.

I estimated I was in the air, in an airport, or prior to arriving in Johannesburg, for forty-seven hours. This included, from LA to Heathrow to "Jo-Burg" and four movies. There wasn't much to see flying from Heathrow in the late afternoon local time to Jo-Burg. Most of the flight took place at nighttime. By mid-morning, we landed at the Johannesburg airport where a driver was waiting for us. My first impression of South Africa was beyond negative. As the driver continued into the city, from the airport, I witnessed ghetto poverty that completely surpassed anything that I had witnessed as a pre-teen while traveling to Guadalajara, Mexico, with my grandmother. Upon landing, I knew I had to prepare myself for a country of stark opposites. How could a country with leading edge technology leave most of its population as poor,defamed, lost humanity?

I knew prior to working in South Africa that this was a country in transition. I was there during a revolution, with the government transitioning to the Nelson Mandela alliance. What struck me as we drove past the segregated poverty were the guard towers at the edge of the barbed wire fencing. With search lights and weaponry on the top of the towers, the local people of African descent were literally living in a concentration camp. I suspect that fenced in South Africans were Bantu, which had been forced off their land after World War II and moved northeast of Johannesburg. After all, the area northeast of Johannesburg was originally Bantu land. The houses behind the fence topped with barbed wire were of primitive construction. They made some houses of dysfunctional cement. Others were made of wood, and some badly deteriorated where it would be a stretch to call them a house. How could hygiene function in an environment like that? Then we passed through modern buildings and roads where only people of European descent lived and worked. The juxtaposition of these two worlds was mind numbing. Finally, we arrived at our first-class hotel, which provided some urgently needed rest.

The two of us tiredly worked during our first day in "Jo-Burg." We finished after applying a known fix to their routers. For the rest of the six weeks, the two of us monitored their network and applied what technical skills we offered. This allowed me the advantage of conversing with the information technology workers, spend time in pubs and restaurants, and to get a first-hand view of what was going on in South Africa. The workers at Rennies would take me and my coworker out "razzling." This almost always comprised drinking large amounts of alcoholic beverages accompanied by food. On account of this merriment and behavior, typically the information technology workers would show up for work at about 9:30 local time and ready to depart by 4:00 or 4:30 in the afternoon.

The African National Congress, ANC, revolution took place while I was in the country. The old regime was being dismantled, but there was the disadvantage of apartheid in the collection of people that made up the Union as they tried to forge a new national consensus. I talked to people who were staunchly reactionary and opposed to the changes taking place. But the direction of the current upheaval doomed such a view. While working in South Africa, I picked up a copy of ANC charter, read it, and then sent a copy to my friend, Jerry, in Chicago, who I knew would have a keen interest. One immediate issue for the government in transition had to do with language. In fact, in 1994 and even now, there are at least eleven languages. The two official languages remain English and Afrikaans, a variant of Dutch.

The employees at Rennies were staunch cricket and football, i.e., soccer fans. I remember one instance where the entire shop emptied, and walked across the street to watch a cricket match. Much of the small talk in the office centered on cricket and football. Myself and my co-worker from the UK would see the Australian national cricket team at breakfast each day. The employees at Rennies would ask us questions about the team. The Rennies' information technology department was at least nominally integrated, to the chagrin of the reactionaries. I spoke briefly with the native Africans employed by the company. They were polite, but did not tell me anything about personal situation. I heard that there were "rescue missions" in some neighborhoods where employees of the company had hired native African tribe members.

After work, many of the employees attended an event that is a variant of cricket called "action cricket." They played it indoors in a screened rectangular area, with rules not unlike cricket on an outdoor pitch. The "Action Cricket Club" had no members from native African tribes. It was all white. I could see the dividing lines were breaking down, but they were still there. Likewise, for some clubs we "razzled" in. Some were all white, others were not.

The food in "Jo-Burg" was carnivore heavy, including at the hotel. I ate several sausages made from kudu, which had an unusual protein that caused an adverse reaction. After eating kudu sausages, I was ill for at least two days. Upon returning to the States, I had trouble with all red meats. When eating red meats, I had a similar reaction as I would have if I ate kudu sausage. It wasn't until I visited

Hawai`i in 2002 where I consumed free-range, grass-fed beef that I could tolerate red meat again. To this day, I will not eat lamb.

The land around Johannesburg is like the rolling plains of Ohio in the US. It is a rich farmland supporting several crops and domesticated livestock. My self and my co-worker took a trip into the plains, or veld, to witness tribal dancing. The presentation was excellent, but I don't remember which native cultures were represented. What stuck in my mind forever, while traveling to the veld, were several lasting mental images. The first was a military convoy of integrated, native, and European armed men heading into what was probably harm's way. Second, when we passed the Afrikaner settlements north of the road where we were being escorted, I saw US confederate flags from the nineteenth century Civil War fly above their farms and settlements. I had always had a strong dislike of the confederate flag as a symbol of a slave economy. From that day on, I considered the flag to be the moral equivalent of a flag with a swastika.

Rennies continued to be magnificent hosts. On Fridays, at four in the afternoon local time, they would open up the company bar. It was a full bar inside their office building. They provided trips to local restaurants regularly during the day and at night. The weekend before myself and my coworker departed for the UK, Rennies flew both of us to Cape Town. This was a holiday. First, we hired a car, and my co-worker drove us to the Cape of Good Hope. I had driven right-hand drives only a few times, but he had driven that way all his life, so he was the natural choice. The beaches I witnessed on the way to Cape were, to this day, some of the most beautiful I have ever seen. The waves and the stunning light azure water are like nothing I have seen since, even in the beautiful waters of the Hawaiian Islands. Along the road, we witnessed tribe members selling stacks of sticks. It emphasized in my mind that South Africa was a land of severe contradictions. When we arrived at the Cape of Good Hope, the weather was cool. It doesn't take much to understand why. To the south is Antarctica. There were several cars parked in designated parking spaces. There were also signs telling visitors to roll up the windows of the vehicle. All over the Cape lived packs of baboons. I believe the correct term for the collection of baboons is a "congress". Think about that one for a bit. We did witness a group of baboons running down the road with a six-pack of Coke that they had nicked from someone's vehicle. Later, back at Rennies, after recounting the tale, our peers in information technology told us of how some foolish visitors had left the keys to the vehicle in the ignition and the baboons had entered through the open window, and wrecked the vehicle trying to go for a joy ride.

For the next day, we signed on for a tour of the wine district to the west of Cape Town. The view of the fields and the wine were excellent. The landscape reminded me of the Northern California wine-growing regions. We drove by, but did not go into the prison where Nelson Mandela was an inmate. It wasn't on the tour, but I would have liked to have seen it. After this impressive tour, we took the fight from Cape Town back to Johannesburg. The flight was uneventful until we landed. The conveyor belt to unload the baggage from the plane broke down, so the passengers and the crew had to form a line like a "fire brigade" to unload the individual pieces one-at-a-time. Eventually everyone gained their belongings and myself and my coworker returned to the hotel, tired, but pleased with a gratis trip from Rennies' Travel. I still have very fond memories of Cape Town. To me, it was a cross between Malibu California, the San Francisco Bay, and Big Sur, if you can imagine that.

Both of us returned to the UK after our work was declared finished. I slept one night at a bed-and-breakfast near Guildford, bid farewell to the UK workers, and returned to LA to witness the results of the 1994 Northridge quake.

Retix sales took an enormous hit. After a few months, they laid me off. Shortly after that downsizing, the company ceased to exist. I followed up on a DataProducts lead with one of my managers, James T. from Citicorp TTI. My friend Zee and former associate convinced me to interview with DataProducts. This company had once been the leader in the production of "line printers," but management had made the unfortunate mistake of believing that desktop printers were a fad. So when I joined DataProducts, I knew it was a holding-pattern job. The manager of the group was a man named Nabil. He was a Muslim who had grown up in Egypt and earned a PhD in economics. He was a fairly decent manager, but got lost in some aspects of software development. I worked on their desktop printer project, which was a designated "catch up to the industry" gambit.

I carpooled with my friend Zee, whom I also worked at AM Jacquard. She had worked at CitiCorp TTI, but not at the same time I worked there. It was probably her good graces and my former manager James T. who managed the Unix Systems, that DataProducts hired me, which was in a serious contradictory economic situation. They were a failing company that owned valuable real estate, which made them a prime target for a hostile takeover. I don't remember all the details, but they had gained the company land in Woodland Hills, an area at the west end of the San Fernando Valley. The company then moved from Woodland Hills to Simi Valley.

From there, things went from bad to worse. Everyone, with a minimum amount of economic common sense, knew that it was the end. In actuality, the company survived by providing a niche product when purchased by Hitachi Koki after surviving several hostile takeovers. By then, the core company was a tiny shadow of its former profile. James T. was the manager I worked for at Citicorp TTI and at DataProducts. He departed, along with other people. One employee, after resigning, had a parting phrase, "It's been real, and it's been good, but it hasn't been real good." SEI Consulting hired James T. He once again recruited me and later the most talented person in the DataProducts software group, Val for SEI.

Some of my more interesting memories of Simi Valley comprised walkabouts and viewing the local populace. Skinhead kids would stare at us through cracked windows. We viewed bumper stickers that said "An armed society, is a polite society." And the Ronald Reagan freeway ran through the middle of the Valley. There was no loss of happiness when I said, "Adios!" to Simi Valley.

CHOST II

•••

I entered the world of software consulting by working part time for a company started by friends, AdMaster. This activity occurred while working at ICL. The system was new to me, Microsoft Windows 3.0. Working with Windows software was new to me. I loathed Windows 3.0. I spent a time giving the computer what we affectionately called the "three-finger salute", control, alt and delete. The simultaneous pressing of these three keys caused Windows to reboot. I completed the work for AdMaster on my days off. As a lesson, I didn't understand yet why it was a bad idea to work long hours and especially when you should decompress and focusing on something non-technical.

Going to work for SEI, a consulting company, officially made me a full-time consultant. Now I was a hired gun for SEI, and something of a software prostitute. In the nine years I worked for

SEI, I initially enjoyed the assigned tasks and was, mostly, paid well. When I first joined the company, the one benefit that worked out nicely was that they paid me the difference to a client's site, in time, not mileage, from where I lived in Culver City to the Los Angeles downtown office. This was a boon given my first assignment with this consulting company.

The year 1995 was the age of the exploding Internet. They developed the Internet Protocol as part of the Apollo project in the late 1960s. After the completion of that project, since it was a government project, no one company could be the owner, so they entrusted the source code to the University of California at Berkeley. This transfer of the Internet Protocol source, along with Richard Stallman's Free Software Foundation and Linus Torvalds' new Unix-like system, Linux, started the open software movement.

My first assignment as a consultant was in Orange County with NavTech, literally across the street from the stadium where the Angels played baseball. There were a couple of instances where I left work and would then walk to a game. When first arriving at NavTech, there was no desk area for me in the open office space, so I ended up in the computer room, with the temperature between 50 and 55 degrees. I would put on a heavy jacket when working in the computer room, and gave it the nickname "Cyberia," to the amusement of my peers. The makeup of the team was akin to the bridge on the science fiction series Star Trek. There were Indian Nationals, Chinese, Nigerians, Vietnamese, Russians, and, of course, home-grown products of US culture. Vin, a Vietnamese Buddhist, went out to lunch with fellow workers as a group and ordered a hamburger. One of us asked Vin, "But you are a Buddhist.

Aren't you a vegetarian? Aren't you not supposed to eat meat?" He answered, "Oh, I'm not supposed to eat Eastern meat. This is Western meat." We were all amused.

I could depart "Cyberia" to a decent work station Sadly, as an example how damaging the stress of technical consulting can be, the woman who now sat across from me, checked into a local hotel near NavTech, died one night from heart failure. She wasn't particularly healthy, but the work did her in. I escaped injury more than once by being near traffic accidents en route from Culver City to Anaheim. This was a drive of over forty miles, much of it early in the morning. During one commute, there was a ten-car pileup to my immediate left in the fast lane, where if even one vehicle squirted out of the sequential wreck, I would have been an unlucky participant.

The work in Orange Country for NavTech continued until 1997. NavTech was a pioneer in processing geo-spatial, satellite data combined with visual confirmation. This technology is known as "direction by direction" route generation. Then, early in 1997, I spent some time in Los Angeles at the home office. When you were there, you were "on the bench". What this meant is the company paid you while you were waiting for your next assignment. I used the time at lunch to investigate downtown Los Angeles. It had been twenty years since I explored downtown Los Angeles. There is a business culture that is a class above what goes on at the street level. It connected hotels and buildings via bridges, so a pedestrian does not have to descend to the street. I would walk the connecting bridges, and then descend walking towards the Grand Central Market, first via Hill Street, looking at how much had changed. Though downtown Los Angeles was a shadow of what it was in the 1950s and 1960s. I saw several fast-food stalls, mostly serving Latino food. Walking up Broadway and back to the office was like walking through a Mexican city. Todos los signos esta en Español. I took trips through the downtown library, checked out a few restaurants, none worth the price, and would return to the office on the ninth floor of a building near Figueroa Street and Fifth Street. I had to work while at the Los Angeles office. Sometimes I was doing research. Other times, I was recruiting or identifying potential clients.

This soft technical existence changed when given recent assignments. They sent me to Chicago in March to do an analysis of Internet use for a huge logistics firm where I interviewed managers. The work was frustrating since the managers, mostly, did not want to be bothered by some rising Internet techie who was being pushy. Of course I had to write a report describing how to use the Internet in the world of logistics. Later, in the spring of 1997, I was sent to Vancouver for a week to analyze the architecture of a client database. Vancouver is an interesting city. I could take public transportation from the hotel that I was staying in and from the client's building. The restaurants and pubs were also entertaining. I had never seen a night club literally underground. For a quick project, writing a report regarding the client's database was a typical wrap up. Next, I received an assignment with a publishing house in Itasca, Illinois. The assignment was to write an "app" in a computer language I had never used before, Java, to translate publishing keywords for the client. If you recollect parse trees for English in school, think of this project as the parse tree for publishing keywords. Up to then, I had been working in a language called C++, so I could get some of the new language concepts of Java, similar to C++, while on the plane to Chicago. I also learned something during this assignment. Never take a consulting job in Chicago and take the late afternoon flight if you don't know where you are going. I arrived at the O'Hare Airport car rental in the dark, and then had to drive to Itasca, Illinois. At about 2:30 AM CST, I arrived at a hotel near the Medinah Country Club, after getting lost at least two times. The attire at the publishers, except for Friday, was a suit and tie. My first day was, of course, Monday. I was miserable. Acclimating, I adjusted to the work climate and the time zone. This work lasted about two weeks. I impressed the Chicago SEI home office with my work of inventing a new computer language to parse keywords. They called me into their Chicago main office for a verbal outline of my work. I impressed the SEI presiding manager. After the assignment at the publisher, I returned to the office in Los Angeles.

I was under the constant stress of being a software consultant, constantly studying and attempting to learn new technologies. In 1997, one SEI Los Angeles senior member told me that there were now 200 new software applications released every month. Given the large number of software packages being developed, which one to focus your attention on became a challenge. SEI management in Los Angeles attempted to simplify the choice. The orientation of SEI now turned to the Microsoft framework and its sphere of control. I had learned some of Microsoft technology, remembering how awful my experience was with Windows when doing software for AdMaster. In addition, I took offense to the remark by Bill Gates that Linux and open-source software were nothing more than "techno-communism". Actually, he was partially correct, and looking back, that is part of the irony.

But my time in LA was short-lived. By the end of July 1997, I had an assignment as a developer in Chicago. The company, NeoGlyphics. com, was an Internet startup with several clients, including Playboy Magazine and Hallmark Cards. They hired me as a Java developer, but often ended up working with the current version of the Oracle database manager and even some visualization work using a new fragile language named Javascript.

During my first week at NeoGlyphics, I stayed at a hotel near Lincoln Park. Because NeoGlyphics wanted me for a multi-week assignment, they provided me a rental unit on North Cumberland Avenue. It was a multi-story building with a furnished apartment. It had a single bedroom, a kitchenette, and a living room. This condo was home until the beginning of December.

Every other weekend, I would fly from Chicago to Los Angeles. Those weekends, not commuting to Los Angeles, I spent in Chicago. During weekdays, I was always in Chicago working for NeoGlyphics. A few of the flights were ominous. Once again, I learned, if possible, to get the earliest flight on a Sunday morning, avoiding the worst turbulence of the jet stream. Just before I moved into the condo, during the flight, we spent two hours circling O'Hare in a storm. The flight controllers would only let one plane land at a time. I have a stark memory of one young child panicking and then running down the aisle with the flight attendant chasing him. That night I didn't get to the hotel until 1:00 AM. This was a nerve-racking flight. Often when flying over the Rocky Mountains to Chicago, the plane would hit the jet stream, often with the pilot asking the flight attendants to take a seat. I hated flying from Los Angeles to Chicago, but once there, it was a simple drive to the condo. I joked at how austere the complex looked from the outside. It looked like a Soviet housing project. It was well constructed inside. There was a bar on the second floor and a gym on the third floor.

NeoGlyphics was a business with a new model that many startup companies later copied. They served breakfast each morning upon arrival. There really wasn't a dress code with the exception that you had to have clothes on. Meetings were informal and held just about anywhere, even in the parking lot. The software engineers were open and shared information freely. At the end of the Friday workday, a cart full of craft beer selections would appear.

I was in a world of every other weekend in West Los Angeles, on an airplane, or in Chicago. My ghostly existence continued. I could ground myself by connecting with my friend from Long Beach State, Jerry, who lived in Chicago. I had a high per-day food allowance supplied by SEI, so we could visit some excellent restaurants. He was still involved in left politics, so I attended their study group in one of the Chicago neighborhoods near Wicker Park. One attendee, older than myself, used to be a member of the Socialist Labor Party, an old, mid-west organization with its roots in the early twentieth century. He was interesting and the conversations in this group were educational. The emphasis at the time was on Third Wave radical orientation a la Alvin Toffler. This study group in Chicago was led by Carl Davidson, a well known nineteen sixties radical. It was interesting that the group often spoke of low road and high road business ethics. The group's ideas had transformed into "market socialism".

The work at NeoGlyphics continued until late 1997. I was happy to depart Chicago in December and return to Los Angeles. When

I first took the apartment, I judged I could walk to work in the cold with warm clothes on. I had never tried to walk eight blocks from the Blue Line station to the facility on Paulina Street. The first slip on black ice taught me a lesson. After that, I drove a rental car. NeoGlyphics ended up as a causality of the initial Internet bust. A conglomerate purchased them, and that was the end.

While back home and while in Chicago, I was working for a second company, Matrix Consultants. The president of the company was an advertising man who could hustle deals, spoke fluent Japanese, and was a drama department graduate from UCLA. Then a manager from Citicorp TTI also ended up the technical director. I first met the president at Raider football games being held at the Los Angeles Coliseum. He was definitely a "party Viking," but seemed easily connected with business opportunities. Matrix Consultants was another home-grown Internet company with, and from the beginning, a flat organization. I would work full time for Matrix Consultants two times in the future.

My next assignment while working for SEI Consulting was once again deep into Orange County, close to where I used to work for ICL. The difference, this time, is that the client, Cendant Corp., was a moving logistics company whose principal business was finding professional transplants a place to live, and then moving all their belongings to the new location. At Cendant, I was an outcast. There were only three people in our group, and we were the only ones in the entire shop not directly using Microsoft technology. Our work was to connect a Java app to their Microsoft application. After two months, they canceled this app project. I took a new assignment in La Brea, Southern California, for Capital Group, the technical development company for American Funds. Later, I found out that Cendant was associated with an accounting scandal in the 1990s because of a report of inflated revenue.

The commute from West Los Angeles was 88 miles a day to Capital Group, Brea. This would make anybody a ghost, since the trading took place on the international market 24 hours a day and 7 days a week. I worked as a consultant for Capital Group from June 1997 until early 2004. The corporate culture reminded me of Citicorp TTI. They made every attempt to treat employees well, with excellent benefits, but the company was your typical corporate oligarchy. They solicited opinions that could trickle up the company structure. Decision making directly affected by those who actually did the work might be possible in a company culture like NeoGlyphics or Matrix Consultants. But I missed the flat and open companies like NeoGlyphics and Matrix Consultants, where everyone was accessible. I worked in the group that handled the transaction stream from the Bloomberg Trading organization. To synchronize with trades from Europe and the East Coast, it was best if I arrived on the job at about 6:30 AM Pacific Time. When I started, I found the software backward and primitive. My entrance test comprised questions associated with a programming language, which I hadn't used since working at Data Products in early 1995. I easily passed the test. They hired me as a contractor. The system used to "safe store" your work that was as equally primitive to the system I used when working for CitiCorp TTI. Database was one technical skill I improved during my stint at Capital Group. My fellow SEI consultants at company meetings warned me, "You will be in Capital Group forever. They will never let you go." I must admit, I was there a long time.

The office was an open environment where your entire group could hear you. Often when arriving in the morning, sometimes I would doze off. The managers seemed to tolerate this. It amazed me that group and department managers would have meetings discussing a single change in the database schema. This was a grossly inefficient was to solve technical issues. I suspected the true power of a globalized political economy when working for Citicorp. While working for Capital Group/American Funds, it materialized before my eyes. As mentioned, this company ran 24 hours a day, 7 days a week. The company did not recognize local holidays. There were a few international holidays, well sort of, that we had off, like the Christian holidays of Easter or Christmas. Most staff received the traditional holidays off in the US. To compensate, someone always had to cover for holidays that were not international, like a Fourth of July in the United States.

My initial work at Capital Group was in a "scripting" language known as Perl. Apps written in Perl were the bulk of my work for the first two years. After the year 2000, management converted their system to "Enterprise Java". This sealed my fate, since I had knowledge of the language. Before the year 2000 "freeze" for the Y2K bug, they assigned me to rebuild the group's source control infrastructure to save the developers' daily work. Initially, I tried to convince them that the best open-source control system at the time was Concurrent Versions System. It was a popular tool and completely free. I argued to use this system instead of having to write a source control system from ground zero. They informed me, "No open source software can be used at Capital Group".

Privately, I told myself, "What a stupid waste of money by this collective bureaucracy." In terms of employment, it was absolute job security. In the four months I built a new source control system using the Perl scripting language and the Sybase database as a persistence store. I changed, maintained, and enhanced this system until 2004, when I departed Capital Group and ceased being an employee of SEI Consulting.

Occasionally, because of requests from my consulting company, I worked for a second client while at Capital Group. The management at SEI Consulting knew that I had to be at work at 6:30 AM, and would often depart before 3:00 PM. SEI managers added additional assignments. The first was for Sparklets Water, at their plant in Eagle Rock, near where I once attended kindergarten in 1950. It was another Java app. I worked there three hours a day for about a month, changing their app, which was to be loaded into hand-held devices used by water delivery truck drivers.

Next, I received an extra assignment to assist a startup in the San Gabriel Valley. I only worked there for an afternoon. The small company had lost their password to their new Linux server configured in San Diego, and they needed to have their new URL registration website up and running. This was a challenge. They were Japanese and barely spoke a word of English. We communicated well enough, so using an open-source package available written in the Perl Scripting language, I could configure a web server on their Windows machine that did what they required. I told them they had to go back to San Diego and get the password, or have their Linux server rebuilt. My parent company, SEI Consulting, charged them two hundred dollars an hour for my labor. I gotta' a gold star "atta boy" from the home office in Los Angeles.

After the Y2K challenge at Capital Group, we converted the Bloomberg Trading Platform System to the Java language and environment. So, my technical background continued to be enhanced. But much like several people who used to work at Citicorp TTI, I felt stale, almost locked into a gilded cage. I monitored the trade system that our group maintained in the last years at Capital Group. Every morning they required me to arrive at 6:30 AM Pacific time in Brea to monitor monetary conversions. These conversion processes transformed the local currency of a European nation to euros. During the final years working at Capital Group, I audited millions of Euros converted and traded to and from every national currency on the planet. That this trading took place before a single euro was printed or minted was stunning. Turkish local currency conversion to euros was a recurring issue. The millions of Turkish Lyra would overflow the arithmetic capabilities of the software. And for each failure, a report had to be sent to the controllers of the feed as a legal requirement.

I decided that my term at Capital Group and my employment with SEI was ending. They split and sold SEI Consulting, with the software consulting group centered in Irvine, California. Of my volition, I departed Capital Group and SEI Consulting. I received an offer from another small consulting company to sub-contract for Yamaha Motorcycles in Los Alamitos in Southern California. Yamaha Motorcycles was strictly a brick-and-mortar shop. They wanted an app to price items at an auction. I should have recognized that their project was way under budget, and with a deficient architecture. I continued at Yamaha for five months and delivered an app with deficiencies from their viewpoint. After that gig, I returned to Hawai`i preparing for my next job search. It was a pleasant break. I sat in a large, beautiful house, reflecting on the past, present, and future. I decided that one of my primary goals was to write this memoir. The Big Island of Hawai`i was the perfect place to write it.

I had retirement in mind, but at the time it wasn't economically workable. I was hired as a post-sales engineer at Intersperse, a startup in Pasadena. Their product was the supposed to be the ultimate dashboard for enterprise applications. Their existing product simply did not work. As the CTO put it, "You are trying to change the engines on an airplane while it is still in the air." I have never heard a CTO curse and swear as he did in the meetings. One reason they hired me was the CTO remembered me when we both worked at Retix. It was an oppressive company. The dysfunctional communication between the various groups was nerve-wracking. My group, now performing technical pre-sales, attempted to install the broken, current release of this ultimate enterprise dashboard at Pfizer in Manhattan, New York. It was a disaster. A couple of days later, they dissolved our group. So once more, it was time to look for a new job.

I still had a good relation with Matrix Consultants, and they were building a "kiosk" station based on Microsoft's "dot net" architecture. They hired me to help with the project. The team member I worked with, Rakesh, lived in India. It amazed that for a small company they were global with their connections and labor force. I was not ready to go to work for Matrix Consultants full time, so as we finished the project by the fall of 2004, I landed a job with

OAO Health Systems. I worked on their medical integration system for about two months. When hired, I told OAO Health Systems that I would spend the Christmas holidays in Hawai`i, to which they agreed . At the time of the hiring, they seemed well organized, with clear goals. I was familiar with the area because they were in the same neighborhood that DataProducts once had their plants and offices. After a congenial company holiday dinner in early December, I returned to my Elysian location, the house on the farm in Hawai`i. I was on holiday for three weeks.

The breadth of the storm stretched across the entire horizon.

While in Hawai`i, I witnessed the strongest storm coming in from the west that I have experienced to date. In the dusk, I viewed this black line approaching that spanned the entire horizon. It hit with force and knocked down all the banana trees on my farm, but there was no major damage to the house. Two water spouts transformed into small tornadoes and made land-fall, tearing up houses in the Ka`u district, just to the south of my farm. After all the excitement, I relaxed and listened to Nat King Cole singing Star Dust and the geckos chiming in as they crawled across the ceiling and walls.

Before departing Hawai`i, I checked in with OAO Health Systems, specifically with our group leader, and he told me, "things are good, I'll be happy to have you back". I returned the car rental and took a red-eye flight on the day after New Year's Day out of Kona International Airport. I was due to work by 10:00 AM in Woodland Hills at the OAO complex. This flight, initially, was a flight from hell, but later became comical. Around me were four babies, and they would wail all at once. After a while, the sound became like a loud, mystical chant. This is my only experience with quadraphonic howling babies.

The plane landed at Los Angeles International Airport. I met with my ride, and took a two-hour nap, then got in my car, and drove to OAO Health Systems. When I arrived at the office, the door was locked. What happened next is something out of the Twilight Zone. The security guard on this floor asked a few questions, and I answered I was attempting to go to work. He acknowledged that and agreed to let me into the office. I stepped in and there was absolutely no one there. I am a ghost. Finally, I saw a light on in the director's office. We met, and he told me that the software company had lost its funding and everyone, except himself, the director, had been laid off.

So again, I looked for work and found it almost immediately. I interviewed with a company in downtown Santa Monica,

Evolution Software. I was once again hired as a consultant. My first assignment was with eHarmony, the date connection site. The intent of my hiring was the development of their core software, but for three months ended up working as their database administrator. The database was a back-end to a somewhat primitive "AI" application to match personality types given an extensive set of questions you answered on their website. After eHarmony, they assigned me to Sempra Energy in San Diego, a utility company, to analyze their infrastructure. That job continued off and on for a few months. Besides Sempra Energy, they assigned me a second client, Workforce, which assisted in employment search for the public and associated with the state of California. A team of Oracle consultants had originally built the Workforce project, but needed several changes. I surveyed the deployed technology. I judged it as "standard" and "off the shelf". A different consulting company in San Diego rejected this project. When I talked to the group at this different consulting company, I asked them, "Why didn't you take the project?" "We didn't have the skills and couldn't spare the people." In retrospect, I believe the real reason was the client was difficult to work with. I should have paid closer attention to that my intuition. On top of these two clients, I took on more work with Matrix Consultants. I was now working with three clients and either working or commuting in San Diego fourteen hours a day or more.

When I completed my work at Sempra, I was assigned as a consultant by Evolution Software to QualComm, also in San Diego, doing Business Process Automation again using an Oracle package. So I continued to work for three clients. I considered the Workforce project completed, but to my frustration and the frustration of the manager of all Evolution Software consultants, the client added new requirements that I was unaware of.

This was all taking a terrific toll on my energy and health. I encountered a dental issue with one of my teeth. It destroyed this tooth from the inside out. My dentist at the time told me that my immune system had literally rejected the tooth. This rotten tooth was a life-changing event. When I returned to Evolution Software's home office and continued to deal with the mess at the Workforce Project. Now that I was in the Southern California area, I wanted to continue to complete the dental work. My current dentist, who had done an excellent job, referred me to an oral surgeon. His staff measured my blood pressure, and said, "It's a little high," but they went on with their procedure. They extracted my eye tooth and completed the procedure on Friday afternoon. They prescribed me antibiotics and some strong pain medicine. By Saturday morning, I was in severe pain, with little or no sleep. I could not eat. This condition continued on until Sunday evening, when I went to the emergency room at Cedars Sinai Hospital on my regular doctor's orders. I was in severe pain, and had not slept for 48 hours. We put a call in to the oral surgeon, and he responded two days after they checked me into Cedars Sinai Hospital. On entrance, the hospital staff took my blood pressure, and it was well over 200, at a lethal level. Their first task was to knock me out and drop the blood pressure. Over a period of several hours and three doses of morphine, I still couldn't sleep because of the pain and blood pressure at a lethal level. Next they gave me the strongest narcotic in the hospital, dilaudid. The second dose put me to sleep. I was a ghost for about the next five days. My doctor, who was in touch with the hospital in the wee-hours of the night, arrived at 7:30 in the morning. For this perseverance, she will forever be a heroine of mine. After many tests, and none really conclusive, they released me from Cedars Sinai after eight days. I came to realize that even though making good money, working two or three jobs in software was literally killing me. Why did I do what I was doing? I wanted to provide for my family, eliminate all debts and be able to retire soon.

I returned to work for Evolution Software and cleared up what we perceived to be the remaining issues from the Workforce Project in San Diego. Shortly after I returned to the office, Evolution Software changed its name to Service Oriented Architecture, and moved to a high-rise close to West Los Angeles. Then they laid off most of my group, including myself. The manager of our group took a job with an Internet start-up. I returned home with a broad smile on my face. It was time for a change.

GHOST III

•••

In 2002, I visited, as a tourist, the Big Island of Hawai`i. I had no inclination to visit Hawai`i up to that point. I had a stereotype in my mind of Honolulu as "Los Angeles" in the tropics. I might have considered Maui, but when reading a National Geographic with the pages describing Volcano National Park, I thought to myself, "I'm there". The Big Island amazed me. While being there for two weeks, I could witness twenty of the twenty-two sub-climates of the planet. Fortunately, I paid off the mortgage for the house in Culver City some years before, since we purchased it when the market was a fraction of the value in 1978 when compared to 2002. I did not have a mortgage tax write off, and originally had considered a second home in the San Luis Obispo region in central California. While driving through the districts of the Big Island of Hawai`i, and after reading a real estate listing on this beautiful island, there were several properties available for one-half of the value of the property in Culver City. So we decided. The next real estate purchase would be on the Big Island. We spent many hours traveling through all the districts on the Big Island. The first choice was a 37-acre estate in the Hamakua district. The house was diminutive, but the property was spectacular, with its waterfalls and greenery. We entered escrow, but the whole deal fell through when the current owner refused to allow a formal inspection of the property. In one waterfall, there was a non-up-to-code electric generation system. As a result, the entire deal fell out of escrow. Another property that I was excited about was a coffee farm in South Kona. That deal worked. I now had my second career in my pocket, but at the time could not live there. The first step to stay on the Big Island on a more permanent basis was to establish internet connectivity, which was accomplished in 2004.

In 2005, after my near death experience at Cedars Sinai and the end of Evolution Computing consulting, I did not search for another job. I was in contact with Matrix Consulting. The employees at Matrix knew I was available. They contacted me and offered me a full-time job. I will accept the offer with one caveat, that I could work half-time, telecommuting from Hawai`i. They formally hired me as a full-time consultant, after they submitted references to the primary clients. I knew managers at Matrix Consultants from previous jobs, like CitiCorp TTI. My familiarity with the Matrix staff made the transition easy, since I had worked with them off and on for years. But one ghost from past would haunt me. The Workforce Project called up the software director of Matrix Consultants and wanted me to fix "bugs" they found after they signed off on the project. I had to explain I no longer worked for Evolution Software and did not even have access to the laptop that I used to develop their system. I told the Workforce Project manager that she would have to deal with Matrix as a new vendor. I never heard from her again.

The Matrix Consultants office was in Santa Monica next to the Santa Monica airport. The company had contacts in Japan, India, and in Big Bear, California. Even a company this small, with about twenty employees, was globalized. A company with a web page knows no national boundaries and no borders other than the language of the company website. Technical people working on software often cuss like a longshoremen. Matrix Consultants hired a Chinese immigrant with a high level of education, but with little "in-business" experience. He did good-to-excellent work as he gained an understanding of the development environment. This was an open office, with only two enclosed offices, so vocalization was heard by just about everybody. English was this new employee's second language, so sometimes he would attempt to cuss and swear like the rest of the developers. He would get it about 90% correct. Those of us listening in the room had to do everything we could to control our behavior, and not end up howling with laughter.

The office space in Santa Monica was tiny and expensive. Matrix purchased a warehouse on Jefferson Boulevard in Mid-City, Los Angeles, and they made the move at the end of 2005. The building formally was an actual warehouse. The ceiling comprised two domed areas with Crisscrossing wood beams covered what was the original warehouse material. Gazing up at the beams rendered a comfortable but amazing artistic pattern. The previous owners of the warehouse, ironically, moved to the Big Island of Hawai`i. They even visited one time when I was present. They were both artists from the Berkeley area, and they must have done something correct to sell a warehouse in Mid-City, Los Angeles and end up on the Big Island. Since the previous owners of the warehouse were artists, the entire building had an artistic facade to it. The front bathroom had a shower flowing into a sunken, tiled enclosure. There were remnant works of art on the walls which remained after the purchase. This creatively converted warehouse was to be my southern California work-base for the next eight years.

Matrix Consultants continued to expand in 2006, but after the move to Mid-City, several employees could not adjust to working in the new environment. There were several issues. Mid-City Los Angeles was on the edge of the inner-city ghetto. The easily accessible food comprised soul food eateries. The closest was Mel's Fish Shack. This establishment was okay for a now and again lunch meal, but employees wanted something a bit more diverse. This meant they had to drive to purchase something more to their liking. Other employees could not fathom the semi-industrial neighborhood.

When first occupied by Matrix Consultants, occupancy of the warehouse was divided in half, separated by a wall. Matrix occupied the east half and a company that manufactured packaging for Apple hand-held devices occupied the west half. They had leased their part of the building before Matrix purchased it. The arrangement worked out nicely until the company in the western part of the building moved to a new facility. At that point, Matrix Consultants constructed a large doorway in the dividing wall, thus giving access to the entire building. The eastern half of our building had a small kitchenette, a single restroom and a very large sunken rectangular area covered with beautiful Spanish tile, where one could take a shower. Now the western half of the building had a full kitchen with a professional oven and stove. These facilities allowed a different approach to lunch time meals. The bathroom area had a two person sauna and an old school bath tub that had a shower with four legs raised on a rectangular structure covered with Spanish tile. If you wished to take a shower, it was necessary to climb up on this rectangular structure. There were four actual offices in the entire building. One in the eastern half of the building where the director of software had her office. A door in that office exited to a conference room. The conference room had a large table that had banquet capacity. The president occupied the second office when present. On a platform, he could view part of the western half of the complex. A ladder existed in his office that allowed access to the roof. From the roof you could view all the way down La Ballona Creek to the ocean at Marina del Rey. Looking to the north, the Hollywood sign was visible. Then, looking to the east, you viewed the Los Angeles central city skyscrapers. Looking to the south, you had a view of the Mid City neighborhood. The president's office was usually open for passage. During the late afternoon, passage to the roof would render these amazing views of the city. The other two offices in the front of the west half were for sales and sales support. They were sound proof. They constructed a local computer complex in the east portion of the building to house development machines. On top of this complex was an office overlooking the east portion of the building. It was the home of operations. A similar area was constructed on top of the small kitchenette. It also overlooked the eastern portion of the building. It was the work area of the quality assurance manager. We built a wooden platform for each employee, along with a desk. The entire layout was open, but also comfortable. At the far end of the western portion of the building, closest to the south entrance, there were several tables to use for such activities as eating, playing games, and impromptu conferences. The company hired a cook to make lunches for all the employees that wanted the cook's style of cooking. This solved the lunch issue for most employees. While in California, the Jefferson warehouse was my most comfortable work environment to date. Matrix Consultants had the talent to build apps for smart phones. We actually built some for specific clients. In retrospect, the company could have diversified as a mobile phone advertising company, but that didn't happen. Matrix Consultants were democratic compared to Capital Group-American Funds and CitiCorp, but not democratic enough. The principals in the company did not have the same vision or even the same goal. One wanted to build a software startup, and the other wanted to land the "next big deal," and then move on to the next one. These differing goals worked if they coincided. Later in the evolution of Matrix Consultants, they did not. This is a classic case of where those that understood the technology should have driven the direction of the company.

* * *

Situations in Hawai`i took a turn for the worse when someone broke into my farm house and stole a strange array of items. The theft included used bedroom furniture, underpants, and kitchen utensils, but left items of value like musical instruments and expensive wine. The farmer who leases the western coffee field called me in Los Angeles and told me he saw someone carrying a chest of drawers through the field. My guess is that the thieves were high on methedrine, or commonly known as "ice". The previous owner had installed an alarm system. I called up the alarm company and had it activated. The person who was hired by the previous and original owner to mow and garden recommended two caretakers to stay and guard the house. I trusted this person's opinion, and I hired Candace and Joyce. Later in 2005, I shipped my car to Hawai`i, picked it up in Hilo after a one-way car rental at the Kona International Airport. I drove from Hilo to my farm and met Candice and Joyce, two gay women, in person. It turned out that while living with them part time, about six months a year, for the next few years, they were the best roommates I had ever had. I felt completely comfortable and not the slightest bit apprehensive about female roommates. They shared their opinions with me, taught me about the ways and means on the Big Island and were never afraid to call me out, if they I did something that annoyed them. "John, wash your beer bottles before you store them for recycling".

High-speed Internet was established with Hawai`i Telcom, and I could telecommute to Matrix Consultants. This meant that I was up at 5:00 AM each morning, Hawai`i Standard Time. During the first few years, while a Hawai`i part-time resident, when I wasn't working with Matrix, I was clearing the cane grass and planning the future of the farm. This physical work usually occurred during my "lunch break", which took place in the morning, varying two or three hours, given standard or daylight saving time on the mainland. Candace and Joyce introduced me to several local friends, most of whom I'm still acquainted with . When I wasn't working on software or working outside on the farm clearing land, I was writing or playing music. My writing comprised science fiction and articles for the amateur press. I was curious about Joyce's and Candice's background. "Where did you did you meet each other"? "Oh, we both worked in the forestry service in Oregon". Joyce was more organizational and serious. Candice was more of a joker and very much like to "talk story". She enjoyed telling me how she was the only female on her high school football team, an offensive lineman, and how at one time she had the weight lifting record for her class in the state of Oregon. Candace was not a massive girl, or particularly large. She was strong as an ox.

When living on the Big Island for a significant part of the year, I was even more of a ghost to my family, old friends and some new Matrix employees. I took part in group meeting phone calls to Matrix regularly. On the other end, there were several new employees. One of the software staff told me when I returned to the warehouse that it was like the old television show, Charlie's Angels. They were talking to the "Charlie" in a box. Of course, this was before the days of Skype on other similar technologies. Later, with Skype, I connected to a party at the Matrix warehouse. Attendees of the party would walk by and look at my image on the monitor. Those who knew that I was "connecting" to the party via the Internet would pause and talk with me. But many others, even a few who knew me, would look at me, and exclaim, "Oh Look! They have a screen saver of John". It was an interesting party. My father and my aunt, his sister, attended. Known or unknown, I was a fly on the wall and could drop in on many conversations like "Why does

Gordy walk along reading a book at work?", or "Jill really wanted to visit Big Bear, but has never gotten an invitation to one of the Big Bear parties".

I was now living a good life, and I had time to turn my thoughts on what was going on with planet Earth. I became very much aware of our globalized economy. It was obvious in Hawai`i due to all the connections to the island in the Pacific Rim dominated by the oil companies. The bank that funded my mortgage for my house was the creation of a dominant oil company. Shipping and tourism directly depended on oil companies. I quickly came to appreciate the local elements of Hawaiian culture. I would pay attention to modern and traditional island music, made, at least, a minimal study of the Hawaiian language, bought a ukulele, took my half-size acoustic guitar or the uke to the beach and would slow down... for a while until I had to speed up and work. I felt I had at least some control and ownership of what I produced. In one sense, I could own much of the technology since I helped create it. It made it easier to be awake at 5:00 AM HST to be ready and online. New local friends would see me sitting and staring at a monitor. They would say, "what is he doing up there"? In 2006, I saw one of the last concerts held at the now dilapidated theater in Naalehu. It was a beautiful mix of island slack guitar and then other artists doing a modern synthesized music.

Cleaning up the native forest, about eight acres' worth, was one of Joyce and Candice's tasks for care-taking rent free. Not only did they do a beautiful job, but they brought in their friend Morgan, who crafted a Frisbee,a.k.a. Disc, golf course. It still exists to this day and is a pleasing but gentle sport that all can enjoy, no matter what skill level they have got. Entering the forest is a treat and a near-magical experience. The curving of the rose-apple trees and the twisted existence of Christmas berry trees (Brazilian Pepper tree), the native and majestic ohia trees, the ancient common mango trees, green agave cactus, the kukui nut trees, the yellow guava trees, flowing lilikoi vines and native Hawaiian guava trees present themselves in the forest, in a way that makes it impossible to walk through this precious preservation and not succumb to its spiritual effect.

A visitor once told me, "John, you could subdivide your land year, develop this forest and..." I said softly, "I like it as it is." In my mind I thought, "Over my dead body." The land was once the "Papa Homestead." There are stacks of rocks, depressions lined with rocks, and other "structures" that no one has deciphered. This land must be preserved.

I reached an agreement with the Hawai`ian that had farmed the coffee on my land for years. I wanted to keep "ke aloha aina" intact. I would purchase the roasted coffee below market price and sell it directly to the buyer or over the Internet on the South Kona Farms website. I didn't like the conventional coffee farming practices of the Hawai`ian farmer. I tolerated them. Using Roundup as an herbicide turned out to be my primary objection. I would prefer a weed-eater, which is labor intensive. My solution was to divide the farm into the conventional part, which I leased for a yearly amount to the Hawai`ian farmer, and to designate the mauka, or up-the-hill portion of the farm as potentially organic. For several years I led this double existence, part-time on the Big Island and then part time in west Los Angeles working in the Mid-City. During the months I was in Hawai`i building and guiding software design, I was back to a moderate, but not the high stress level. On the good side, I had a great corner office with a view of coffee tree fields, the Pacific Ocean to the West and, once in a while, a rainbow. The stress was easy to counter. Joyce and Candice introduced me to several locals who played music. My music activity, with local musicians, continues in Hawai`i to this day. When going to the beach, where the temperature is ten degrees warmer than the average at my farm, I would turn into a lizard, strumming my guitar or my ukulele, mesmerized by the sound of the waves. It was and is, easy to calm and readjust.

When on the Big Island, I also studied agriculture. The Agriculture center in Kainaliu offered several extension courses sponsored by the University of Hawai`i. The courses ranged from pest control to irrigation techniques. Sometimes the classes were held on a farm where the techniques were presented as a live farm model. This differed totally from studying history or computer science. The classes were always a real treat and enjoyable. The classes at the University of Hawai`i mark my last association to an institution of higher learning.

After a return trip to my farm, I was shocked to find out that my two excellent caretakers were moving back to Oregon. Another person with good intentions in my extended ohana, or family, suggested a new candidate to take over the watch. Linda was several years older than me and could not do the physical tasks that Joyce and Candace were capable of. After an interview, we hired her. She moved her belongings into the house, along with her three cats. But she had several positive qualities. She had a genuine concern for people. Inside the house, she did an excellent job of keeping the place clean. As time passed, issues developed. Linda had severe boundary issues. She operated like an owner, and did not have the responsibility of a hired employee. She took many actions without mutual consensus. This tense situation existed until 2014, when I retired from corporate USA and moved full time to the Big Island. Linda introduced me to several good locals, many of them oriented to New Age concepts, which I find amusing, but I have little truck with. Often it was a glimpse back into the Age of Aquarius popularized hippies in the mid-1960s.

Given the Great Recession that occurred from 2008 on, eventually Matrix Consultants lost its primary account, and could never recover. Late in 2011, I lost my Matrix contract job and was now on the open market. The time was not yet ripe for my exit from Corporate USA, so I had to search for another job. There was a last party at the Matrix Consultants warehouse. I considered it an insane expenditure of resources. Several former contractors which worked at Matrix attended. I was searching for a job at the time of this party, and had been contacted by a game company on the north side of Oahu Hawai`i, where I went through an initial interview. But one contractor with whom I had worked closely in the past effectively offered me a job on the spot. Grindr was the company which was building a gay male connection site. Having interviewed with the technical director and my former Matrix Consultants associate consultant, and I was hired. I informed the game company in Oahu that I was hired elsewhere and would not continue with their hiring process. I had not convinced myself that I wanted to work on an on-line variant of Dungeons and Dragons as a permanent job. It would pollute the nerdish, but fun memories of working at Honeywell. The

Grindr application was a challenge to the extreme.

I purchased a Toyota Camry, since my original vehicle was on the Big Island, with low mileage, and went to work in Hollywood. The company had gays and straights, and probably some bisexuals. It was a very difficult leading-edge project. Over a million gay men were connecting to find dates and relationships each night. Grindr attempted to partition their target audience into gay "tribes". I don't know if it was a successful marketing strategy. Having found the "tribes" like "bear", "twink", "otter" to be interesting. I had not heard of gay male tribes before working at Grindr. To construct a million connections in a single night effectively amounted to a distributed database of a million smart phones with a two gigabytes of memory in each phone. This was a daunting task. The original contracted system was failing each night, so our job was to re-engineer the system, so it was secure, fast, and reliable. They fired the chief technical officer after I worked there for about seven months. They hired a new chief technical, originally from Israel, and a seasoned veteran from MySpace. He changed the way we were doing things. It was a nice fit nicely into Grindr's culture since he was a gay male with a steady partner. He gave out monthly awards to those engineers who had made significant contributions. It was an "atta-boy." He introduced these awards as a theme that would capture both the geekness and the gayness of the company culture. The award turned out to be a golden statue of Star Wars' C3P0. The response from all the employees was hilarious.

The architect who was my primary contact went on holiday for two weeks. He left me with a specific design to implement. There were several problems with it, and he was not around to answer questions. I attempted to come up with creative solutions on my own. The project ended up over budget, a typical experience in software work. After working in Hollywood for over a year, myself and other team members were laid off, and the responsibility of the project handed off to a second consulting company. Before that, I got to experience Hollywood culture on a day-to-day basis. This included street performers, Scientologists, local restaurants, narrowly missing skate-borders dressed in black riding in the dark, and the aggressive Hollywood traffic patterns. On being laid off, I celebrated. I could return to Hawai`i and make sure all was secure on the farm in South Kona.

My plan was to collect unemployment as a gateway into "retirement" from corporate USA. After signing up, which had to be completed with the local office in Marina Del Rey, near the harbor below Venice in California. I attended a class, which was required, but mostly useless. What wasn't useless was the direct phone line to Sacramento, which was required for the sign up. There was a public number and a website for the state of California. I could enter the basic information on the website, but to complete the process, they required a call to the center in Sacramento. The call center opened at 09:00 AM. At 08:59 AM, there was a message that the center was not open yet. At 09:01 AM, the message explained all the lines were busy. You could try many times after that, but the lines were always busy. Hence, I visited the office in Marina Del Rey, where you could get a direct line to the center of Sacramento. I successfully signed up for unemployment for the first time in my life. I played the game according to the rules and headed back to the Big Island.

What happened next is your standard bureaucratic blindness.

I was applying for jobs in both Hawai`i and California. The unemployment staff workers would call periodically to get the status of my job search. They called me at Kona International Airport while waiting for a plane to return to return to Southern California. They thought I was on a "Hawaiian vacation" and canceled my unemployment. I had to go to "unemployment court" to contest their cancellation. I found myself alone in a room with a judge where I explained I could telecommute from any location on the planet that had an Internet connection. The judge was sympathetic and explained that the employees that worked for the department did not understand computer technology. She reinstated my unemployment.

For several weeks, I remained in California preparing for a move to the Big Island. I followed the rules of job search, but after a few weeks a company received a copy of my CV, and called me in for an interview. Given the rules, I could not reject the interview. The job was close to where I had been living in Culver City. And after the interview, they hired me. I knew why I was hired. One of former Matrix Consultants employees worked there, and had recommended me.

PriceGrabber.com was an Internet marketing optimization company. I told them I was in permanent transit from Southern California to Hawai`i. After quizzing me, the hiring manager, actually an amiable person, told me it didn't matter since it was a three-month contract. They hired me in 2013 and the three-month contract eventually turned out to be a sixteen-month contract. The company was not democratic in the slightest way, a few managers made the critical decisions. On the bright side, the company culture was excellent, with leniency in work hours, infinite not-so-healthy food, copious interaction among the employees, and an outstanding corporate environment. There were pool tables, ping-pong tables, pin-ball machines, and digital TV in the large lounge area. Stepping back into one square, this is a trend for software companies in the twenty-first century, but it can become something of a gilded cage.

PriceGrabber.com let me telecommute from Hawai`i, so for several months I split this into two trips. On the first trip, the person who I worked with at Matrix Consultants became annoyed with an individual that was the leader of our group. She was angry because that employee that started the same day as I did, according to her, took credit for my work. I could not care less. Yes, perhaps, this new manager was not a core technical person, but he was doing what was in his self-interest, projecting successful status based on my work. This behavior is typical of several managers in all technical industries. So my former associate at Matrix Consultants found a new job and resigned. I was disappointed, but continued with my contract.

During this time, we made preparations to move from Culver City to the Big Island of Hawai`i. The house in Culver City was to be rented or leased. Culling through belongings, I had to decide what to keep and what to sell or jettison. We held two garage sales on the front lawn, with neighbors asking what was happening. The selling continued for some time, until a vast number of material items were sold, given away, or donated. The lesson I learned was "not to collect stuff," and if you collect material objects, make sure they are meaningful. After going through this process, I decided to only give people presents that would "go away" and not persist. That might include tickets to events or entertainment, something you would consume and then it's gone, gifts for restaurants, for example.

My contract finally ended at PriceGrabber.com in September 2014, and I once again briefly worked for Matrix Consultants at the twilight of the company's existence. They paid me in computer hardware, which I shipped to Hawai`i. For this brief period, I took the new Expo line train to work. Finally, Los Angeles was developing a semi-reasonable mass transit system. The curse of General Motors and real-estate developers dismantling the Los Angeles Red Car rail system in the beginning of the 1950s was finally being reversed. Before departing California, I took the new rail system to concerts, baseball games, and other centrally located events.

The last items were finally shipped to the two-story farmhouse on the Big Island of Hawai`i, the house leased, and we donated all noteworthy items not shipped. This was a transition from being a ghost to a second life, in a familiar and very different place. I established a new daily routine of hard work on the farm and relaxation to the schedule set to my preference, only mitigated by the real world around me. The ghost had finally settled on a large island in the Pacific. I realized I will be likely be spending the afternoon and twilight of my life on the Big Island. Sometimes I considered these feelings as heading to the end of the line. As a result, new conscious archetypes emerged. Entities that were once in the background of my perception moved from less important to more important. The animal friends, your cats, the mother wild turkey nesting with her eggs under a ti plant, become a bond that reduced worry and enhanced good feelings. Helping your friends around you moved to the forefront of your consciousness. I noted I paid more attention to my immediate environment, which leads me to thinking more about the state of the planet that you live on.

I paid more attention to my dreams. Sometimes they were fun night escapades of a mesmeric mix of old friends and workers, often where we told stories and played games. Some archetypes from the past haunted me in my dreams. I didn't consider them nightmares, but during several dreams I had anxiety. Working on the mainland as a software engineer was a typical dream pattern. Sometimes the work dream was comical, like building the initial foundations and charter of a new company. Finding myself at a critical juncture of a of a project and when the company asked "please don't return to Hawai`i yet..." was a typical theme of anxiety. When I had conversations with the dead, I would wake up in a cold sweat. Some of the deceased characters included my father, mother and my old roommate, which had passed because of cancer. The talking dead dreams always freaked me out. Then there was my nuclear war dream that I considered a return to the start of my life story. Somehow, I survived while in my old neighborhood at Culver City. I stepped outside after the destruction. Many of the houses had vanished. There were no vehicles except buses. It required myself and remaining survivors to use them as the only remaining transportation.

All these entities that formed a kaleidoscope of my new and changed reality lead me on as an active ghost of my former self.

META-WORDS

•••

eta-words are a list of word choices or invented words
I describe outside the flow of my memoir. I define
any "techno-speak" words that sneak into the main
memoir.

I am reluctant to name the spread of the United States empire as
the "American empire". America includes all of North and South
America. Thus I invented the term "USA-sian", pronounced "you-
shay-zun". I could have used the term SPQA, meaning Senatus
Populusque Americanus, something of a pun on "SPQR", the symbol
of the ancient Roman Empire, but is abstract and unless you know
some Latin, you won't understand it.

A legend that is not part of formal Christian scriptures inspires
the title of the Harrowing "book" in the Atomic Baby Bible. Jesus
descending into purgatory and Hades makes up the legend. The

word "Hell" never appears in any of the Christian Bible. Jesus referred to Gehenna, the burning trash dump behind Jerusalem, an actual place you can locate on the Internet.

Fortran is one of the first computer languages. They designed it to look and feel like algebra.

"Heavy petting" is where each partner has an orgasm, but does not engage in intercourse.

"Bennies", "whites" means benzadrine, a stimulant.

"The Hollywood Ten" refers to the writers that refused to testify in the House Un-American activities Committee starting in 1947, that were "black-listed".

Wilhelm Reich was a protege of Sigmund Freud. He combined the theories of Karl Marx and psychoanalysis. Having wrote books on the mass psychology of fascism and sexual freedom, it discredited him when adopting the pseudo-science of "orgone" technology. In my opinion, Herbert Marcuse from the Frankfurt School of socialism did a much better job of integrating the theories of Marx and Freud in Eros and Civilization.

Computer Operating System is the core software that lets a human or other computers send and receive information via devices the "OS" manages. This would include the hardware where information and data is stored and retrieved.

C Language is a computer programming language developed at AT&T in 1972. It is not dependent on any hardware or Computer Operating System. The language was influenced by earlier languages, like Pascal and Algol. It allows the software engineer to author code, which can manipulate computer resources in a structured way.

Unix is a computer operating system that was developed at AT&T

in 1970. It was one of the first operating systems that could run on different hardware platforms. Almost all of it was written in the "C" language.

Linux is a computer operating system that behaves like Unix. It is completely free and the source code is available to anyone who desires it.

Object Oriented computer programming languages have the common concept that collection of source code has a common theme. The algorithm and data are associated with that theme.

C++ is an Object Oriented language that attempted to be compatible with the C language.

Java is an Object Oriented language that in some ways resembles C++ but with its own self containing structures that execute on a virtual machine, a machine that only exists in software.

Scripting computer languages have the characteristic that you can immediately execute the program after entering them on a consol or in a file.

Javascript is a misnomer. It is a scripting language that is more "C" like and has little to do with the Java language.

Perl is a scripting language with extensive pattern matching capabilities. Later versions had optional Object-Oriented capabilities.

Relational Databases give you the same answer to a query where the position of the row of data or information in the database doesn't matter.

AFTERWORD
(REVELATIONS)

•••

Now for a cross-examination. Where maybe myself, God, or Lucifer, or nobody, depending on your Big Picture orientation, is going to cross-examine me. Yes, let us ask the difficult questions that I answer in a relaxed and easy frame of reference. Sic et non?

Why did you write this memoir?

It is important to understand history. This is a history from a subjective view. The purpose of the writing is to leave a record for someone interested in the decades of my lifetime to analyze and digest.

Are the people in your memoir real?

Yes, they all are. I have changed a number of names. For friends and peers that are openly public, I have not changed those names.

There is a lot of rebellion and even anger in your story. How do you perceive that now?

I am still angry when I perceive injustice. These days, my response is to struggle against social depredations, in all forms, in a calm, non-violent, but with a determined acumen. Yes, I have what many would perceive as "dark side" emotions. I use the feelings to motivate myself in several endeavors.

So you are, even to this day, a revolutionary?

Yes.

What is a revolutionary?

It is someone who questions the root, the basic causality of what human beings do and realizes that there is a potential for humanity at all levels to achieve something much better.

That's quite a stance for a farmer in Hawai`i.

Don't confuse aloha with weakness.

Where do you want this so-called revolution of yours to take place?

A global revolution to democratize the capitalist infrastructure and where organizations controlled by those who work for them to operate and compete in a market economy.

So you are anti-capitalist?

Yes.

But you just referred to a market economy. Isn't this a contradiction?

No. Market economies have existed since tribal humans could collect enough useful things, whether food or tools, since the dawn of human history. Capitalism is tied to a particular period in European history. You can label it with a number phrases, but it ushered mass society into the environment of factories, cities, and the emergence of the nation state where a powerful few controlled the alignment of the newly developed machines of mass production, and extracted value from those who worked in the new production line systems. A market economy is about trading "things" of equal value, whereas capitalism is about power of a few over many. It's that simple. I say "things," since as we move into the twentieth century and beyond, many conceptual entities transform into a commodity, something of value.

Conceptual entities? What are you talking about? New Age skylarking with the planet Mercury in retrograde, so you stay home and read books and not do business?

To start, as world society entered the information age, with its start in the 1950s, in what we once named "First World Society," status or your reputation became a commodity. Of course, you could trace the origins of "what you did" and "how many people knew you" back to radio and motion pictures. In those 1950s cases, in terms of the overall economies of the industrialized world, it was a niche factor. By the post-modern twenty-first century, information is the commodity that dominates what nearly all people do on a twenty-four-hour day. As of 2016, there are approximately 40,000,000,000,000, or 4.0 to the 13th power, units of information transferred planet-wide on the Internet every second. You have globalized information controlled by globalized businesses. Control and processing of the source and destination of these units of information, let's just refer to them as messages, is a vast business.

But we have ignored the basics of what makes the life possible on the planet. Things like food, machinery, automobiles, airplanes, electricity, oil, wood, plastics and other such hard commodities. These are of primary importance compared to "information commodities."

Now, let me present some core principles. These things of value mentioned are directly associated with the physics of the actual material world. Food must come from crops, where labor as a human being or a machine transforms seed, dirt, and fertilizer into something that a person can consume. Machinery itself must be produced from common and rare materials, often built by other, older machines, and often humans assisting in terms of corrections and control. So we have automobiles, airplanes, and other such devices, large and small, produced on a global scale. Wood is a finite resource, and introduces scarcity in the economy, just like gold, but not to the same extent. Plastics are a combination of many elements and are both a useful and destructive force. They often replace metal and wood because of their resilience. They are also an incredible danger, since they virtually never dissolve and go away in the actual material world. Oil is the dominant hard commodity on the planet. It, also, is a finite resource.

Yes, oil, petrol in all its forms. You object to this?

I'm not going into a long declension of alternative energies, but petrol from the perspective of the home planet as a resource, we should use another energy. Okay, not nuclear, unless in the radiation-filled vacuum of space.

Tell us, what was the best moment in your life so far?

There are many, depending on whether physical, emotional, or social. For a social happy I would cite the ending of the Vietnam War. For emotional and physical, it is where I am today.

Then, what are some of the worst moments in your life?

A suicide that I might have prevented.

Do you believe in God?

It depends on what you mean by "God." First, if you mean a higher power in the universe, you cannot prove or disprove it. There is an amazing consistency mixed with randomness in the universe. Where did this originate? If you go back to the Big Bang, and then stipulate the conditions from where it came, then you ask, "Where did those conditions originate?" The ontology of everything is an open question. For me, the greatest evidence of a higher power is the consistency of the universe as it transforms to and from matter and energy, and vice versa. One attribute of a higher power, I would state God is not a male or female. If I were to fictionalize God, I would say it is pure energy in several dimensions we don't understand.

So you are not an atheist?

I leave the question open. I know several atheists who are more "Christ-like" than a number of people who claim to be Christians. Thus, I have complete respect for atheists as human beings.

Now you have done it. You've pulled Jesus into this mix. So who is Jesus? Is he the son of this higher force?

Why not? And what follows is that I am too. But you, since you are a creation of my imagination, perhaps Lucifer the "light bringer" that is cross-examining me, pushing me to confess... you are a meditation of my mind and thought. You only exist in that context.

You didn't answer my question. Go ahead and designate me as Lucifer, a chunk of your fantasy creation. Again, who is Jesus?

Okay, here is your answer. Jesus Christ was a revolutionary. He championed the outcast, the least capable and powerless individuals in the society that was dominated by a religious hierarchy and an expanding Roman empire. He had a vision of a new society, radically different from the one he lived in.

Since you embrace this vision of yours of humanity, what is good and evil given that revolutions in the past are violent, where peoples of the dominating class are killed, even murdered. Answer me that one.

First, in a society where most of the society or even a large plurality are struggling to attain the basic life needs, those needs supersede a culture of non-violence. When a society becomes so dehumanized that the negative utopia becomes positive, that former negative utopia delivers the bare necessities of living at the cost of losing everything else. Think of it as the recognition of necessity at the cost of losing all that is optional. The base definition of evil is physical. It is the loss of energy and the deterioration of matter as entropy and death. The base definition of good is anti-entropy, life.

But there are fewer societies, on planet Earth, where the necessities of living are missing from the majority of the population.

True. The classes that rule the planet can create a mass culture where everyone has the base essentials plus some devices that fixate their attention, while the select few have power and wealth, in some ratio that vastly supersedes the base, planetary socio-economic measure.

To end with, what do you think should be done?

A decade-long revolution that creates centers of democratic enterprise where those enterprises compete in a market economy. This means the slow flattening of all business hierarchies, so the top is tangible from the bottom. Manage the consensus and conflict in corporations, so they become more democratic over a long period.

Cute. How utopian.

There are many unknowns ahead of our global planetary human species. One that we will all face is how we interact with the forces that we face daily. If we deal with these forces, many optional, others as base necessities, we can develop a common goal implemented by a flexible and consistent program.

GEEK
APOCRYPHA I

•••

1971-1978

At United Computing, they introduced me to the PDP-8 minicomputer. It had a 12-bit word size and 8 instructions at the machine language level. The PDP-8 was the first machine that implemented United's Programming Language (UPL). In retrospect, it was far, far ahead of its time. The founders of the company, John Wright and John Palmari, had invented a virtual machine. We implemented it on several other minicomputers, including the General Automation SPC-16, Varian, and on mainframes at the time of 1973. The PDP-8 could produce a numerically controlled tape for a Boeing 707 part in less than two days. Of course, the PDP-8's cost was a fraction of a large computer, so that's how the company made its money.

UPL was a "virtual assembly language." It was not a high-level language. We programmed it using instructions that were like IBM 360 assembly language.

They introduced me to a slightly more powerful minicomputer, the General Automation SPC-16. It had a 16-bit word, what became the standard for minicomputers until Motorola 68000 microprocessors and Intel x0086 microprocessors, where x in the name is 2, 3, or 4.

We ported the UPL virtual machine to a DataGeneral Nova minicomputer and then a DataGeneral Eclipse in 1974. I authored programs in this virtual machine language and eventually mastered it.

On the other side of the house, United Computing had bought a minicomputer graphics system from a product developer named Patrick J Hannratty. He led the development of CAD/CAM systems using the Fortran IV language and low-wage students who were novices in software development. His system was completely re-engineered and re-written at United Computing.

The DataGeneral Eclipse is of interest, since it supported the Algol language, very popular in Europe, but almost unknown in the United States. Pascal existed, but was the domain of new Computer Science departments. PL-1 was the only other well-known high-level language at the time that was reasonably well-structured and invented by IBM.

For the PDP-8, all the software engineers had to key the bootstrap program through the front panel of the minicomputer.

The DataGeneral Eclipse was an exception, but for the DG Nova, General Automation SPC-16 and the Digital PDP-8 that was the rule. Typically, the program you keyed in was a minimal driver that would read "paper" tape (in most cases, it was a Mylar tape). And that paper tape would then boot the operating system. There was a technician who worked for Digital Computing with only six fingers. His thumb and little finger were missing in each hand. He was the master of keying in octal codes. The keys on the front panel of the Dec minicomputers were in octets. We nicknamed him "Doc Oct." No one could key in a bootstrap faster than Doc Oct.

Programs running on minicomputers had no memory protection. At United Computing, high-level source code was written in Fortran IV. If you made a mistake in a "for" loop and accidentally wrote across the "constant" one with a typo, your program would explode in mysterious ways. Fortran IV is primitive compared to modern languages. There were no structures, objects, or classes. There was a "common" segment of global memory that all programs read and wrote data.

Remarkably, the Unigraphics System worked as well as it did on the Tecktronics 4014 graphic terminal. There were strict rules for Fortran program structure. "Gotos" always had to flow from top to bottom in the program listing. This was an early implementation of the d.r.y. principal (don't repeat yourself.) Unigraphics still exists today, though in a radically different implementation. To make this more treacherous, several low-level modules were written in the native assembly language of the hosting machine, especially those controlling any graphic devices.

I spent a few months developing the entire operating system

and application for a DataGeneral Nova-attached processor that controlled a digitizing table. Imagine this hardware as a huge laptop, about the size of your dining room table. I wrote the timing and interrupt control in DataGeneral assembly language. There were no "high"-level languages in this system (if you want to call Fortran IV a high-level language).

1978 – 1980

Packet switching networks were relatively new. We partitioned information into pieces or packets. This was nothing new in 1978. They based the original Internet Protocol on packets, and were a derivative of the Apollo Project and a backbone of the original Arpanet. We built the entire TranTelecommunications switch on banks of physical memory, which at the time gave the company a low-cost alternative to a machine with equivalent power.

Probably because a recruiter did a slick job of luring me out of TranTelecommunications, I went to work for Cybertek. This company used Perkin Elmer minicomputers, which, except for the Program Status Word, had an assembler instruction set identical to that of the IBM 360. In addition, Cybertek had a minimal minicomputer-based office automation system. I wrote these and other applications in what was a de facto IBM 360 assembly language. I inherited a program written by a young person who was a COBOL programmer. What a mess. The last project I engineered was a report, written in Perkin Elmer assembly language. Because it was a report, with repeating idioms with headers and pagination, I wrote it using recursive "calls."

1981-1982

When I hired on with AM Jacquard, they placed me into the communication group. This was probably because of my experience at TranTelecommunications. The maintenance of existing software that supported IBM's BiSync protocol was my task. If you implemented it exactly as written in the specification, the end points would "deadly embrace," that is, would go into an infinite loop trying to acknowledge the most recent message. After nearly eight years of programming in assembly language, I imagined a little creativity. I was now familiar with Algol and Pascal, so I would design my algorithms in these high-level languages and manually compile, that is translated, into this symbolic machine language using my own mental capability. I would actually place operators and operands similar to a construct in a high-level language as "arguments" to routines and then build tiny interpreters "on the fly" to use them.

AM Jacquard's machine was like the popular minicomputer the Data General Nova, so I was familiar with the instruction set from my days at United Computing. Another manager had me work on a development project called the Limited Inter-processor Link. It mimicked a new protocol called "Ethernet." The idea was to connect the minicomputers using the same hardware as BiSync, copper wire with synchronous control like Ethernet. Ironically, the same project was completed at UC Berkeley four years later and called Serial Internet Protocol, or SLIP, thus bypassing the whole requirement of special hardware, which, back then, AM Jacquard had developed this serial link as a prototype.

Jacquard had several competitors, but it didn't make that much difference in the marketplace. The IBM personal computer would wipe them all out in two years. And once Ethernet technology became widespread, all the home-grown hardware for office automation became history. At the end of my Jacquard tenure, the management was examining the "C" language. It didn't make any difference, the horses had already left the barn.

1982-1985

After Jacquard crashed as a company, I went to work for the Honeywell Los Angeles Development Center. CP-6 was the follow-up to Xeroxes CP-5 operating systems. The senior staff at LADC were intensely loyal to the CP-5/CP-6 project. When hired, my primary goal was to make what I might call an inverted index for the CODASYL, id est, a network database manager. I was now dealing with two similar, high-level languages, PL-1 and a PL-1 subset, PL-6, which had been developed in Los Angeles Development Center. They modeled network databases after a standardized structural hierarchy. The database was navigated by drilling down the hierarchy, starting with a parent and cycling through the children. There is nothing wrong with this mode, but by the late 1990s, it had absorbed the parent and the child nodes into object-oriented design. The network database had graduated to what was to be known as the "middle tier" or the "back-end." I did some work in General Electric assembly language, but this was my initiation of using a structured language in a professional environment (sorry, Fortran IV doesn't count).

Of course, there was a database project, "Aires," but I was not part of that. I decided it would be best for my future career to learn Unix and the C language. It turned out to be an excellent decision. The project started with a small group of developers who were breaking from the core culture of the Los Angeles Development Center and learned the Unix system. A company called Charles River Data Systems had built a real-time version of Unix called Unos. It conformed to AT&T's System V specification and had significant advantages. The most important of these was an extent-based file system. The original file system supplied with System V Unix from AT&T was not robust. A hardware crash could easily corrupt it. It could be reconstructed, but would take minutes, not seconds. The project requirements needed a recovery time in seconds for a crashed system.

During this transition, I learned the C programming language, basic Bourne Shell scripts, Unix library and system calls. It would not only be a passport out of Honeywell, but a set of technical skills that I would use for the rest of my working career in the software industry. An interesting anecdote presented itself. In Phoenix, where the project was centered, the developers used Intel 286 desktop computers, which all ran Xenix, a version of Unix built by a new company Microsoft. We connected these minicomputers via USENET, a sibling of ARPA Net. The USENET was one of the connectivity tools that pre-dated and influenced the Internet. I sent messages and newsgroups from "inhp4," a heavily used core service that connected much of the continental American sites.

While at Honeywell, I was introduced to John Lion's line-by-line documentation of the Unix version 6 kernel. This landed him in big legal trouble with AT&T, which owned the Unix source, lock, stock, and barrel. The required public domain ownership of the Internet

Protocol transferred to the University of California Berkeley, along with the Free Software Foundation, was to be the inception of the open-source movement. The open-source movement would change the course of software economics several years later.

Towards the end of my stay at Honeywell, they sent me to a class to learn relational database systems. It was an excellent class, with lectures by Chris Date, one originator of relational database systems. I wanted to know what computer languages could perform transactions against IBM's brand new relational database. Also, at Honeywell, they introduced me to two brand-new languages, C++ and Objective-C. I paid little attention, but these would loom large in my future.

Here is a real "gem" using the C programming language I took with me from Honeywell:

```
int(**toolbox)() = (int(**)()(end_of_memory-0x300))
```

It is the equivalent of a high-level assembly/machine language statement. The C language at the time was a huge step forward used in writing systems, using "level functionality." Unfortunately, development organizations tried to use the C language to develop large-scale business applications.

1985-1991

Working at Citibank TTI, they introduced me to several technologies. I have mentioned UC Berkeley as the keeper of the Internet Protocol. The university worked with version 7 Unix, which they licensed from AT&T as an educational institution, and added "Application Interfaces" for the Internet Protocol. There were two basic camps at the Citibank development center. The first did not want to use the proprietary hardware, but use off-the-shelf hardware and a system derived from Berkeley Unix, known as BSD. The second group was to port the latest Unix from AT&T, what is now known as "System 5." System 5 had a validation suite and a well-defined interface, so management loved it. BSD was technically superior, but less well-defined. System V had a remote file system named RFS (Remote File System) that was only usable with other System 5 systems and had only one working implementation.

The lack of a reasonable source-version control system hamstrung all technical groups. Unix came with a tool called SCCS, but it was only useful if one person controlled all the changes, additions, updates, and deletions. BSD used Resource Control System, a set of programs somewhat superior to the source control system used in System V Unix, SCCS, but had many of the same issues as it related to SCCS when considering concurrent development. A single-user control of source versioning was impractical in a group of several people. We manually constructed the parts list which described the versioning of each module in the build. What was worse, they built entirely the control program in the Bourne shell scripting language, which caused a slow build. Often it took several builds to even get the parts list correct. This was a before CVS and Subversion. The effect of the inefficiency is that it generated wasted waiting time for excessively long builds. The technical workers who did not have to attend the never-ending-meetings often used their private offices to entertain their businesses during these long build times.

My group tracked the Unix releases from UC Berkeley. This put us often at odds with our group manager, who honestly believed that System V from AT&T was more stable and well-suited for enterprise software. Often what would happen is we would "port" modules from the BSD system into our product, and not break the AT&T validation suite. What we ended up with was a hybrid system. The most important of these modules was the Network File System, which had been developed by Sun Microsystems. To support NFS, I ported the entire Internet Protocol stack into the AT&T source, which was the original base of the product.

Also, we ported the development environment to the same hardware as our product. This is what we knew as "native development." We evaluated two different C-compiler technologies. The first was from a company in Santa Barbara known as Greenhills; the second, a new "open source" Gnu C compiler. This also generated heated discussions in the group. Many didn't like the Greenhills compiler, since they wrote it in a language called Pascal instead of C itself.

I spent many hours in meetings while employed at CitiCorp TTI. People around me would see me writing many notes on my paper notepad. I was taking notes, but preserving my sanity. Legends in Norse mythology have replaced the names of real people in these images. The images contain several cartoon-like depictions. Sometimes these were thoughts animated on paper. Acronyms and jargon appear along with the images. Sometimes they are organizations or projects external to Citicorp TTI. For example, OSF is the Open Software Foundation, or Posix, which defined an early Unix-like standard. Other acronyms and jargon are specific to CitiCorp TTI. For example, TTM was a communications protocol stack. PDB was a version of the processor which powered Citibank's ATMs (known internally as CATs or customer activated terminals). CMS was a hideous home-grown source control system with Bourne shell scripts. And some jargon is local to the group. For example, a "fig" is a promised date for the target completion of the module or project.

Much of the odd alphabet soup has to do with the naming convention. For example, SYS had to do with the operating system and the libraries that went with it. CDE was the common development environment. The digits in the name referenced the year they started the project (not completed) and a sequential numbering system. CM and CMS are acronyms for configuration management systems.

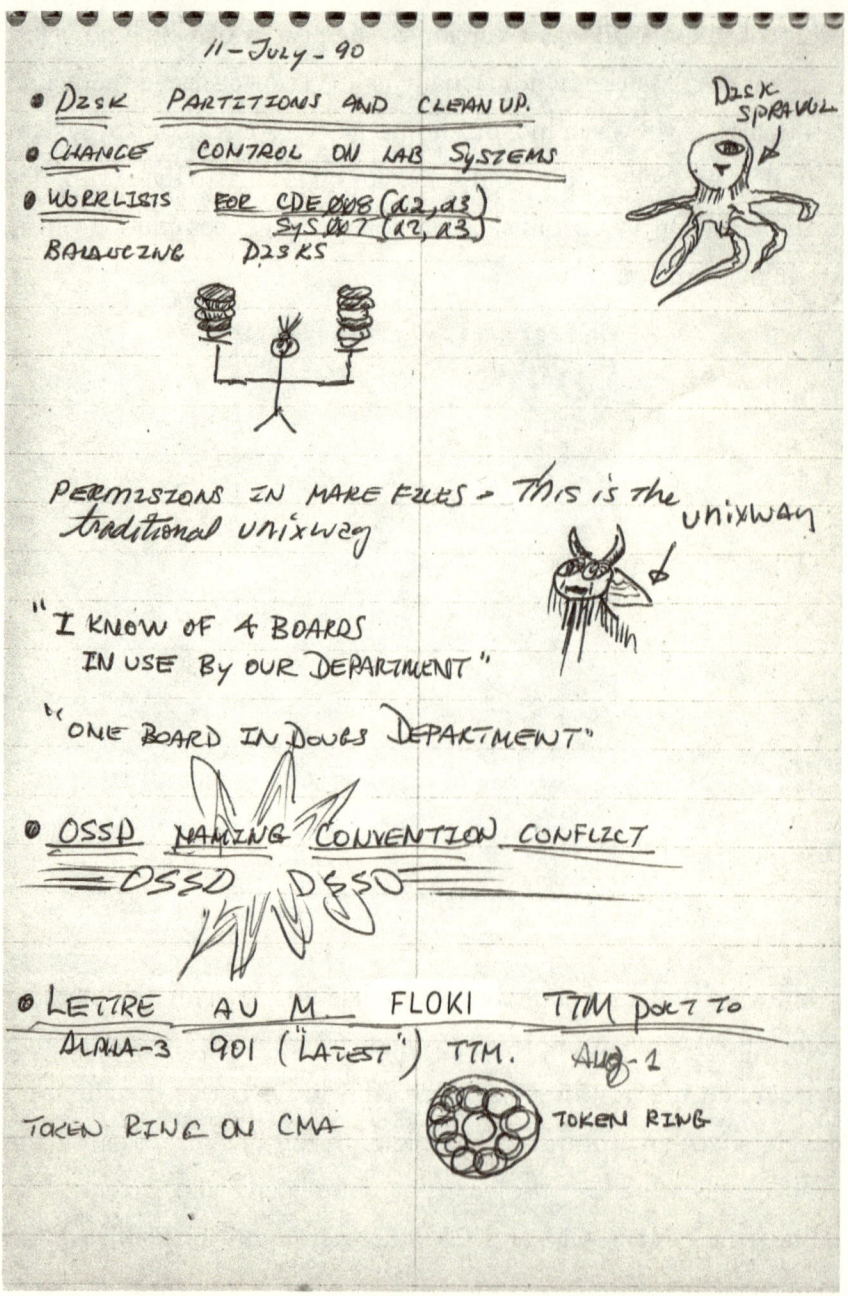

11 – July – 90

- DISK PARTITIONS AND CLEAN UP.
- CHANGE CONTROL ON LAB SYSTEMS
- WORKLISTS FOR CDE 008 (d2, d3)
  SYS 007 (d2, d3)
  BALANCING DISKS

DISK SPRAWL

PERMISSIONS IN MAKE FILES → THIS is the traditional unixway

unixway

" I KNOW OF 4 BOARDS
  IN USE BY OUR DEPARTMENT "

" ONE BOARD IN DOUGS DEPARTMENT "

- OSSD NAMING CONVENTION CONFLICT
  OSSD   DSSD

- LETTRE AU M. FLOKI   TTM DUE TO
  ALPHA-3 901 ('LATEST') TTM.   Aug-1

TOKEN RING ON CMA   TOKEN RING

298

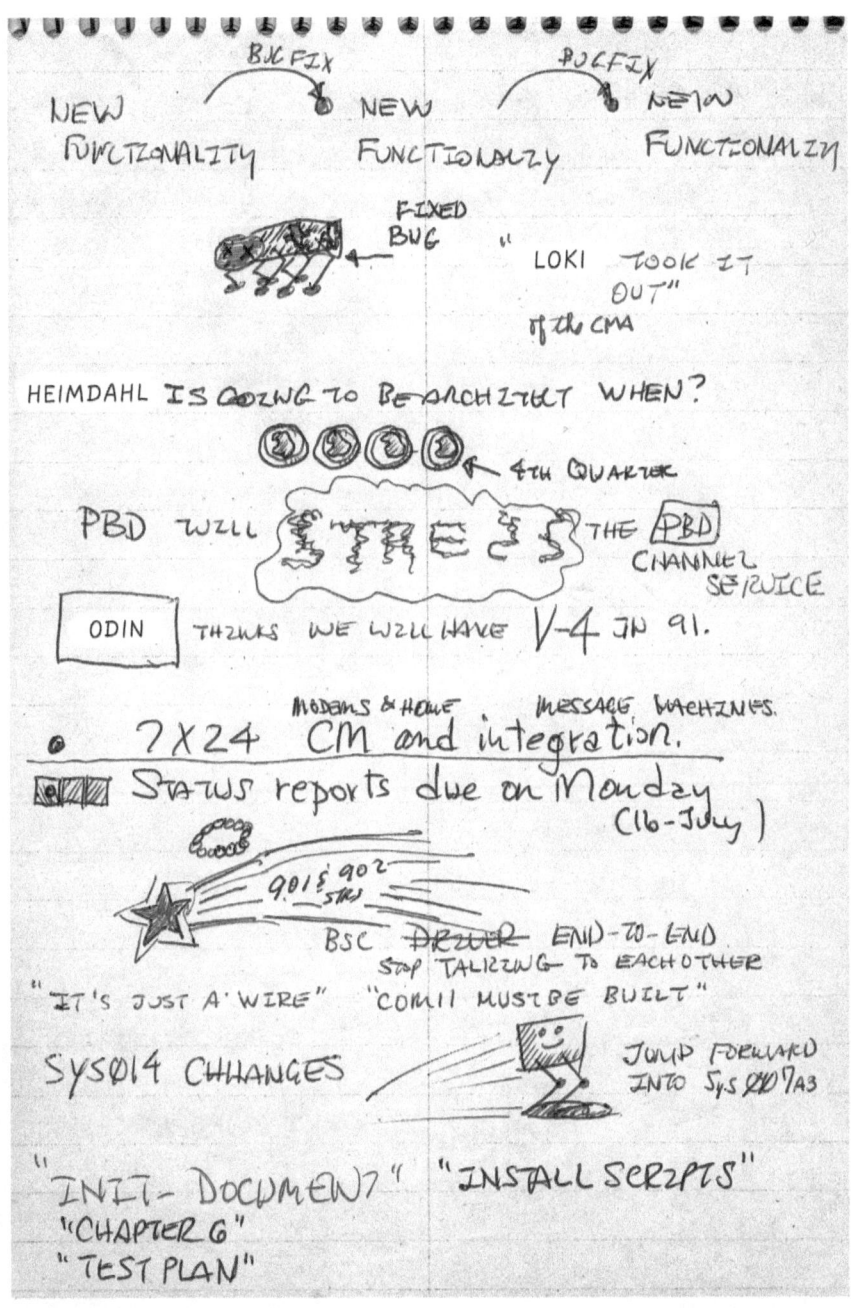

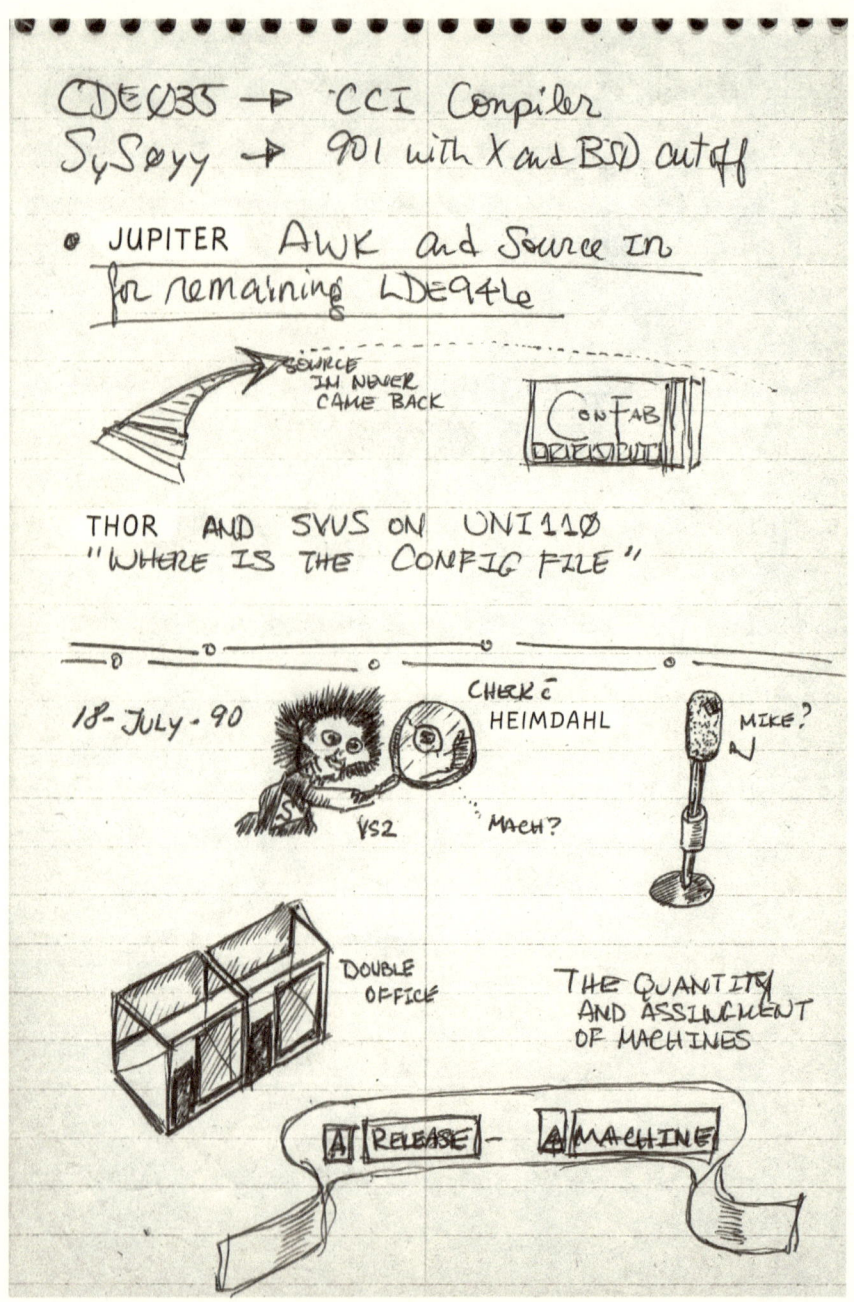

DIRECT ACCESS TEST TOOL

TEST PLAN FOR LARGE DISKS.

"IMPLEMENT DISCONNECT RESELECT" for disk and tape running concurrently. Single and Multiple disks. Configuration

LARGE DISKS available for the PBD.

THE REMAINDER OF PROM WORK. FOR PBD.

TEST PROGRAM HANGS

NO CHANGE OF THE PROGRAM TO IGNORE ERRORS.

 PLANS

○ CALLS TO FREY SHOULD BE LOGGED - JOURNAL

○ Ln sdb to gdb - add sdb commands

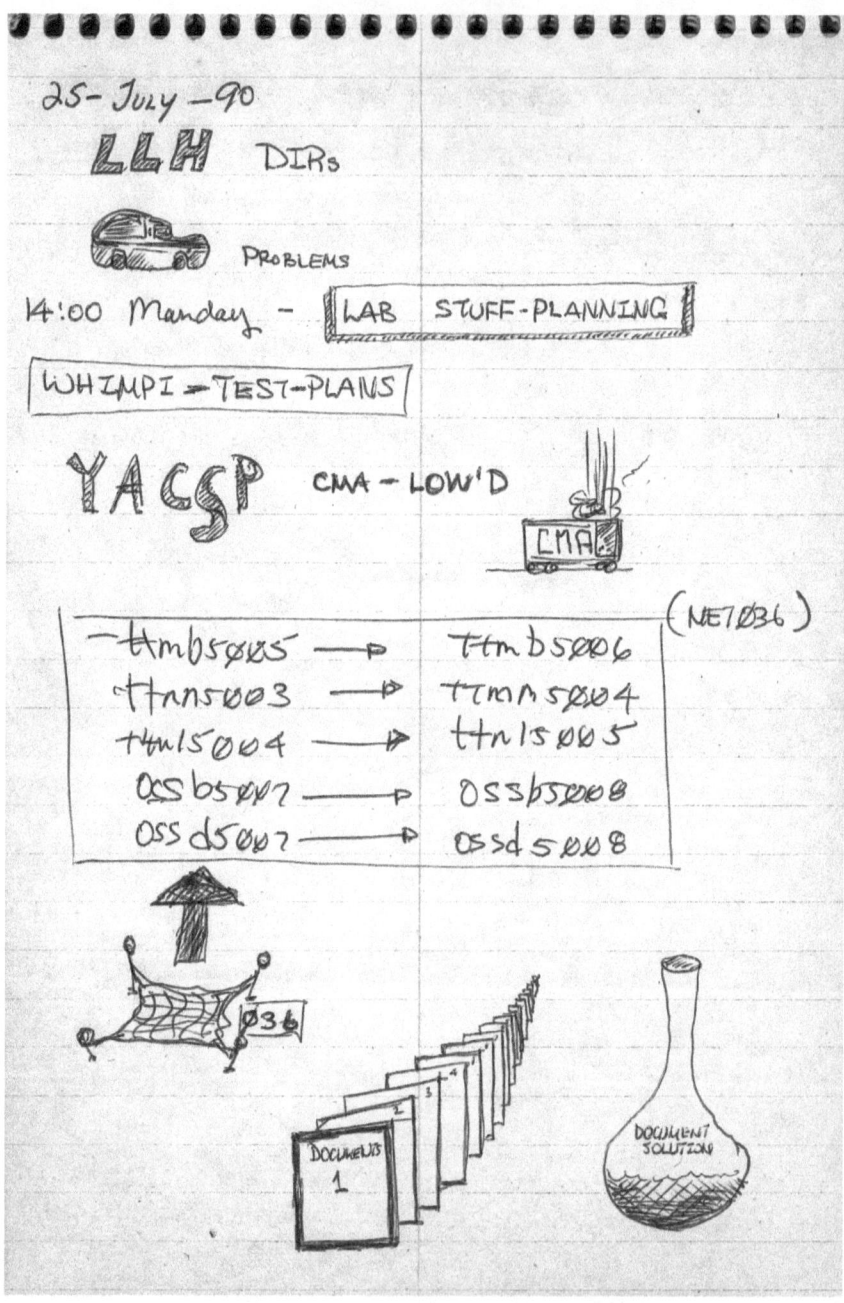

CONFIG FILE

 LARGE DISKS

TEST OF NEW SCSI FIRMWARE

TIME OF FSCK ON 502

	PBD
MINION OF THE GODESS HEL #1	UNIT-RUN OF NATIVE 800 CL
MINION OF THE GODESS HEL #2	GDB ISSUE RESOLUTION LIVE VACATION
MINION OF THE GODESS HEL #3	33% TEST OF KDUMP UNDER alpha-1
MINION OF THE GODESS HEL #4	TEST OF UTILS FOR CDEROB/SYSDATAI HANDOFF HELO / INSTALL - UNDERWAY
MINION OF THE GODESS HEL #5	CLEAN COMPILE OF AS/EDFF CONVERT FOR SHARE LIBS CDEROBA3

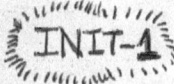 INIT-1 UNMOUNTS ALL USER FILE SYSTEMS.

PBD PROMS HANDED OFF ← FROM CM

FREY ARE YOU COMMUNICATING TO BULDAR?
READ THOR DOCUMENTS- COMMUNICATE
TO THOR

TCPB5- Stubbing for Sysønn ØYY
ASK FREYA

1 – AUG · 90

- PBD probms – write/read multiple Blocks to disk – LOKI ACTION.

- Bernies – PBD EPROM evaluation.
  Some of these seem to be STRs.

- LLH directory – Has HEL been getting updates.

YACSP => IDENTIFY HARDWARE FAILURES in messages.

014 → 901 NING CHANGES for COM and CSP
↳ BEGAT "YY"

<=> UADMIN KDUMP
REBOOT

BATCH FIG ESTIMATE FOR LLH TO UNICOM

OSF 1.0 ANDREW FILE SYSTEM CAMELOT MACH

- Greenhills mess. [INFO NOT FROM LOKI]

[JOHN ■ – Compiler error does not return Generate an STR.] ★

OSCb5 → OSab5 !!

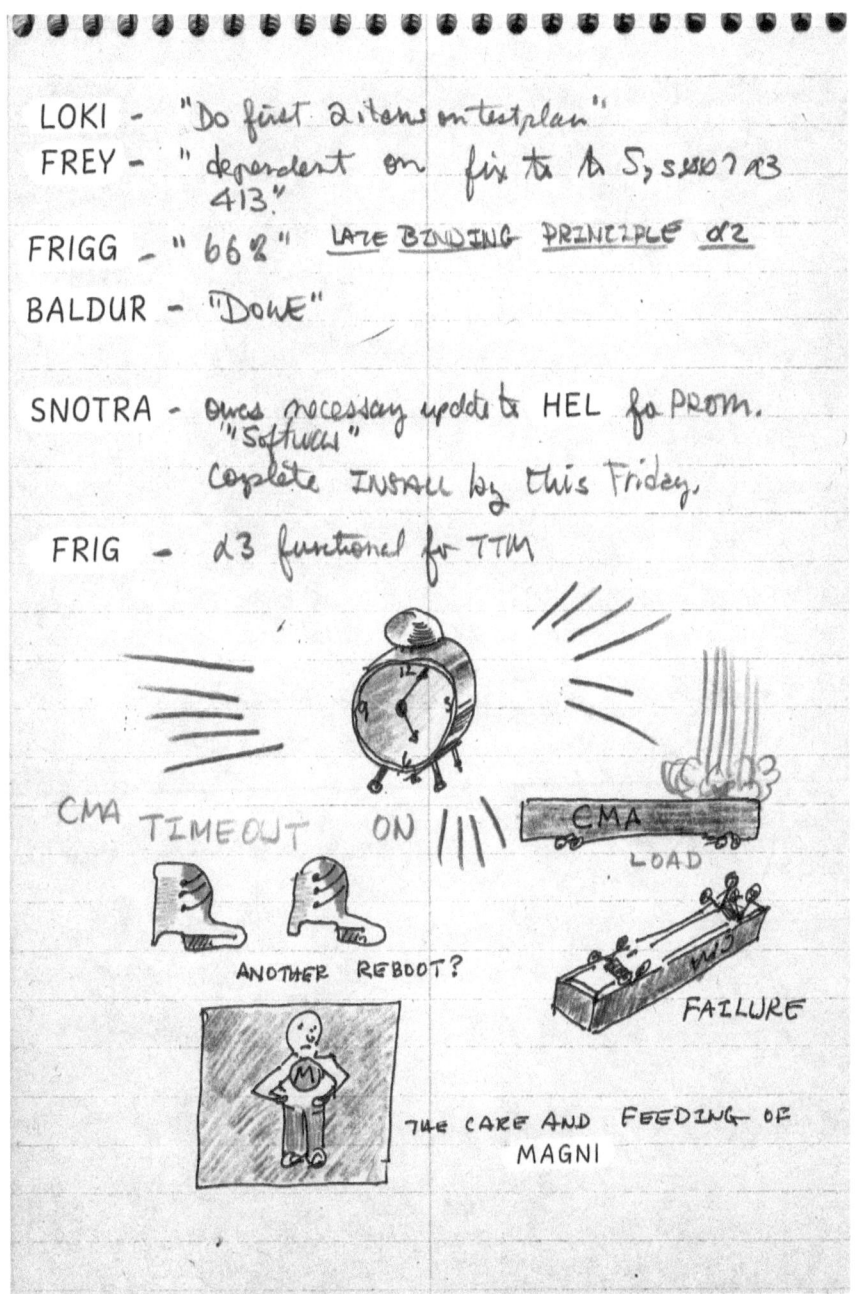

LOKI - "Do first 2 items on testplan"
FREY - "dependent on fix to Δ S, sses7 Δ3 413"
FRIGG - "66%" <u>LATE BINDING</u> <u>PRINCIPLE</u> α2
BALDUR - "Done"

SNOTRA - owes necessary update to HEL fo PROM.
"Softwell"
Complete INSTALL by this Friday.

FRIG - α3 functional for TTM

CMA TIMEOUT ON /// CMA
LOAD

ANOTHER REBOOT?

FAILURE

THE CARE AND FEEDING OF MAGNI

FAMS? NIH?

PAPER ON PROMs
CHANGED FORMAT OF PROM MENUs.

PRO-Ɱ-ENU

4 A   NIT DEMO

"ENDOLENT"

———•———•———

8-AUG-90
- VERZFY KDUMP works seamelessly with THOR SAW THOR working c̄ FRIGG

- TCPB5 α3 - How much More stubbed out - How much time
SENT MAIL TO FREYA

- SCRs and SAC? How to handle
WHATS THE PURPOSE?
SO THE USER CAN KNOW
WHAT-WHEN   Str fixer

- Sys Ø14 → 91; m2

↖ Channel Service

———•———•———

15-AUG
• Backup of /sparc on Bedrock   automatic procedure
                                 THOR   ./v2
• Large Disk capacity for PBD.
• Final version Dissy / LUE add on
   Backup / Restore of Unicorns in Lab

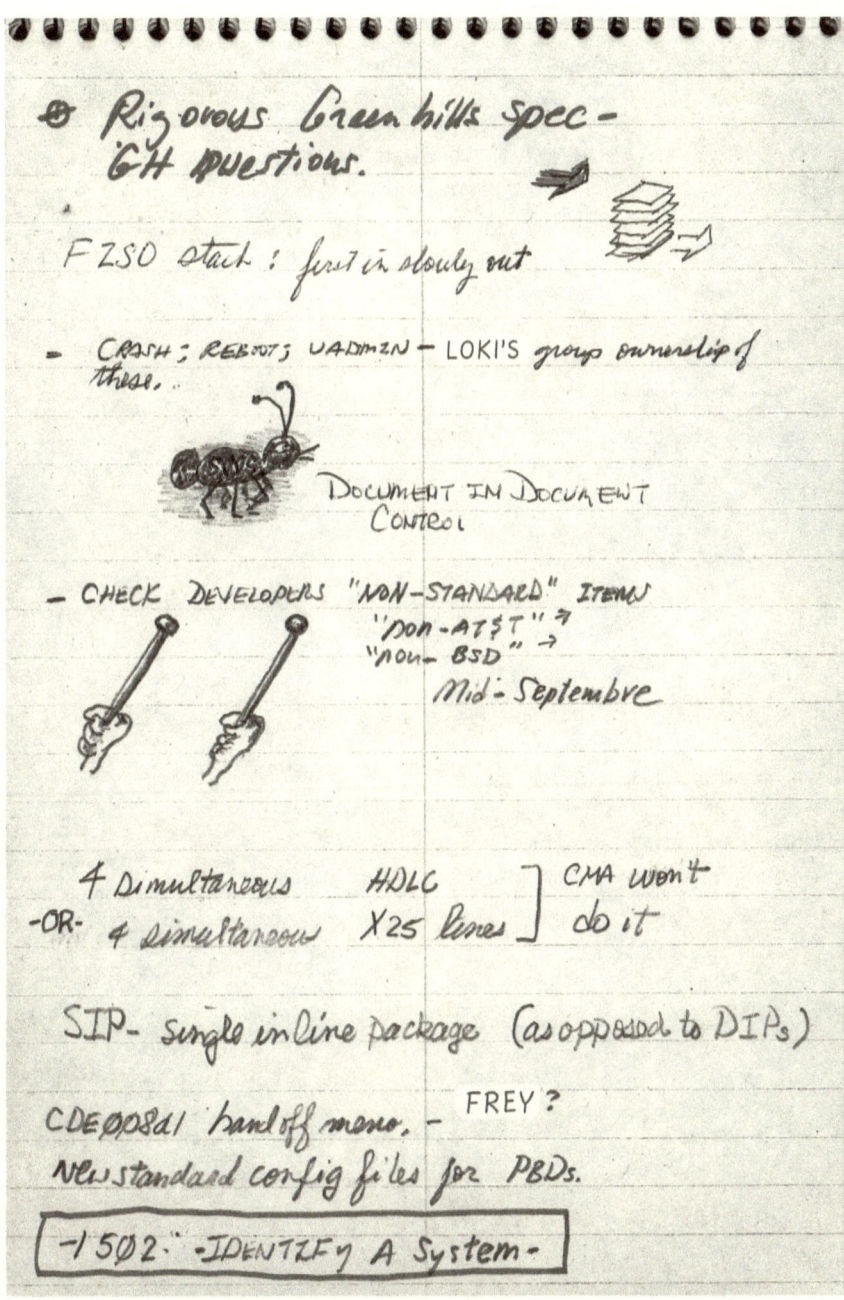

⊕ Rigorous Green hills spec-
GH questions.

F ZSO stack : first in slowly out

- CRASH; REBOOT; VADMIN — LOKI'S group ownership of
these.

DOCUMENT IN DOCUMENT
CONTROL

- CHECK DEVELOPERS "NON-STANDARD" ITEMS
"non-AT$T" →
"non-BSD" →
Mid-Septembre

-OR-
4 simultaneous   HDLC   ⎤ CMA won't
4 simultaneous   X25 lines ⎦ do it

SIP- single in line package (as opposed to DIPs)

CDE008d1 handoff memo. — FREY ?
New standard config files for PBDs.

-1502- -IDENTIFY A System-

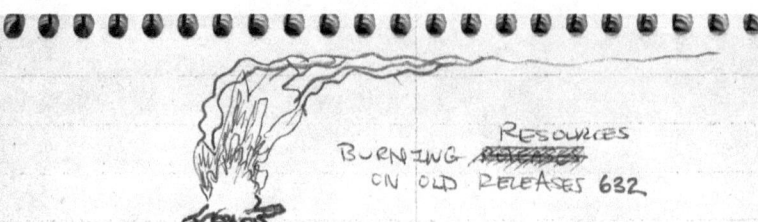

BURNING ~~RESOURCES~~ RESOURCES
ON OLD RELEASES 632

SERIAL NUMBER *for board on loan to*
EOSTRE

∪∪ ∪ *limit* * 2

∪
→ *limit*

REMOTE
BACKUP

12-SEP-90

BULDAR - "UNIT TESTING - DEBUGGING" SHARED LIBS.
MID NEXT WEEK START CDE 008 α3 NATIVE
PAPER ON GREEN HILLS REP FOR SPARC.
NOTE: DIVERGENCE OF ALPHA 2 PROJECT DIRECTORY
AND CM α2

FRIGG : α3 *project directory integration* - CLASS?

FREYA ! GDB and "KDA" mode - only native CLASS.

FREYA : SS PROBLEMS VIA SVUS for α3
SVUS g RATL 4, No EXEC " " →3?

HEIMDAHL : VA GS.
STATUS OF COMM?

PLANING

NEED to have vacation plans in advance

OSSUCS → 44
6 → 901

"MAS

COMØ11 → 44
Ø12 → 901

OSSB5008 → 44
009 → 901

OSAB5001 → 44
002 → 901

UTLB5005 → 44
6 → 901

COMB5003 → 44
4 → 901

'NCF15001 ⎫
IUTT5001 ⎬ 901   NEW
NCC15001 ⎭   TIER 3,4

[S]B5   DISSAPEAR   USE 44 VERSION.

CDSB5017 → 901   Xdev 11   Ø44
↓ 16 → Ø44   ↓ 12   901

No Sibs until SVVS is close for A3

- CHANGE TO LINKER for d2 008 caused world to change. - PLEASE LET BULDAR KNOW.

- WEEK OF TESTING - d2 007/008
- TEST MAKE FILES FROM VENDORS UNDER CMMAKE

WRITING MEMOS ⟶

timing of instruction scheduling in compiler effects the performance of the chip.

19-SEP-90 ——————∘——————∘——————

BULDAR completed "unit test" of Shared Libs for d3
        Start CDEP07d3 native

THOR   802 Done DEBUGGER support for Kdump - in same
        format as Core.

FRIGG   Finish changes to support THOR
        Start init2

HEL   - All changes are forwarded to FRIGG
        Start presentation

LOKI   Handoff memo - End of next week - Debug
        Signals in SVVS

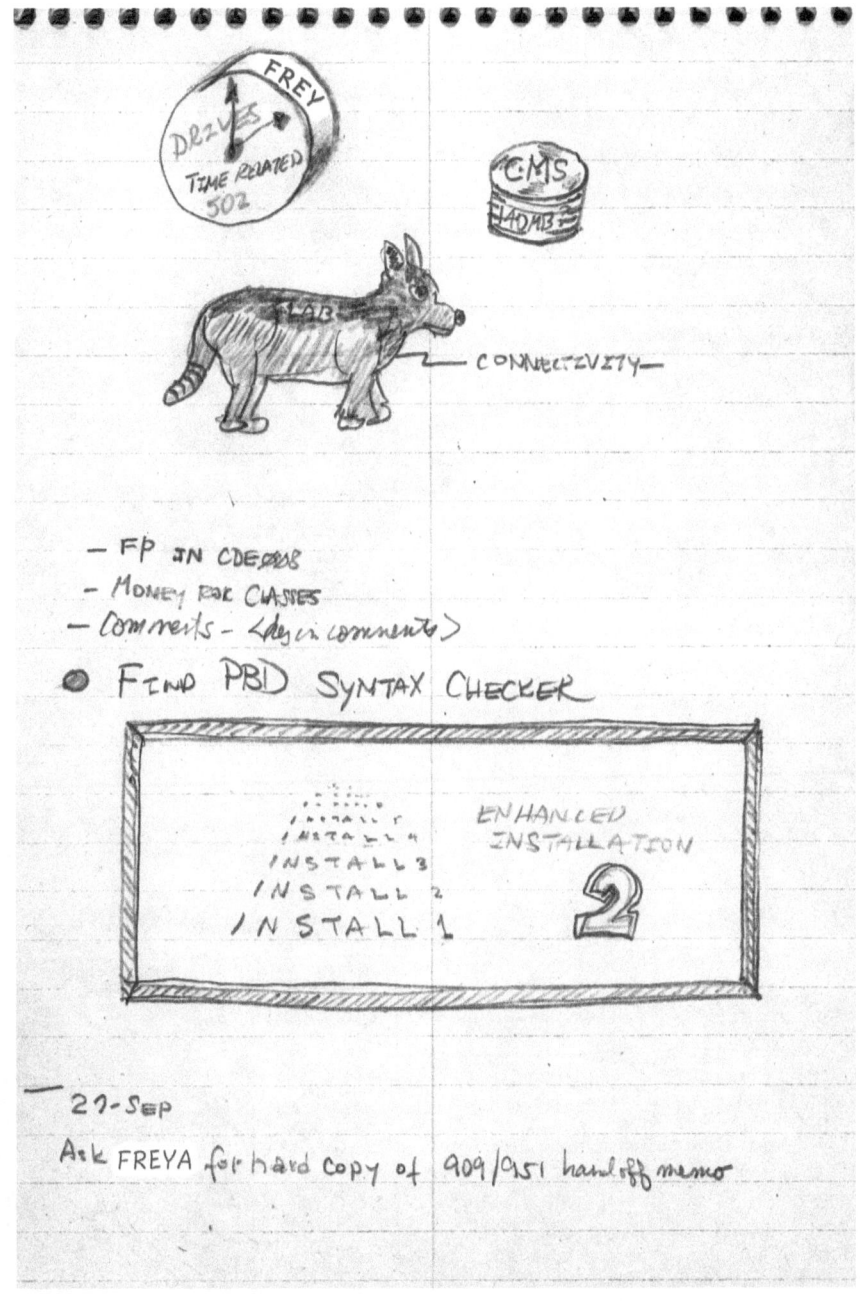

- FP IN CDE??8
- MONEY FOR CLASSES
- Comments - ⟨dev in comments⟩
● FIND PBD SYNTAX CHECKER

27-SEP

Ask FREYA for hard copy of 909/951 handoff memo

JOHN REDDEN

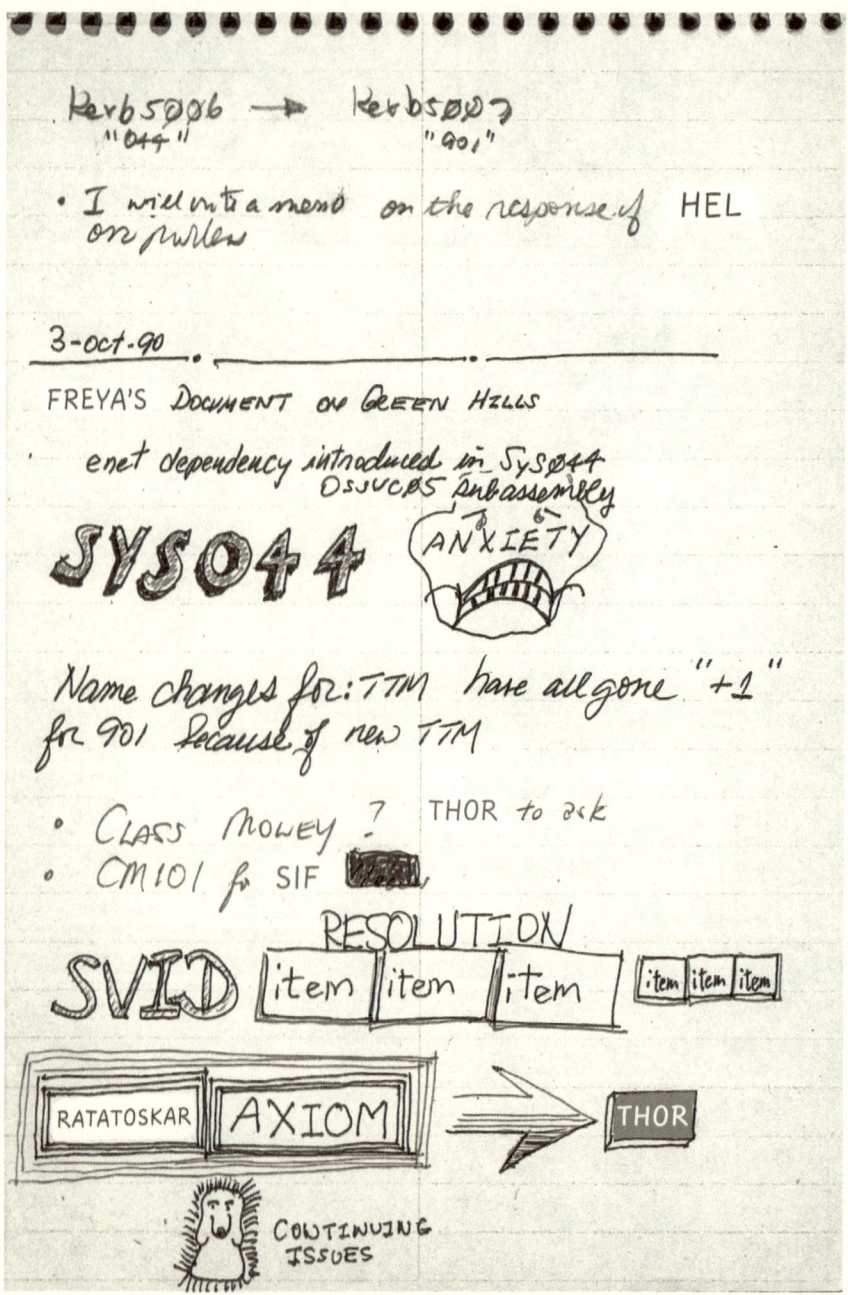

312

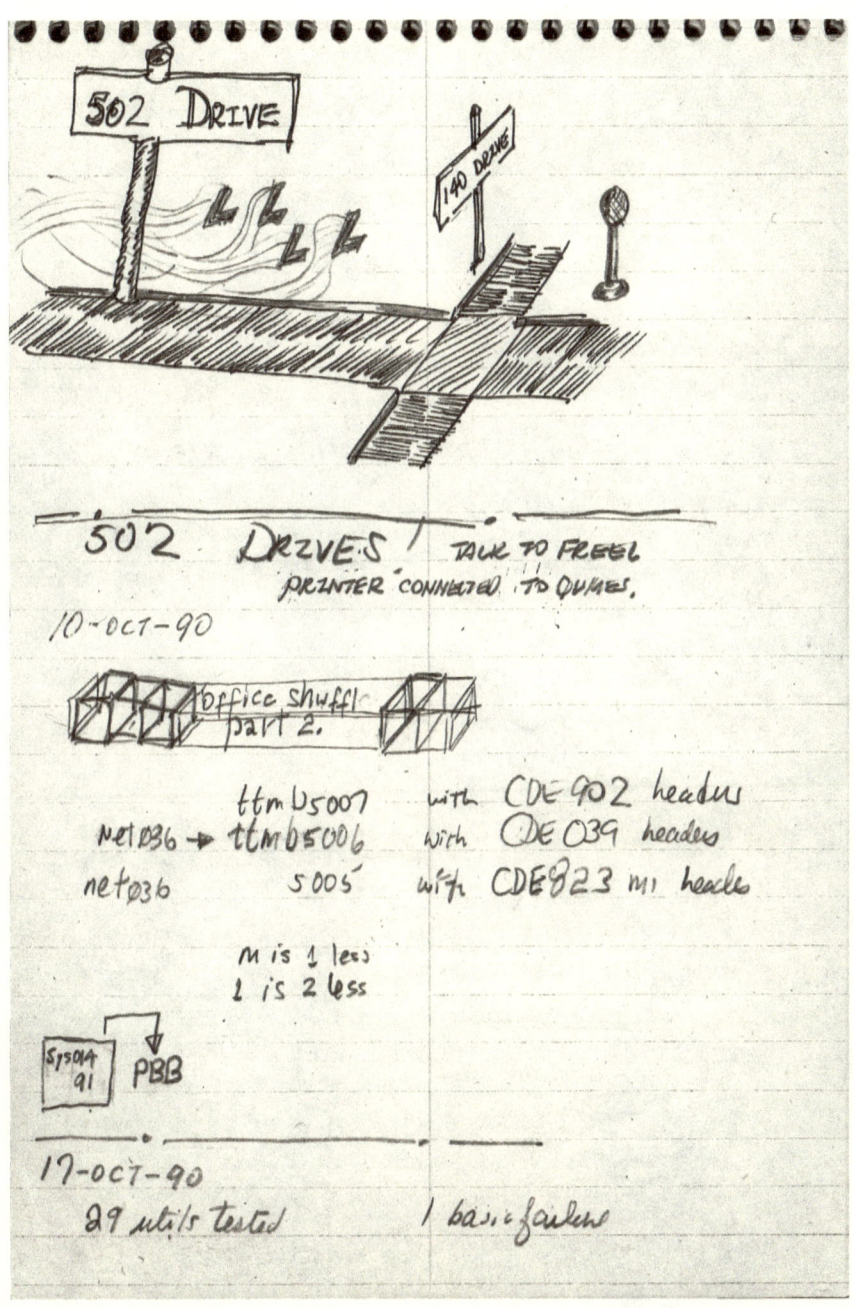

502 DRIVES   TALK TO FREEL
        PRINTER CONNECTED TO QUMES.
10-OCT-90

office shuffle
part 2.

              ttmb5007   with CDE902 headers
net036 → ttmb5006   with CDE039 headers
net036   5005   with CDE823 mi headers

              M is 1 less
              L is 2 less

S150A 91 → PBB

17-OCT-90
   29 utils tested   1 basic failure

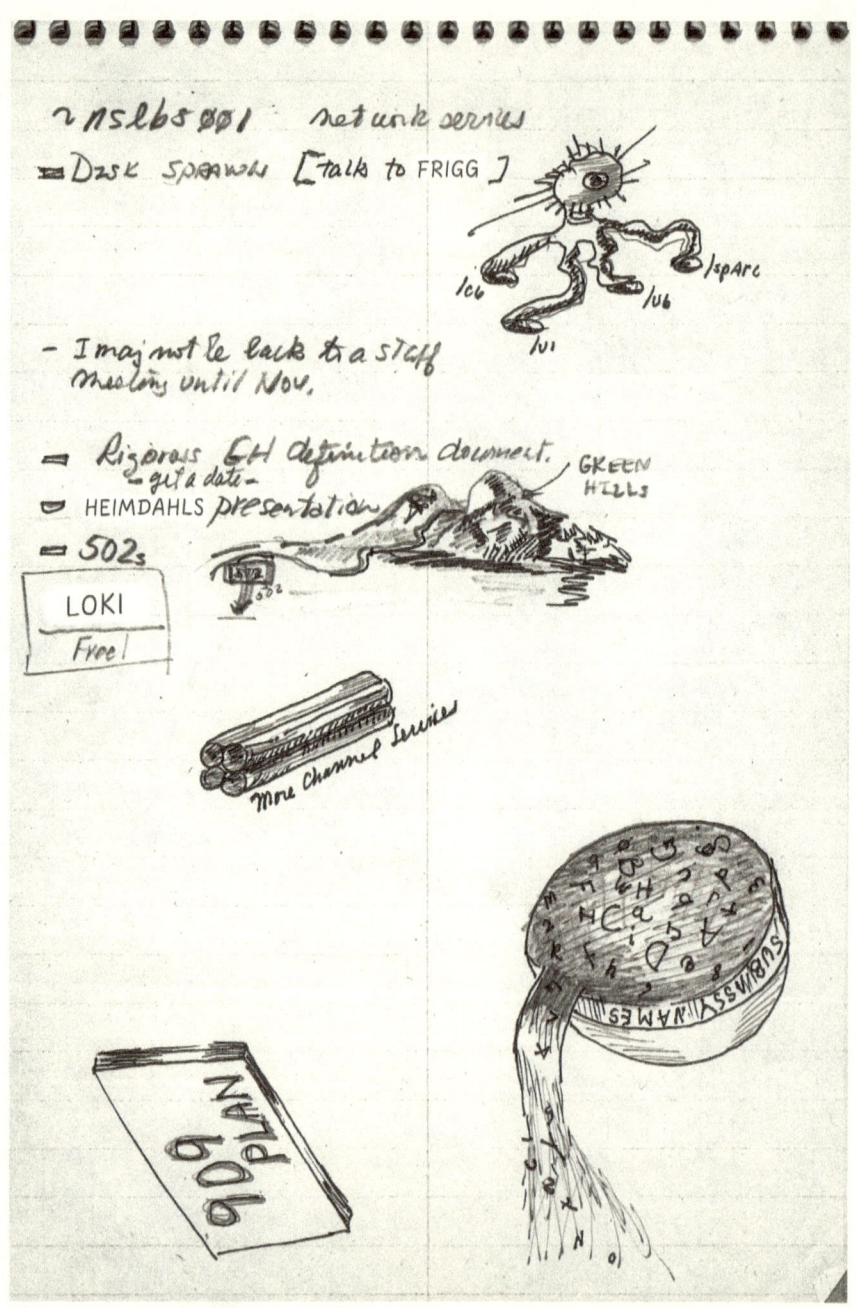

Special TTM software of <u>CMA</u> } MUST BE A COMMON
built by FREYA } ~~name~~ on 807, 901, 909

don't want to have special case CMA software.
→ Requirement Documents -

LOKI   BULDAR   HEL   systems

24-OCT-90

039 ← 029 {complete swap of subassy}
                              names

Nov - 7TH
        UPDATE info on subassy changes -
(name moving)

HEIMDAHL what are the hardware characteristics of the Chip
          → for time keeping

o — deluges
o — priority s interrupts   Sys 909   P88
o — K&R / have ANSI   Sys 1nn   P8D

ALSO - TYR commits TTM by end of Nov.
. New port pass. wd for "controlled machine" CMA 030

14 - Nov 7H   WHY ISN'T
    ASK lee about CLOCK Chip   LOKI using
                                   streamers.

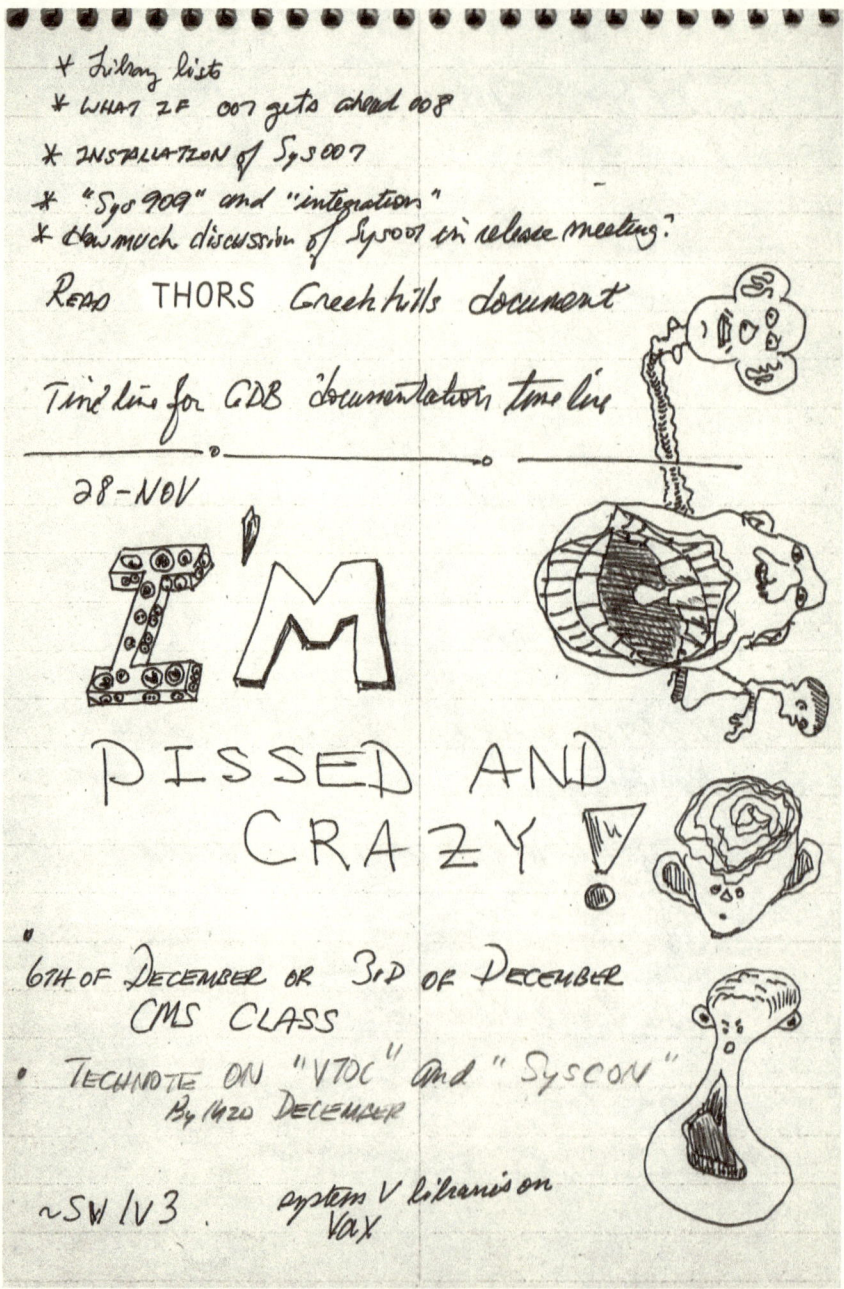

* Library lists
* WHAT IF 007 gets ahead 008
* INSTALLATION of Sys007
* "Sys 909" and "integration"
* How much discussion of Sys001 in release meeting?

READ THORS Creekhills document

Timeline for GDB documentation timeline

28-NOV

I'M

PISSED AND CRAZY!

6TH OF DECEMBER OR 3rd OF DECEMBER
CMS CLASS

TECHNOTE ON "VTOC" and "SYSCON"
By 14th DECEMBER

~SW/V3.   system V libraries on Vax

5-DEC-90

Lp software - questions

YOU'RE OUT
ON CMS.

CM Class 15:00 12-DEC-90

9- DEC-   SJOFN
WED-19TH SECT X-PARTY

11-DEC-90

rxterm — a shell script invoked rsh on
remote client.

CONFIG, generic CDD file man page
Performance analysis task #5 in CBUOS.

                TYR
• CDE008—   CDE839 sync— never don't plan to
                                        do.

20-DEC-90
"COMM" requirement document coming
• new releases "1XX"
• SYS909, project chi.
• "SPEC" to FREYA

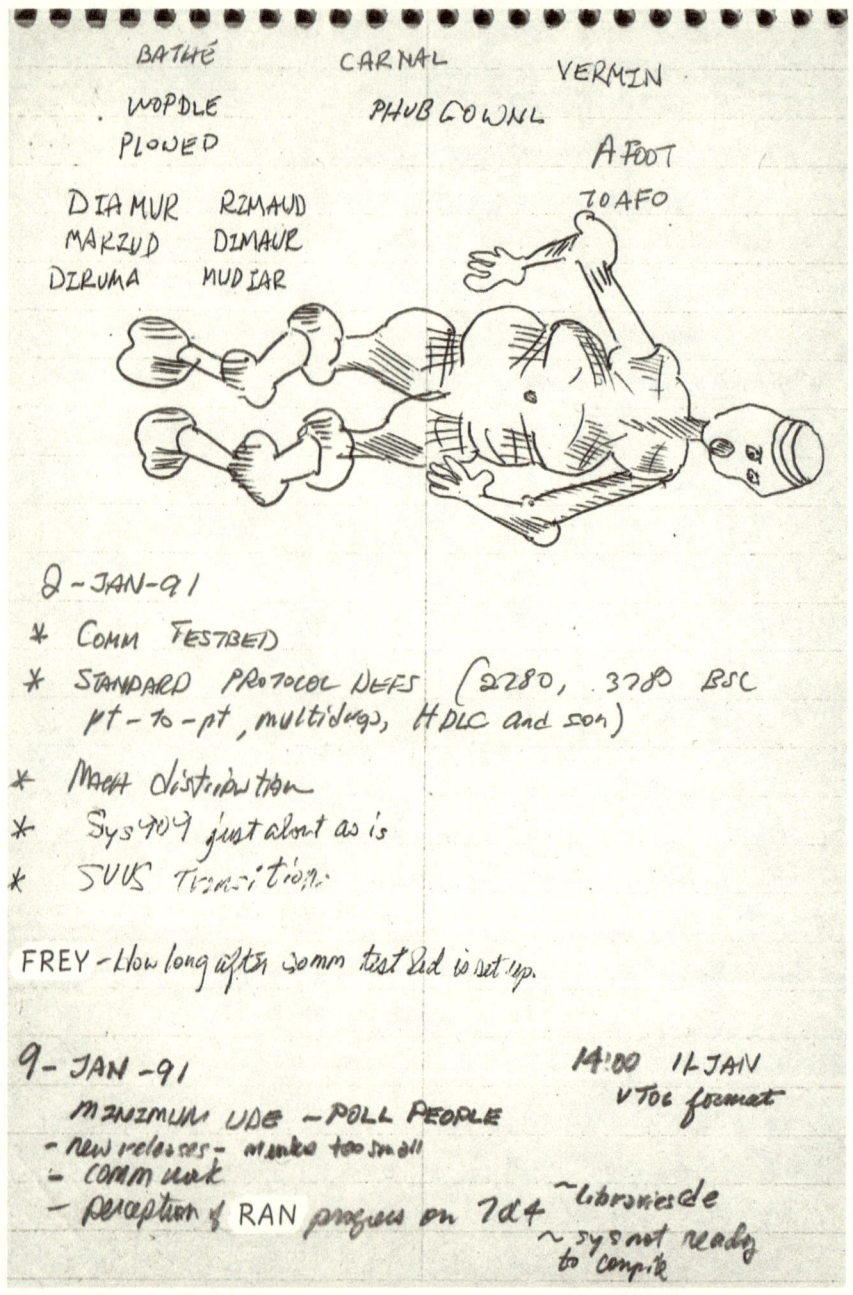

BATHÉ   CARNAL   VERMIN
  WOPDLE   PHUB GOWNL
  PLOWED   A FOOT

DIAMUR   RZMAUD   ZOAFO
MARZUD   DIMAUR
DIRUMA   MUDIAR

2 - JAN - 91

* COMM TESTBED
* STANDARD PROTOCOL NEFS (2280, 3780 BSC
  pt - to - pt, multidrops, HDLC and son)

* Mach distribution
* Sys 404 just about as is
* SVVS Transition

FREY - How long after comm test bed is set up.

9 - JAN - 91   14:00 IL JAN
  MINIMUM UDE - POLL PEOPLE   VTOC format
  - new releases - manks too small
  - comm work
  - perception of RAN progress on 7d4 ~libraries de
                                        ~ sys not ready
                                         to compile

16-JAN-91

SCHEDULE BALDUR

Help menu 2 wks

New disk/tape support 3 wks

SRS 4 wks

New disk - tape Don't support new tons

"New logic drive on hold"

• U3 - LOKI stuff

remove C8 - to U"n"

WED - 23 is cut off date for Sys 002d4

TACWE: ACUTE

KROOB: BROOK

NUPWOT: TWOPUN PUTNOW NUTPOW

TWOUNP WONTUP POTNUN PUNTOW

UNWOPT WPTOWN

ENKASH: SHAKEN

                    CHUNK
           NOT CUKHA
C U O Ŗ T N H A   CUT NOKHA
‐‐‐ of ‐‐‐‐‐

FRIDAY: 2:00 VAR paper

WEDNESDAY: Lunch and schedules

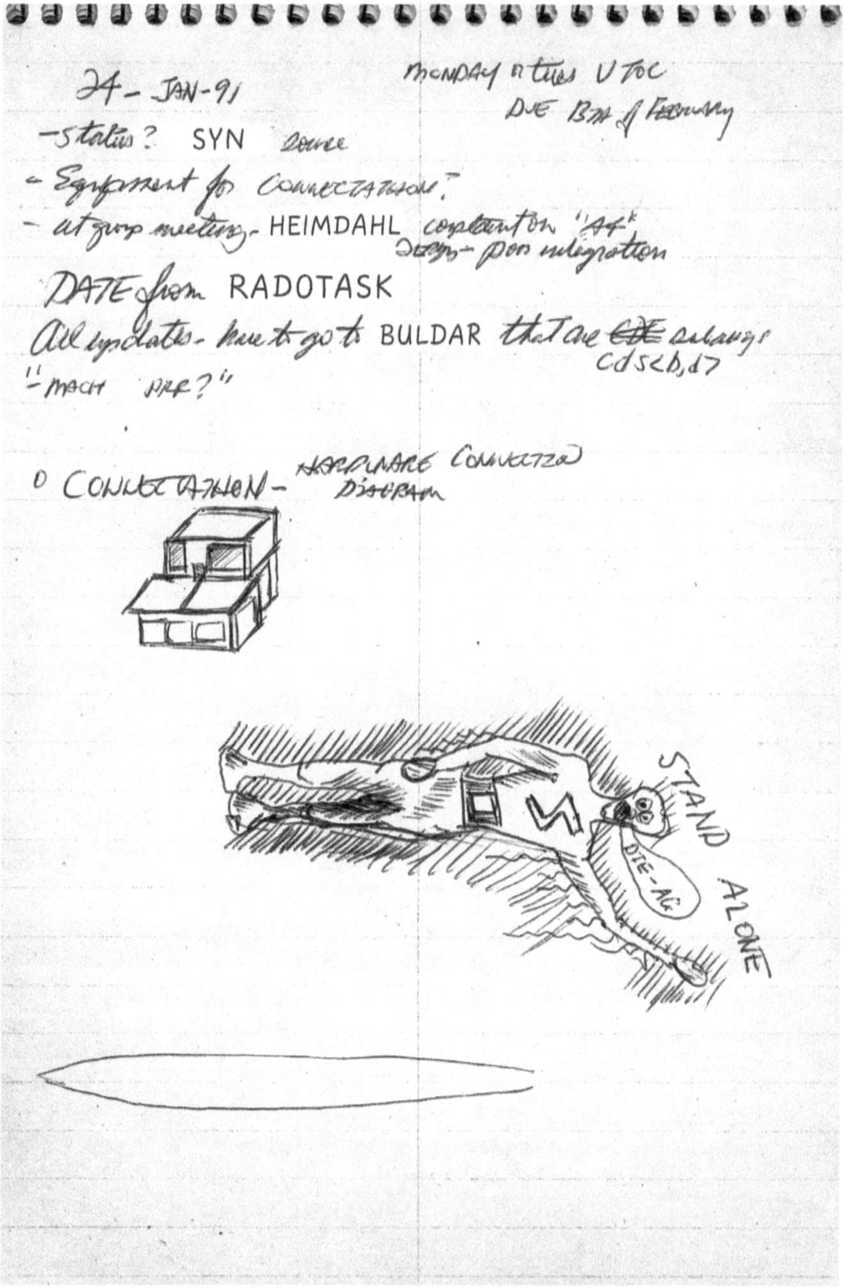
24-JAN-91
MONDAY or TUES
DUE ... of February
-Status? SYN
- Equipment for CONNECTATION?
- at group meeting - HEIMDAHL
DATE from RADOTASK
All updates - have to go to BULDAR
"-MACH PRE?"
o CONNECTATION - HARDWARE CONNECTION DIAGRAM
STAND ALONE
DIE-AG

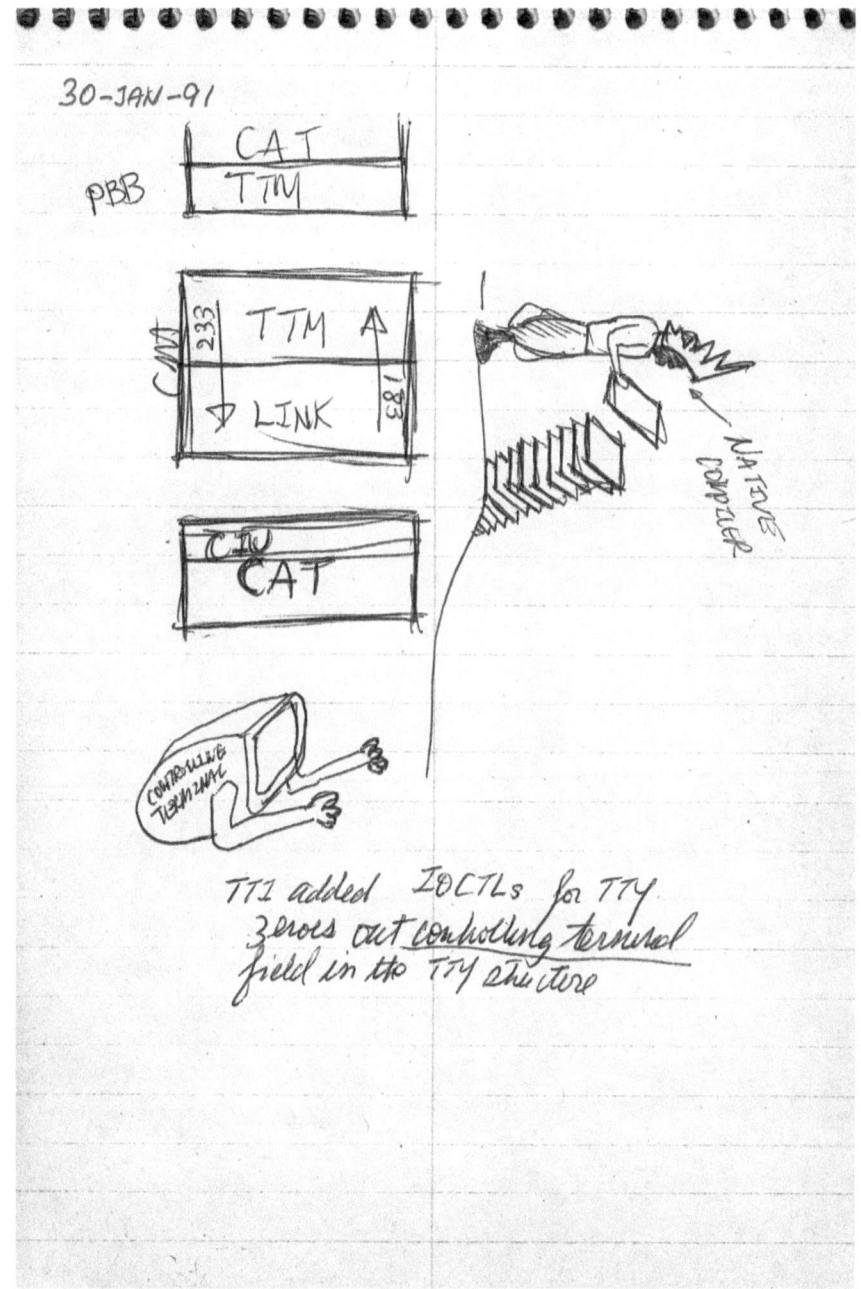

30-JAN-91

PBB

| CAT |
| TTM |

| TTM △ |
| ▽ LINK |

233 / 183

| CAT |

CONTROLLING TERMINAL

NATIVE COMPUTER

TTI added IOCTLs for TTY.
Zeros out controlling terminal
field in the TTY structure

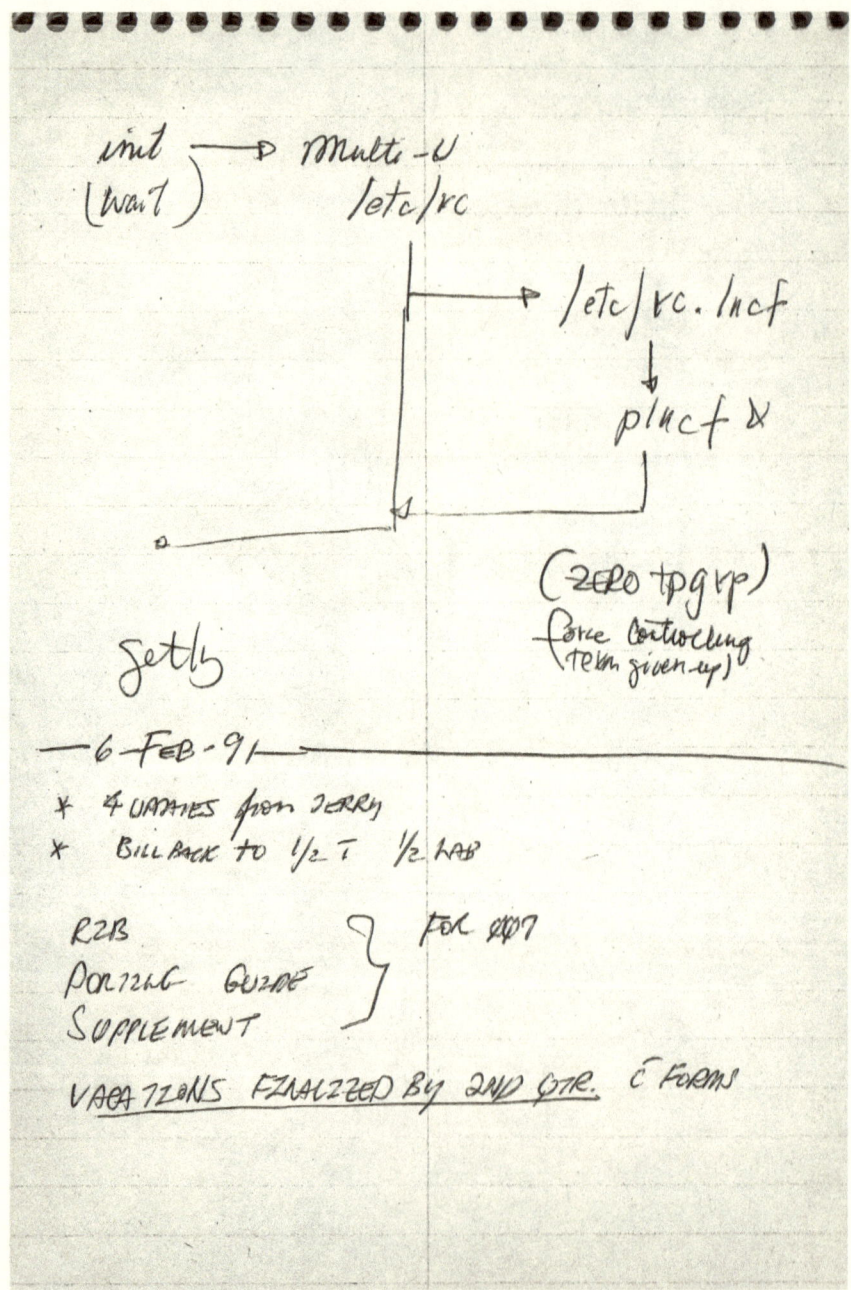

13-FEB-91
d5/v3 -   vax version of the libraries
          for the cross tools

20-FEB-91
VRC DRIVERS MODS, WHO?

27-FEB-91

6-MAR-91
Sys115- VRC Notes—}   }Any kind of Notes}
By END OF WEEK   }on VRC—}

13-MAR-91

WOE BE THE LAB
   new stabe need to INSTALL3
INSTALL3 will be rolled Tior2   will inish Callin.sh
                    part
THOR sw can for YGG

FLOATING
POINTS

3—APR·91

1 JR needs a name
TALK TO Bill

} COMM
LINE PRINTER
INIT/STARTUP

} Beat up D. Howard.

/ CMS / SYS

17—APR—91

JERRYS four STRs

6116 — VAX — toss (Kirk)
10436 } X. test suite
10458
84889 — regex bug. — toss (kirk)

* Compiling test list for D. Howard for SYS115
* Jerry on Plans? (vs. SWS).
* New guys on the Block. — where do they go?
√ * Compiling 115 optimized? when? how?
   Try OO optimized? first? **Done**
* difference in phil of Sys 909 and Sys 125

24—APR

* WANt L CHEN to look at ~~last~~ possible int priority problem
disccovered at connecta thon — ASAP

* Testing of Sys 115
* Disk & memory options vol Plans. difficulty

1-MAY-91

* Network addresses "Class B" for
     Cos unicom

* Simp liked Hites decision to capture DD7

8-MAY-91

— Seperate External phys system is clean
method for "votus to add for V toc". Don't
like hacks inside existing unix kernel.

— Want to fix errors in Steam based log sig
in Sys125.

29-May

    mount bedrock on unit
      cp from unit to bedrock using NFS
     other way will not work.

• Sys5dev

• Things for UDE—Sys125
      named
      routed

X ominous for M stonka Sphere
+ dump and restore

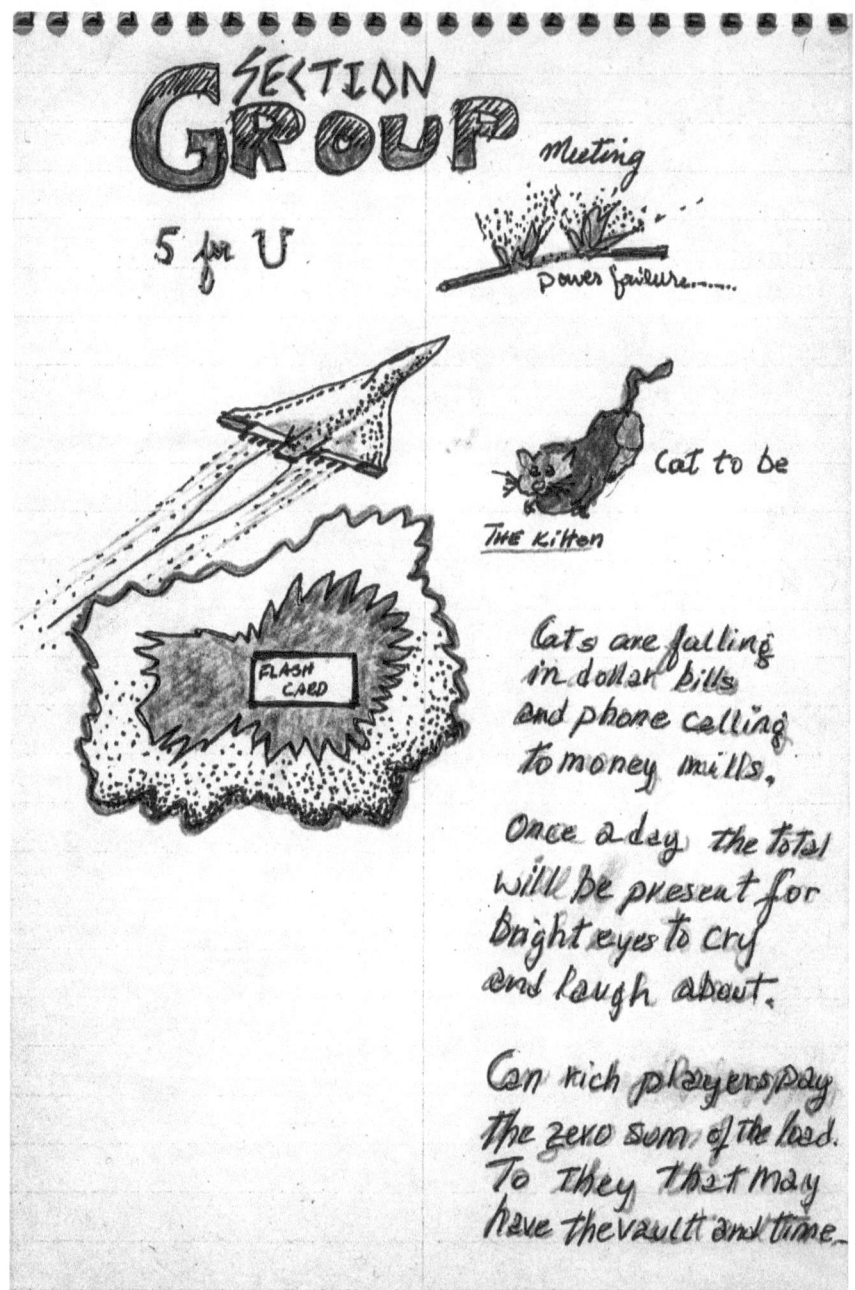

1991-1993

In October 1994, I began working for International Computers Limited (ICL). Originally, the company, Computer Consoles Incorporated, gained fame by donating their Tahoe processor to UC Berkeley, which hosted a major release named "The Tahoe Release of BSD Unix." To interject another level of international control, Fujitsu purchased ICL, a British Company that had moved from mainframe production to high-end minicomputers.

They hired me to work on their Unix system, not the release from UC Berkeley, but a re-engineering of System V.4 from AT&T. My initial efforts were what they named "fourth line support." What this meant is the group that I was in, and which I ended up being the technical lead, would analyze system failure memory dumps provided by various customer sites. The SysV4 Unix Kernel from AT&T did not support multiple physical processors and standard Internet communication protocols. However, Berkeley distributions supported Internet protocols, but did not support multiple physical processors. The Unix system ran on a single processor with attached devices. As multiple processor architectures appeared, it was difficult to synchronize data transfer to external devices and preserve data integrity. I had already experienced this at CitiCorp TTI with their failed experiment with the Pyramid multiprocessor system.

Using the System V.4 source base with the AT&T source license, ICL attempted to engineer a tightly coupled system using from four to sixteen processors. The implementation locked internal data structures in the Unix kernel, typically with short-term locks, which allowed a separate processor to access that data structure.

Any locking has to follow a particular order of priority, or you end up with the possibility of over one processor waiting longer than it should to gain access to that data structure. I would hope, by the time I write this, that this challenge has been thoroughly investigated and solved. Thus, the ICL architecture used short-term and long-term spin locks. Long-term spin locks are rare, but more often used to isolate access to data-structures used in slow communication devices (a keyboard input, for example).

Besides cracking kernel failures posted by customers, they involved me in several other projects. FDDI was a spin-off of token ring technology, but using two counter circulating tokens. Writing I/O subsystems for the System V.4 Unix kernel, one had to pay close attention to top-half and bottom-half interrupt control and processing. In the bottom half, the interrupt and the subsequent stream of data had to be queued as fast as possible because of latency of the I/O system. In the top half, the stream had to be extracted and presented in a file-like format.

One of these projects I started myself. Analyzing system dumps from the various customer sites was tedious and time-consuming. Using standard Unix tools, YACC and LEX, which still exist on all major platforms, I built a set of tools to decompile the crash dumps from the field and present them as "C Language" data structures. YACC is an acronym for "Yet Another Compiler Compiler" and LEX is an acronym for Lexical Analyzer. I called the tool MapGen.

ICL had available test and development servers. I would often build a server from scratch, depending on the system bug. The environment was hands-on, so I could play and test the system in any way I chose.Int the industry of technological development, there was no standardization for reported trouble report and bugs. At CitiCorp TTI, they labeled them System Trouble Reports (STRs). At ICL, we labeled them Rabids. I forget what the acronym meant, but as reports came in, we stacked them on top of each other in what was a z-axis file system, where one collection of data would elide another below it. This was also how they handled source control, distributed across two continents. It was impressive and worked reasonably well. Within the source control, the label "SCN" or referenced the current overlay in the z-axis file system source control number. This system was vastly superior to what we used at CitiCorp TTI.

In tightly coupled multiprocessor systems, performance was often application-dependent. For some application scenarios, the app would actually perform better if "glued" to one specific processor selected from sixteen processors. Processor affinity was the feature that was added to allow this. When an app was instantiated and executed, it could select one processor to be the "master." It was an interesting idea, but added complexity to the product that we were developing and supporting. A special option controlled the affinity with the Unix "ps" command. Remember, this was before the dominance of GUI admin visualization.

In some ways, the AT&T Unix kernel source attempted to mimic object-oriented design using the C language. For example, in the Unix file system, a subset of the previous file system had all the data structures embedded (or encapsulated, using the correct OO term) in the virtual file system (VFS). Likewise, the traditional "inode," the controlling structure of the Unix file system, was now embedded in a "vnode." This overall architecture worked up to a point, but still did not address the vast sources and syncs of data in the networked environment.

ISO9000 certification is another project I became involved in at ICL as the project lead. The primary requirement for ISO9000 certification is providing an accountable audit trail for all work done. Since we had a fairly good source control system and associated documentation, it was not an arduous task. ISO9000 was more important in Europe than in the US. And yet another project I worked on was Simple Network Management Protocol. Of course, before improvement, this was the earliest version. It was an Internet Protocol, using UDP, a basic, high-speed protocol that has existed since the earliest days of the Internet Protocol developed for the Apollo Project in the late 1960s.

When I look through my notes from this period of my professional career in software engineering, many have references to hardware addresses of input and output devices. There are many notes with classical C-language data-structures (see my description of "MapGen" used for memory dumps). Some examples are:

```
struct{
Sema_t mon_lock;
int * mon_proc;
int * mon_oproc;
int mon_lckcnt;
int mon_space[4];
} mutex_t;
```

or

```
struct kernel{
int kernel_pend; // initialize for "p" and "v" spin lock
usage (P and V come from Multics)
int kernel; // "owned" probably an affinity for one processor
int kernel_cpu; // all those CPUs in a multiprocessor system
int kernel_next; // CPU requesting a semaphore
} kernel_t;  // ha! From abbreviated notes.
```

This source code example is brittle, with hard-coded values, but was typical of the C language. Oh yes, there were #defines and then with ANSI C constant (static and unchanging data definitions) to replace "defines."

Development for the Unix SysV.4 kernel in the ICL shop was segmented into specializations. There were a few developers who had a broad scope architectural perspective, but applied this perspective to the projects at hand. I pleased a developer that specialized in memory management when I showed him "e-Lisp" in the Emacs editor. It was something finally... different.

1993-1994

Retix, as mentioned in my memoir proper, was at one time a competitor with Cisco. Retix built a multiprocessor... router based on the 80960 (or i960) Intel processor. It was the fastest router in the market. There were significant bugs in the software that were difficult to isolate. Working for Retix was like working for a reincarnation of TranTelecommunications. The president of the company was a department manager at Tran. He remembered me. The primary protocols they dealt with at the time were IP, the standard Internet Protocol stack, (the Internet Routing Protocol being a paramount component) and IPX a popular protocol used by IBM and supported and developed by Novell.

Programming the Retix Router firmware was like the code style of the Unix SysV.4 kernel. Again, my notes from this period contain many C-language structures. Fundamental to the architecture are interrupts at different priorities and the ordered access to data structures associated to the priorities. There were several modules written in Intel i690 assembly language, which were invoked from the C runtime package. I would look at the assembler language code and see several NOP (no operation operators, as opposed to arithmetic, conditional, and branching operators) machine instructions in the source code. When asking one developer of the original system, "Why all the NOPs", the answer was, "So we could align machine instructions to memory cycles so the response time for reads and writes would be faster."

The network routing algorithms were interesting, "open shortest path first" as an example. And there were many methods that they would try to establish this the shortest path. The router not only dealt with in-house, Ethernet protocols, simply named local area network protocols, including AppleTalk and Banyan Vines, but also wide-area network protocols. Of course, by the time of the ubiquitous Internet, the wide-area protocols were first eclipsed and then became obsolete. Smart, fast routers were required to support all existing wide-area protocols, including X25 and LAPB (a wide-area packet-switched network), Point-To-Point Internet (PPP). Think of PPP as a predecessor of "DSL." A significant quantity of in-house authored testing software existed, including several tests to create connection and transmission storms. As the Internet became ubiquitous, it transformed transmission storms into a test for a denial-of-service attack.

At this point in net e-mail development, there were still mixed modes of the up-and-coming Internet style and remnant Usenet style e-mail addresses. An example: "felder!gedsoft!rej@telebit.com." This made the parsing of e-mail addresses confusing.

Like previous work at ICL, they supported Retix Simple Network Management Protocol (SNMP) and the structures of Management Information Base (MIB). I could configure the router using SNMP and MIBs. Towards the end of my tenure are Retix, they assigned me to evaluate a code coverage tool for the C language. I thought little of the capabilities provided by the selected tool, but it didn't matter. Retix was non-existent three months later.

1994-1995

I contacted my old manager from Citicorp TTI working for Data Products, at one time a dominant leader in line printer technology. Like Retix, the project they hired me for was their new high-speed laser printer line with multiple processors. The source was all written in the C language. The architecture of several modules was deficient, with many seriously violating the DRY (Don't Repeat Yourself) principle. Along with development, which were usually bug fixes to support the existing product, I ended up being the "build master." The existing convention for building the objects from a source used a technology named "Imake." Imake dynamically generated make files from templates, so the build process could be easily customized. The imake-to-make stream allowed a unique collection of configurable parameters, include files (a cornerstone of the C and C++ languages), and source modules. So imake-driven product builds were one of the prime points of technology at Data Products.

There were several others. I began building utilities in the C++ language instead of C. C++ attempted compatibility with the C language, but allowed the developer to build objects instead of the cascade of procedures typical of a well-designed, C-language-based system. I and another developer downloaded a manual for a new language, Java 1.0, from Sun Microsystems. This was my introduction to Java, but I didn't use it for another two years. The examples in the manual were awful. A poor example detected the end of an array of objects by intercepting a "null" pointer exception. And I was introduced to the SlackWare distribution of Linux. The downloading from the Usenet was free and written to over a hundred three-and-a-quarter-inch floppy disks. I took the disto home, and loaded it on a spare partition on my i486, which was still running Esix AT&T System V.4. I had to rebuild the Linux kernel, so it could interact with my ESDI hard drive, which at one time was considered a large storage device on this Intel server. This was the last time I would do kernel-level programming in C. Following my experience at DataProducts, I once again was recruited by my former manager to join a consulting company in 1995, SEI.

GEEK
APOCRYPHA II

•••

During my tenure at SEI from late 1995 to 2004, I experienced a litany of projects. The first project was a stay at the home office. After some orientation at SEI on how to be a software whore consultant, they contracted me out to a subsidiary company on the leading edge of the Internet explosion in 1996.

NavTech

NavTech was probably the first company to publish map discovery and route directions on the exploding Internet. In Orange County, California, next to the local major league baseball stadium, they collected consultants from all over the SEI offices and placed in Orange County. They split the group into basically four groups.

There were managers, other administration and operations, some dealing with database, but the majority were C++ software engineers generating the front end and middle tier for Internet navigation technology.

I was part of the C++ development. Not being an accomplished object designer, I was still learning the basics of Object-Oriented Design. Concurrent Versions System (CVS) was the source control system. It is concurrent within a single source server and a single local development environment. When performing reads and updates at our single development location in Orange County, CVS worked. If we had been using multiple development locations, CVS... would not have worked so well.

Common Gateway Interface (CGI) was introduced into my technical vocabulary. CGIs define a specific protocol between the browser running on the visualizing device and a server using an HTTP protocol. The HTTP protocol was stateless, and still is. The communication from the browser or the visualizer and the server could take place in any order after being started from the browser. Embedding a unique token in the transmission solved the simulation of a state-full protocol. The server would recognize the token, or "cookie," to know what the state the "stateless" protocol was in. Software at the server and client, aka browser end, would key off the cookie to vector the current state.

EnRoute, the internal name of NavTech's system, depended on both satellite data and ground-based observation, id est, an employee driving around in an automobile adding to and verifying satellite data. As I worked with the source and the connections via Internet Protocol sockets, issues repeated themselves. Memory leaks plagued the C++ runtime environment. An infrastructure used by an individual developer controlled memory management. There was no common memory manager, other than that supplied by the C/C++ API. So many of the bugs we, as developers, encountered were leaks and orphan pointers in the source that were very difficult to identify.

A second issue that emerged was unsafe thread source. This was not as common as fundamental memory leaks. Concurrent access of structures and classes was new to C/C++ developers at the time and error-prone. So terms like "serially re-entrant" defined a potential solution. It was not accidental that many of the developers at NavTech took the new language from Sun Microsystems, Java, that provided a vast simplification of the issues regarding concurrent access.

The architecture of the system was new at the time and a glimpse into the future, where all the networked connections are homogenized into an entity called the "cloud." NavTech's EnRoute was not a cloud, but a collection of servers with a back-end connection to the exploding Internet. What was apparent was the "system" was now the net itself, not on a single server hosting applications. This was a major fundamental change.

Specifically, the website hosted on IBM RS/6000 servers connected to a firewall router, a Telebit TrailBlazer for example, to an Internet Router connected to the Internet via Frame Relay. Frame Relay is a precursor to DSL, and used in some remote Internet connections as of 2017. The IBM RS/6000 servers running EnRoute software were hosting the street-by-street route generator visualized for the Internet user. I visualized each turning point for the user first with the start location with a visualized direction sequence continuing until the specified destination. Our web interface was pure CGI. The browsers, Mozilla and Netscape being popular, invoked the CGI, which was the portal to the machines that provided the drive-to-location instructions. The <Form> HTML statement with a CGI invocation statement sent a stateless request to the server and waited for the stateless response. Of course, Internet Explorer later easily eclipsed Netscape since they tied it to the PC Microsoft Office systems.

Search engines were now in their infancy on the Internet. The most popular in 1996 was AltaVista, which is now something of a footnote in Internet history. It was helpful when looking up technical data. The richness and complexity of the query results were primitive compared to what is in common practice in the early twenty-first century.

The development environment at NavTech was primitive. The testing and debugging tools of C++ classes was primitive compared to what was available even two years later. C++ classes were tested by attaching individual "main" programs and running them under a debugger, or with primitive logging print statements. The actual routing algorithm for EnRoute was complex. The selected region, which could transition to a state of origin and destination or to a final state, error, resetting the state to its original context. Origin and destination could transition to an invalid origin location, which could transition back to origin and destination or to the final state, which was an error. The origin and destination state could also transition to the final error state. Additionally, the origin and destination state could also transition to an ambiguous origin and destination state. The ambiguous origin and destination state could transition to the final error state or to the successful route state, which meant the route was visualized on the website. Testing in this environment was an afterthought, and difficult.

Several contributions used C++ nested classes and virtual classes. Nested classes are source class definitions nested inside another class. Virtual classes were fast, did not allow multiple inheritance, and used fewer resources. I must admit that Microsoft ended up with a superior C++ development environment. SEI, the parent consulting company, had a MSDN (Microsoft Developer's Network) license, and we could load it, of course, only under Windows 95. Some development continued under AIX using the open-source GNU C++, which was the Cygnus open-source C++ compiler. UUNET, an early Internet provider, was integral to the development process at NavTech. Given the Internet new paradigm, any single server became another resource. UUNET was eventually gobbled up by Verizon.

I spent much of my time and the time of my fellow developers on configuring the NetBlazer and Cisco routers that came along with the explosion of the Internet. The difficulty of configuring a Cisco router in Fargo, North Dakota, remotely from Orange Country, California, was a real treat. These were the days before secure connections, so we used the original IP utilities like FTP and Telnet to connect to a particular port number. To make matters worse, connection ports below 2046 in Unix-like systems were governed by admin and root privileges, but in Windows they were completely open. These systems were completely open to attack.

As developers, we were aware of security, but it was in its infancy.

There were passwords, but that was about it. Equipment was primitive compared to what was available in five years after 1996 all you had to do was attach a sniffer, like WireShark, which could reside in any laptop or desktop with the Internet protocol stack, and you could capture just about any data transmitted or received.

This technology was primitive compared to twenty-first century Google Street View. Intersections of streets visualized in primitive graphics were the focus of drive-to-location visual instructions. One of my tasks was to generate the graphics for multiple converging avenues, typical of the East Coast, where five or more streets would meet at a focal point. I used trigonometric functions to translate the EnRoute data, part satellite and part verified by drive-by-validation (Google still uses this technique). I could implement a mathematical algorithm, and it worked most of the time. A peer suggested a mapping into an array of bits. That might have worked better. The methods I implemented were complex and used math vector cross and dot products.

Vancouver – Arc Service

Early in 1997, they contracted me out to a startup Microsoft shop. Database schema analysis was my task. The Microsoft SQL Server was a fork, i.e. a clone of Sybase, an established and popular relational database product. The vernacular of the schema definition, Structured Query Language (SQL), and stored procedures were a virtual copy of Sybase. Within two more years, they diverged, and MS SQL Server completely eclipsed Sybase. From an architecture viewpoint, stored procedures made it easy to embed "business logic" inside queries, and thus became later to be known as "middle-tier" software. Middle-tier software embedded in SQL is the antithesis to encapsulation. After authored, one had to plow through stored procedures to expose the underlying decisions made embedded in the database.

Riverside Publishing

In spring 1997, with my new laptop, they sent me to Itasca, Illinois via Chicago to write an app, which extended an HTML web page, in the new Java language. I loaded an IDE (Integrated Development Environment) on the laptop and spent the plane ride to Chicago learning some basics of the Java language. Given designated questions, the app was a timed quiz that could run on the Internet. I designed a language with a formal grammar, which I named Application Definition Language. A test designer could load a set of questions given the structure of ADL and then the test would sequence on the Internet as the test taker would answer the questions. I wrote the ADL app in Java 1.0, which I found brutal to use as a developer. The IDE was flaky, but the project was more or less completed. It was a two-tier application, with the app as the visualization component and the back-end a series of uploads to the client answering the questions.

SEI, Los Angeles, and Chicago

Shortly after returning from Itasca, Illinois, the consulting company I worked for effectively became a Microsoft shop. The preferred development environment at the time was Visual Basic. Microsoft introduced what was the last version of Visual Basic before it became VB.net. I considered VB in 1997 to be akin to COBOL. It had an IDE for rapid development, an IIS web server with its quirks like Active Server Pages (.asp), and the emerging database server, MS SQL Server. It was like COBOL in the sense that it had a learning curve with a low bar. I focused on Visual C++.

They based the Microsoft C++ platform on their set of objects. However, these objects were a thin skin over their previous non-C++ development environment. The encapsulation was shallow, so as a developer, I had to learn all the quirks and idiosyncrasies of this new and the previous Microsoft C environment. It was like learning a submarine with many switches and buttons within which one needed to memorize or at least be familiar with. To test out this new favored company technology, I wrote programs using the Microsoft C++ for a logistics company in Chicago to analyze customer Internet traffic. In retrospect, the IDE or Microsoft C++ was the best and may well still be. The key for successful action was to just leave most of the Microsoft proprietary framework alone.

NeoGlyphics

In late July 1997, I received my next assignment as an SEI consultant at NeoGlyphics, an Internet-startup company in Chicago. They hired me to design, implement, and validate a website for the "Turnaround Management Association." Their infrastructure comprised Java version 1.1, CGIs (Computer Gateway Interface), which used an interface written in C++ to send and respond to the CGI stateless protocol defined by the Internet specifications. An API (application interface) for Java for the Internet protocol didn't exist and wasn't released until version 2.1. The servers that processed CGI post and get messages used C or C++ language-coded CGI modules. The NeoGlyphics solutions were creative. On a different or on the same server running the CGI module, Java objects existed that used a different Internet Protocol port number, below 1064, to communicate with the CGI. Port numbers below 1064 were privileged, so this solution was secure on servers running Unix or Unix-like systems. Like I said, Java 1.1 did not have the equivalent CGI interface, but had a TCP/IP interface. That made the implementation possible. Then the extension written in Java would process the messages and feed POST or GET to the CGI written in C++, and wait for the stateless response.

Electronic mail was an important part of the Internet project and the solution was to use a C++ interface that used Unix-named pipes to broadcast e-mail messages to the appropriate listening servers. The database definition language conformed to Oracle 7 standards. The Java modules handled all reads and writes to the database. This was before the existence of a solid database framework. You built "raw" SQL using format objects and passed them to the JDBC Java module. This is the first time I had to do a "full-stack" implementation with minimal help from graphics designers.

For a short while, they involved me with NeoGlyphics Hallmark site. It was so popular that it crashed the Oracle database. I analyzed it and deferred to Oracle consultants who had better knowledge of what was a going on than I did. This also ushered in the era of the shopping cart, or e-commerce. Because e-commerce technology was in its infancy, they built the shopping cart from the ground up. Eight years in the future, many plugins, e-commerce systems were available. But this was in 1997, and e-commerce was a new technology. HTTPS secure links existed, but Internet companies were embedding them in their web pages using round-trip technologies. NeoGlyphics had their shopping cart technology, home-grown comprising Java 1.1 source code, Oracle version 7 database, CISL (a C like scripting language that NeoGlyphics built), and fledging JavaScript source. JavaScript had subtle differences on each browser, rendering it difficult to use. In the future, the European Computing Manufacturing Association standardized JavaScript. This was a progressive contribution by the Microsoft Corporation. Home-grown, e-commerce solutions continued for a decade in the future.

During my work a NeoGlyphics, I also developed software for Matrix Consultants. I implemented during off hours a dealer location algorithm. This was specifically for Suzuki Motorcycles using geodata. The software would locate dealers by zip-code. The software would "draw a circle" and then using a zip-code mapped to geography data to "see" if there were any dealers in the circle. If not, the circle would expand. I gave it the nickname "the expanding atomic bomb algorithm."

While working at NeoGlyphics, I studied Design Patterns, Elements of Reusable Object-Oriented Software. It was a bold attempt to identify pattern creation objects in the C++ and SmallTalk languages. What it did was enlighten me to software engineering at a new level as a discipline. In the real world of software design, I only ended up using a few of the patterns, notably singleton, little language (interpreter), builder, factory, and abstract factory. Composite was one of the most difficult to implement, since you must maintain a uniform interface for each object in the collection.

Cendant

It was an experience working in a Microsoft Shop, where me and three other software engineers were the only ones developing in a non-Microsoft language on Windows 98 workstation base interfacing with the current release of the Windows NT server. We had quite a hoop to jump through. I could access the C/C++ native library through the Java Native Interface of Java version 1.1, and fortunately, I was familiar with this kerfuffle while working at NeoGlyphics and Matrix Consultants. The encompassing architecture of the Cendant system, which was used to identify housing areas and compensation for folks that were required to relocate from one location to another, usually distant from the original location, was well-thought-out. Its design included a presentation layer, which I would associate with visualization using web pages, and Microsoft NT server with their IIS web server. An NT server and the IIS web server interfaced with client-specific business objects written in Visual Basic 5-interpreted source code, which then communicated via the VB5 API with a pure business object server. The business object server interfaced with an API developed in-house with the data-access-layer. The data-access layer invoked the SQL-server, which still similar to a Sybase database server. They typically based database access to stored-procedures.

The overall architecture impressed me, and I made several mental references to it later in my work as a software engineer.

A visualization layer, later implemented by HTML5 and JavaScript (actually ECMA script), which was resident in the browser. Of course, the Internet provided the transport between the NT/ISS server base. (These were flagship products from Microsoft).

Very thin request and response handlers to receive and send messages to the browsers.

A logic layer that implemented core logic along with pure domain objects. Sometimes referred to as the business logic layer.

Database associated logic, for preparation associated with the data access layer. This layer would handle any translations given different data access APIs.

The architecture was mandated and enforced by what developers called the "architecture police." What was our tiny group of three doing with the API? Evidently, one of Cendants clients required a Java API (1.1) interface. The architecture police treated us with disdain since we were the only non-Microsoft module in the system. I delivered a raw version of what they required.

American Funds / Capital Group

My first experience of Capital Group comprised taking a C-language programming test during the interview with the project lead. As I remember, I made one error on the test, using a programming language I hoped I would not use again. They hired me to work in the Bloomberg Transaction Processing Group.

The feeds would arrive at approximately six in the morning,

depending on the local time. Feeds were parsed, validated, and broken down, then stored in the Sybase database. Most of the processing took place during the batch cycle, which was initiated at noon local time. There were several feeds, some of which were sent to other processes via database-to-database transport. This was a common architecture. They persisted transactions to the database and another group's process would then read the transactions in the database, and act upon them. It seemed primitive compared to a direct-IP connection with audit trails. Capital Group reminded me of the technical culture at CitiCorp TTI. Manager meetings made basic technical decisions at a high level. There would be a manager meeting to decide whether to change a column in the database schema.

Hewlett-Packard's HPUX was the base operating system being used by Capital Group. It was the worst Unix-like system I have ever worked with. You never knew exactly how it was going to behave. Sometimes it operated like AT&T Sys V.4, other times like BSD 4.3. You never knew which mode you would get, or maybe a hybrid. IBM's AIX was superior to HPUX.

The next hurdle, which was source control, put me in a time machine. We built a manually constructed parts list explosion on top of RCS. This source control system had similar deficiencies to the source control system used at CitiCorp TTI. The manually defined parts explosion was error-prone. The Capital Group release cycle comprised the classic waterfall model. Each stage of the release is a cascade to the next process. It doesn't mean it does not involve all the groups in all the steps. Passing the complete product to Quality Control with a release candidate was often the worst-case scenario.

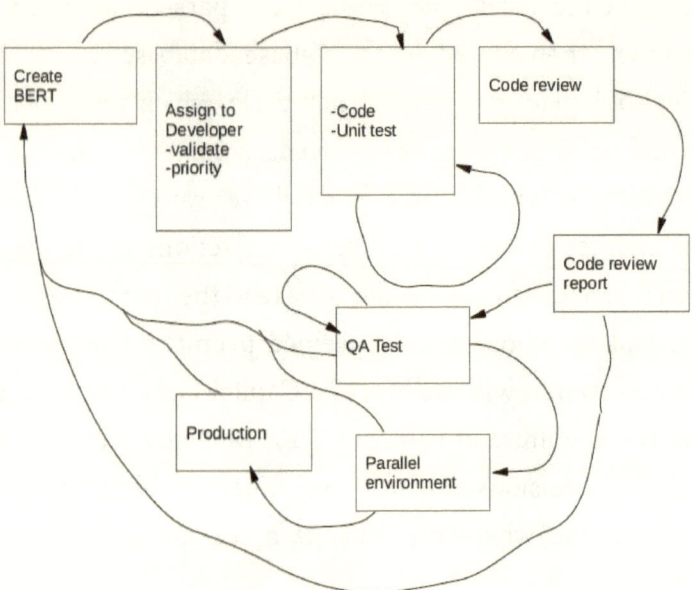

Classic Waterfall Development

I would encounter this fundamental technological process within most of the companies with software projects. Of course, most companies where I was employed in the future would minimize or even skip steps in the classic waterfall model. Typically, there would be a minimal test inventory or a complete lack of repeatable unit and system tests using this model. Code reviews were lacking tools that would allow asynchronous, free-time reviews, and these reviews were held in a room with a projection of the source on the wall. Management would often see this as an expensive step (how much money does it cost for all the developers to walk into the bar at lunchtime? Slightly less than a conference room.) In this diagram, a "BERT" is a system trouble report (BTPS error report). In other systems, it took many names.

Another tool integral to the production process at Capital Group was Autosys originally developed by Sterling Software, which ironically, was located up the boulevard from DataProducts where I worked in Woodland Hills. The Autosys product was the classic Unix cron and crontab scheduling system on steroids. The configuration files had the postfix ending of "jil." It was an integral part of the system developed, but controlled and owned, mostly, by system administration. The developers could not use Autosys. Of course, this was a source of discrepancy between the development and production environment and a source of errors. I do not know if it was due to license issues, or a deficiency in the tool.

A serious deficiency of Capital Group's system was because most business logic and control, including data-structures, were all handled by Sybase-stored procedures. They derive part of this architecture from a classic two-tier architecture used by Power Builder, which influenced critical business logic that existed in Capital Group's system. The limit of skills was another delimiting factor. There were people who only knew how to code stored procedures. There were others who primarily developed in the C language. Often you ended up with a mixed conjuncture of both.

The Korn shell was specific to AT&T proprietary technology. Several shell scripts to install production software at Capital Group depended on the features of the Korn shell. I found this odd, given the number of other shell capabilities under HPUX. Capital Group used Lightweight Directory Access Protocol (LDAP) for access to the file systems by all developers. Normally, LDAP is used to control access from web-based transactions. At Capital Group, the tool was being used in an internal environment that had little to do with web access. Different developers would have fine grain access to data. No other company that I worked for used LDAP in this way.

As work progressed through 1999, the BTPS group adopted a coherent unit-testing strategy. They divided batch processes into short-term and pay down divisions and real-time processes into five meaningful states. I was attempting to delve deeper into object design patterns by designating generative versus non-generative design patterns. A good definition of a pattern: "The abstract form which keeps recurring in specific non-arbitrary contexts." The concentration of examining software patterns continued with an analysis of several pattern archetypes. Some archetypes include a hierarchy of architecture patterns, design patterns, and idioms. Another pattern hierarchy comprised a set of parent conceptual patterns. Besides software patterns, software anti-patterns were identified. These included analysis paralysis, creeping feature-itus, design by committee, kitchen-sink design, rape-and-paste programming, and violation of the d.r.y. principal (don't repeat yourself.)

By April 1999, Capital Group was gearing up for the Y2K bug-fest. I used the simple command line search:

```
find . -name '*.c' -exec grep -n sprintf "{}" /dev/null ";"
```

or

```
find . -name '*.c' -exec grep -n 'strto|' "{}" /dev/null ";"
```

We were looking for buffer overflow exploits. After a study of software patterns, next came Universal Modeling Language (UML) diagrams, of which, the most important, are System Sequence Diagrams. Rational Rose invited Capital Group developers to a demonstration of their UML suite, which included class diagrams, sequence diagrams, and collaboration diagrams. Collaboration diagrams, later renamed Communication Diagrams in UML version 2.0, resembled old-school flow charts with some structured decorations. For the next fifteen years, I found class diagrams and then sequence diagrams to be the most useful. I suspect formal UML ran aground later and became less important when the software development culture turned to an agile methodology.

Inheritance of one class by another is a canonical idiom of object-oriented design. An alternative to inheritance is delegation, where a link, message, or calling sequence is established to another object where the original object provides the functionality. Sometimes, delegation presented a more simple architecture where using inheritance designs another object as a child, or subset of a parent object, instead of using an object. As I dealt more and more with objects and patterns, a well-designed object has a clear and recognizable purpose.

As the freeze for Y2K approached, they assigned me to automate source control, which up to this point required manual editing of the parts list. Initially, I attempted to convince management to use what was a new open-source tool named Concurrent Versioning System (CVS). This approach was flat-out rejected. "Capital Group does not allow the use of open-source software in production." I ended up reinventing the wheel. Using Sybase database as the back-end, and with a command-line interface, I wrote the parts explosion in object-oriented Perl 5. I had three months to complete the project and by the beginning of the year 2000, it was complete.

Initially, each source control operation was implemented as a Perl command line request. Thus, I could get each operation working before the next build and the command with the modules that supported it. Each command was distinct from the next. The "migrate" command was mig.pl. The "release tag" command was rag.pl and so on.

After the Y2K bug interlude, Java and JDK version 1.2, alongside the first release of Enterprise Java, were introduced to our group at Capital Group. Enterprise Java Beans were supposed to be the silver bullet of middle-ware control. A developer could reconcile transaction isolation and object encapsulation in a series of magic containers. In retrospect, no. Also, an initial version of JDBC emerged for the Java language. JDBC is a database vendor independent data-access control module for relational databases. I mapped objects to relational schema definitions. Unfortunately, there is always an impedance mismatch between an object-oriented design and the relational model. These mismatches are well known and intractable. Years of experience have showed that simple object models and simple relational tables provide the best solution for the impedance mismatch.

While the object-oriented Perl source control system was in production, simple object-to-table mapping seemed to work with no major errors. Alongside this system, I implemented a Java 1.2 web interface that provided a visual environment on top of the Perl application. I was lucky in that much of the database complexity hid in Sybase stored procedures.

At the beginning of year 2000, the Bloomberg Transaction

Processing Group (BTPG) started a transition to an application software control using Enterprise Java Beans (EJBs). We perceived them as a "silver bullet," solving dependencies between layers of software, solving database deadlock issues, and so forth. Sure.

What actually transpired at Capital Group was one part of the business logic was developed in stored procedures, since is all some developers knew. The next layer outside the stored procedures was a set of EJBs. Yes, it worked, but only marginally better than the previous two-tier logic of C-coded business control and application logic backed by stored procedures. Were there better solutions? Yes. EJBs were not well-designed. What they needed was a simpler set of objects to map from messages to business logic and then to the database.

I used a Java-build tool, vastly superior to the command line scripts I had been using up to this point. Ant was a build tool designed for Java compiles that allowed runtime substitutions. I used it for several years until I started using a tool even more powerful, called Maven. Both tools are, until now, free and in open source.

Later in the year 2000 and early in 2001, Extensible Markup Language (XML) was being introduced into Capital Group development groups using the Java language. XML was derived from Standard Generalized Markup Language (SGML), a very complex and difficult document-definition language designed by committee as an ISO standard in 1982. This was a period of inception for XML. It is simple when compared to SGML, but as a language, it is dynamic. One feature that was derived from SGML was the Data Definition Language (DDL), a meta-language. It defined the language semantics for a particular instance of XML in a preamble.

However, DDL is a distinct language than XML. Later, DDL was replaced by XLST, which was written in XML. Developers struggled initially with XML because the tools did not know the XML syntax. Of course, this changed with the first smart editors like EMACS and later Integrated Development Environments (IDEs), which could parse XSLT, and detect errors in an XML file.

To run the new enterprise environment, Capital Group installed the WebLogic application server. It supported the new Enterprise Java environment. Given all the configurations that took place, WebLogic J2EE was far too complex for what it provided. BEA supported the server originally purchased (named after the initials of the three founders). Oracle Corporation later purchased BEA. WebLogic implemented a complete, but tightly coupled set of server tiers. I implemented visualization using Java Server Pages. The middle tier was where most of the domain and business logic was implemented using Enterprise Java Beans. The back-end, or persistence layer, comprised an interface with the EJBs and many databases. It is still in use until now, but not with the fervor that existed in 2001. The main performance issue with the WebLogic application server and its open-source cousin Jboss, which showed up a few years later, was the heavy resource usage for the functionality that it provided.

The issue with J2EE technology is when implemented on the server, you ended up with not just the modules necessary for implementing your project; you had everything that the framework provided. It is difficult to use one module without knowledge of others. The software tightly coupled J2EE technology. However, J2EE was a known standard and consistent.

In 2001, I worked with the Apache Web server. One system administrator told me later that they named it as "A patchy server." This may be apocryphal. The official history says they named it honoring Native Americans. It was much easier to deal with when compared to the BEA WebLogic server. It was easy to start an Apache web server in any environment, including Windows 2000 on the desktop. Using an instance of the Apache web server, I could build graphic web pages into the configuration management environment I authored during the year 2000 freeze. By late 2001, after JMS (Sun's Java messaging system) was designated as insufficient, Capital Group used Tibco, an IBM messaging system. Later it was JMS compliant. Using a key-value architecture with data type constraints made it easy-to-use and robust in that it validated data types.

While working at Capital Group, I attended several classes sponsored by Microsoft. These were mandatory given the orientation of SEI Consulting. By now, the company I worked for was primarily a Microsoft "shop." I completed the classes and became a certified project manager. They broke the topics down into seven basic categories. These were envisioning, planning, developing, stabilizing, work-in-progress, expertise, and standards. Then each of these topics was broken down into sub-topics. For example, we broke envisioning down into project kick-off, detailed minutes, identify risk, assess risk, vision statement, project structure, and component/client checklist.

Also, about this time, I took the responsibility to configure Microsoft's web server Internet Services Server (ISS) for the SEI Los Angeles office. ISS was and is parochial. It is specific to Microsoft

Shops. I found it much more difficult to configure than the open-source web server, Apache, or even BEA's WebLogic server. And trying to use Microsoft's source control system, SourceSafe, well, forget it. Microsoft wisely abandoned it at a later time.

The other technology that came into vogue was Unified Modeling Language (UML). UML is a visual language to design object-oriented systems. I have used UML for years and even for my personal projects until now, which are not associated with corporate USA. The diagrams I find useful are class diagrams and sequence diagrams, and possibly package diagrams. The rest I consider being detailed fluff and "over engineering".

By June 2002, Capital Group moved to a reasonable source management system, Perforce. I no longer developed a bevy of Perl scripts doing builds and persisting data in a Sybase database. I built a Java program to load definitions into an Excel spreadsheet, which connected the new technology to control requests.

Because of all the pieces, most of which were not replaced, the configuration management process grew in complexity, as represented in the above schematic.

New technologies were slowly being adopted. Extensible Business Reporting Language (XBRL) extends XML, and was introduced for pilot projects at Capital Group. Later, it became a communication standard for globalized companies. By now, they installed Microsoft Windows XP company-wide. I installed Cygwin, a runtime package I used for most operations. Cygwin presented a Linux-like environment on Windows.

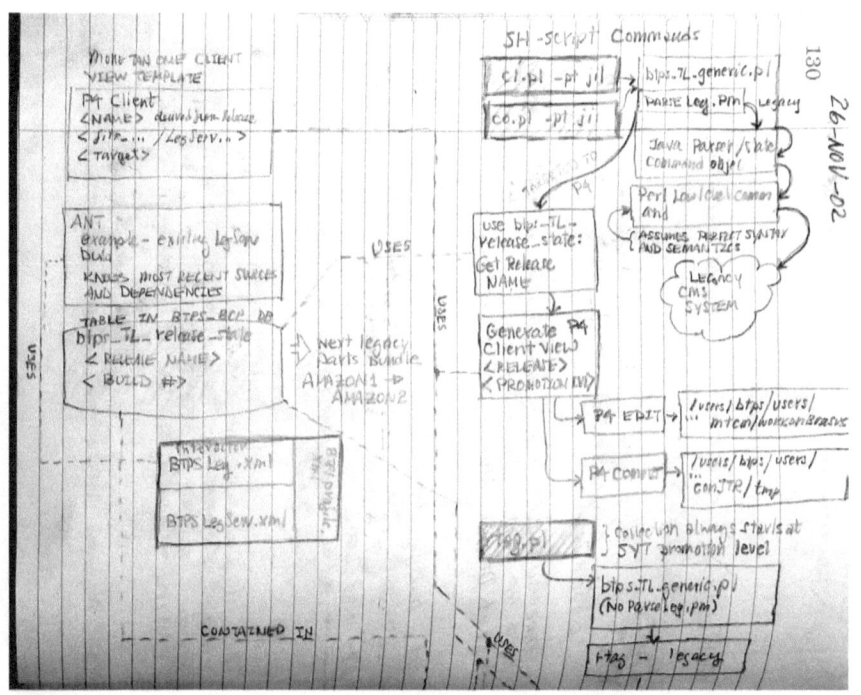

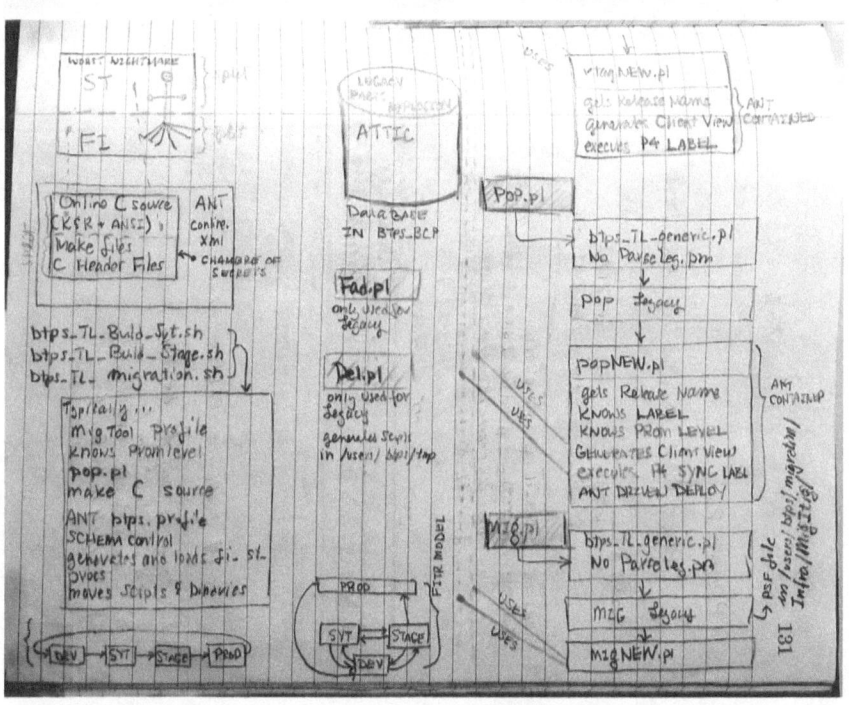

GEEK APOCRYPHA III: WANDERING THROUGH TECH LAND

•••

After departing SEI and Capital Group, I took a contracting job at Yamaha Motorcycles. They hired me to replace an auction system written in Microsoft Visual Basic 3.0. The existing package was used to automate auctioning of Yamaha products provided by various Yamaha dealers. The new project had a limited budget, and I actually didn't complete it, but built and tested all the components.

The general specification required a Java 1.2 application constructed on a PC laptop, interfacing with a scanning device that scanned data from a known tag on an auction-able item, entering it into a database. Besides all that functionality, they had generated reports that provided the details of the transactions and the inventory. This project was to be completed in five months.

Typical software components of the project included the Apache 1.3 web server, the Tomcat 5.0 Application Server, and Oracle 9i lite database server. The Apache web server generated the visualization. The contents of the page were to be written in HTML version 4, JavaScript, which was browser dependent, and Java Server Page (JSP) tags version 2.0. Besides more tags, additional XML files were used to configure how the web server interacted with the application server.

The middle resident software ran on the application server, in this case, a set of modules that handled servlet requests and responses. All these servlets were visualization-centric. Another set of modules that held data objects with rules that perform decisions on what takes place next. Then finally a set of objects that were database-centric. These modules were to be written in Java 2.0, the popular object-oriented language. Finally, we had the schema, all the tables in the Oracle database that are defined and played "transparently" with the database-centric objects handled by the application server. I was designing and implementing what later would be named a "full-stack project."

But there was more. A Telelogix scanner was used to scan the items in an auction and then send a message to a module running on the application server and read the information. It turned out that to interface with the Telelogix scanner; they required a Microsoft C module on the laptop that received the messages from the scanner.

The group that I worked with were not web page, middle-tier, and database developers in themselves. They were mostly COBOL developers used to dealing with a nightly batch process. They conceived this project at a high level as a batch project, but it was anything but. I built a framework from scratch. Much of it worked as it should. In retrospect, I designed and built too much of it, using interfaces instead of "plain old Java objects" or POJOs as they came to be known. While working at Yamaha, I attended an early MySQL conference in Orlando in 2004, where I was introduced to the first version of the Spring framework for the Java language. If I had known about it when starting with Yamaha, I would have used it. It became my "goto" framework for the Java language until 2014, when I ceased to work with software professionally. Ironically, at the MySQL conference, I attended a seminar on an early version of PHP. PHP was an acronym for "personal home page."

The project continued at Yamaha. A Concurrent Versions System (CVS powered the source control and configuration management), an open-source management system. After forty-five "tagged" commits (reproducible collections of software), I departed Yamaha when money ran out. I completed most of the project.

For a short time, I worked for Intersperse, a company attempting to build an application-monitoring dashboard. The technology included the current version of Java, MySQL, and a host of graphical elements representing the process that the system was monitoring. The dashboard would "splice" itself into the virtual machine runtime, and "seamlessly" visualize a dashboard with many controls, monitors, and event generators. When I was hired, I worked with pre-sales development while the system was being completely rewritten. As the chief technical officer would say, "Change the engines on the airplane while it is in the air." After four months, it was time to depart. This startup company seemed to be destined for failure. Another company whose name I don't remember purchased

Intersperse, then Intersperse disappeared.

After that failure, OAO Healthcare Systems hired me. Knowledge of data objects in the Java Language was important for the modules in their software. They had their certification test, which I passed with relative ease. OAO was building a medical system that would replace "green screen" applications. The BEA application server supporting Java 3 and the current Enterprise Java environment was the foundation of OAO architecture. Database-centric objects, business logic objects, and webpage centric objects were part of the architecture. Their back-end database was IBM's DB2. The testing was well organized and partially automated. The web pages used the current Java Server Page technology, JavaScript and the current release of Cascading Style Sheets for the web page screens.

One of the more interesting aspects of the project was the partitioning of the distributed databases. The domain configuration mapped the data sources for distributed databases. Every transaction required a domain value. Using the domain value as a surrogate key, they could distribute transactions across multiple databases. Later, when working for Matrix Consultants, I used a similar scheme to engineer replicated databases using MySQL. I viewed the development at OAO Health Systems as well-organized and geared toward success. When returning from holiday on January 2, 2005, the office was empty. The project had lost its funding.

By the end of the month, I was working for Digital Evolution, once again in the consulting organization. DigEv.com was in Santa Monica, so to commute to the home office was an easy from where I lived in Culver City. That short commute didn't last long. They designated me as a consultant to eHarmony.com, a male-to-female match-making company. Hired to do work in the Java language, I ended up doing mostly database administration. The Jboss open-source web server and the Struts framework made some pieces of technology at eHarmony. Jboss is the heavy-weight sibling to the much lighter and lean Tomcat application server. Both servers are freely available and open-source options. Eclipse, later to become a dominant open-source and free IDE, was the integrated development environment. CVS, another open-source product, was the source control system. To counter the open-source trend, eHarmony used MySQL server, a Microsoft product, for their database. This made sense since MySQL, the leading open-source database product, was just introducing robust transaction control. The actual application would pose several questions to the applicant, then map them to several functions, not unlike later AI-programming applications.

After this assignment, I worked at the home office for a few weeks, working with salespeople and experimenting with one of Oracle's database to object mapping tools, TopLink. At the time it was a proprietary package, but since that time, is now in open source. The best comparison would be with Hibernate, an open-source package that also mapped Java objects to a SQL database schema. In retrospect, TopLink was more complicated and powerful. But did I need this?

They centered my last three assignments while working for Digital Evolution all in San Diego. The first was at Sempra Energy, doing an analysis of their customized dashboards that comprised "portlets," controls, and web parts. Sempra had their own technical terminology. There were Web Access Controls, Web Services Integration, and Application Service Agent, for example.

I was there to analyze the taxonomy of theirs, mostly web-driven knowledge base. Later, this transformed into an analysis of their use of Microsoft's SharePoint server. The managers of the SharePoint project disliked my recommended approach. I argued for a self-organizing project, but they wanted it built with a prior structure. I left Sempra for another assignment, but returned from time-to-time at their request, which made the next assignment more difficult. I had to provide and follow up with use cases for the categories in their taxonomy.

By the middle of May 2005, they offered me an assignment, through Digital Evolution, at the San Diego Workforce Project (SDWP). Technically, they were an Oracle shop. An Oracle consulting company had written their system, using Java, which required several changes as per the standards of the State of California. SDWP's system used the Struts framework, with which I was familiar. The current consulting company employed by SDWP, abarvstech.com, declined the project, and passed it to Digital Evolution. I was familiar with all the components of their system, so I took the assignment.

Unfortunately, the SDWP ended up being a project from hell. The first thing I discovered was that they kept all the passwords in the Oracle database in clear text. The Oracle Integrated Development Environment at the time was a version of Jbuilder, originally a Borland product, that was repackaged as Jdeveloper. This early buggy version running on SunOS removed the last five lines of the source code modules in the IDE. Fortunately, I could rebuild the mutilated modules using JAD, a Java decompiler, from compiled object modules.

Normally, the Struts framework has a long and somewhat messy configuration file, but once you master all the pieces, you are ready. That framework coupled to the web page, named view in the architecture, with actions mediated by controllers and then used model objects to interact with the database. The original Oracle developers had changed the Struts framework with no documentation of the changes. The changes interfaced with the specific JavaScript elements on the web pages of the application. These were mixed in with custom Java tag lib modules. It was a nightmare, but I eventually got the system working.

To complicate the project, I had to export selected contents from the prime Oracle database to Informix, a database mandated by the state of California in real-time. In soft real-time, it was a rather simple database replication. While working with the Workforce Project, for a short while, I also worked at QualComm using the Business Process Execution Language (BPEL). It tried to define a graphic job flow with various small Java applications operating on graphically defined input streams and output streams. When reviewing their design, I told them it was too complex. That did not go over well. I was also picking up more work from Matrix Consultants. At this point had four different jobs. Shortly after that, I hit a wall and ended up in the hospital. Next, Digital Evolution moved, changed their name to SOA Software, and they disbanded the consulting group.

GEEK APOCRYPHA IV: THE END GAME

•••

fter the 2005 episode in the hospital, Matrix Consultants again hired me. The first two projects were all Microsoft-based. The first was a C++ project that attempted to mix streams off the Internet, much like a mixing board in a studio. It required an "NT" server and Visual Studio, which was purchased. The visualization took place in the browser, in this case Microsoft IE. It was a disaster and never took off for several reasons. The internal operations required for the data streams were unclear. Even when the person who was knowledgeable in the Microsoft Codec API worked with me in tandem, the result was not what the client wanted. Besides this challenge, the test streams were the original demo streams, so the demo frame sequence modeled in the software.

For the second, I assisted on a VB.net project with added components in C#. Regarding Microsoft's virtual machine and object library, C# and VB.net were the same object API under the hood. This project was completed and actually deployed as a "toaster" device in dealer showrooms. This Microsoft project, as a complete application, which was distributed to the end-point systems in show-rooms using Cygwin, which was a virtual Linux environment on Windows.

Next, I worked in Java to create middle-tier and back-end modules for automotive dealer websites. This work often used the open-source Tomcat application server and Struts mapping framework. It was common to use HTML web page elements to access database-centric elements. This was common in several frameworks. In retrospect, it suffered from being a tightly coupled visualization of middle tier architecture. Besides working on back-end modules, there was the development of e-mailing and faxing brochures for various vehicle products.

Much of the work for the next eight years comprised importing external vehicle data in some form from either a vendor or a dealer of identified vehicles. I completed the vast majority of this work using the current Java virtual machine framework, Eclipse development environment, and MySQL as the database server. The how-to-map objects to a relational database became an immediate conundrum. In the past, it was all done "manually." We performed a query on the database using Structured Query Language (SQL) and the result was like using a direct query from a command utility or a graphic tool. The "answer" was picked apart piece-by-piece and loaded into the object or set of objects according to specific rules defined by the developer. The process was tedious and error-prone.

Object-to-relational mapping frameworks appeared. I had

used TopLink from Oracle. Hibernate, an open-source mapping tool specific to the Java framework, emerged as an open-source alternative to object-to-relational mapping. It didn't matter using any framework, there is always an impedance mismatch. At the highest level, in a relational database, the order of the data, row-wise, does not make any difference. In an object-oriented model, ordering makes a difference. The first simple solution is to create a table for each object, or even for views, which are mutated tables, but still relational. The ability to have nulls, undefined data in a database wreaks havoc with this approach. Given these issues, we developed tools. I used Hibernate. Instead of SQL, I wrote the queries in Hibernate Query Language (HQL).

In-house, Matrix Consultants had two distinct runtime environments. Java being the first with Enterprise Java extensions, including Java Server Pages (JSPs). The second was PHP 4. I first encountered PHP at a MySQL conference in Orlando in 2004. The creator, Rasmus Lerdorf and enhanced by Zeev Zuraski and Andi Gutmans, all seasoned Common Gateway Interface (CGI) developers, created an easier-to-use alternative. I was critical of PHP. But I understood the advantage. An Apache web page server was the standard at Matrix Consultants. A simple plug-in to Apache could activate the PHP environment. The bar to produce source code was much lower than the Java Enterprise run-time environment. This allowed development to focus on web page visualization and less on middle-tier logic and database requirements. My chief complaint was that PHP 4 had poor support for object-oriented design and data modeling.

I favored a Java environment. Java Enterprise of J2EE was the standard. In retrospect, J2EE was consistent, but difficult-to-learn and to use. The Web Page component was complicated by a tag that interfaced with the middle tier and an element language that was, at least initially poorly documented, made JSP pages an order of magnitude more difficult to develop than the PHP web pages. In retrospect, I ditched J2EE for a simpler Java framework. No matter what Java environment you use, you need a Java application server. This separated the visualization from the middle-tier logic. A separate application server complicated the runtime environment. Initially, I tried to use JBoss, an open-source J2EE server from RedHat. JBoss used too much of the in-memory resources. So later, we used a much simpler server, Tomcat, also an open-source server for the J2EE environment. However, the connection configuration was more complex. For all the GET and POST operations to be honored from the Apache Web Page server, a particular configuration had to be in place. Later, when the Java side of the house switched to the Resin Application Server, requiring a similar configuration.

During the design of several projects, I spent much of my time drawing class diagrams and interaction diagrams as part of the development cycle. Using these diagrams as a model, I would build the source code. Often, class diagrams and interaction diagrams would be updated given review and changes to the source code. During this period, the Java team attempted peer-to-peer communication with an automobile vendor's application server. The project was a disaster. The application running on the vendor's application server had broken multi-user threads and processes.

Subversion, an open-source, source-control tool, was in use for all the projects. Large graphic files had to be backed up on large storage media. All this was done in-house. Collections of sources were "tagged" before the quality control hand-off. Development was driven by regular and ad hoc meetings, but I could classify the overall process as the "water fall" method. Problems often occurred when trying to synchronize software with all the web graphics. This became even more of a problem when visualization and front-end developers used Action Script, also known as Flash. By 2010, some visualization experts predicted that HTML 5 would replace Action Script. Originally, the configuration control tool was a collection of Ant scripts. Ant, along with JUnit, was an adequate configuration tool set. To construct a build, we required paths defined in a build files reference that all the JAR or Java archive local.xml file. This was an Ant deficiency, although some might consider this an advantage. In 2007, I proceeded with a demonstration of Maven. One deficiency of Ant was it was often difficult to determine what version of a JAR file was being used in the build. Maven had strict version control of JAR files. But the great advantage of Maven as a build tool is that public accessible JAR files, with a specific version number, could be automatically accessed from the Internet and localized for the build.

By 2006, I directed much of my attention to what I knew as a dealer dashboard. The visualization tier, middle tier, and data-access tier became increasingly complex. The concept of this dashboard was to allow dealers to customize their website by selecting and manipulating controls. As with all the projects, connection to a client server, middle-tier development, and dashboard, I spent much of my time designing the database itself, including the tables, schema, and queries to access the database. I have already mentioned Hibernate, which supports its own HQL, Criteria Object interface and, if you needed it, native SQL. I found the Hibernate Criteria API to be too limited. For simple queries, HQL was acceptable. With more sophisticated JOINs and sub-queries, it was easier to revert to native SQL. Since MySQL now supported views and stored procedures, I started using them to simplify the development. Stored procedures were useful to ensure that complex queries were "atomic."

We adopted PHP version 5 as the current version in the development environment. It encouraged me to see that this release had a more complete object implementation than PHP version 4, but it disappointed me that the new implementation of objects seemed to imitate Java's paradigm. I tried to introduce Ruby, a scripting language with a unique and interesting method of implementing object-oriented design and programming. This was to no avail. Part of PHP's attraction was you could embed it on an HTML webpage. So other scripting languages like Ruby or Python were not popular candidates.

Hessian from Caucho was another technology, an open-source web service protocol that continues to be widely used until now, (as of writing in 2017). Java developers started a project to build "apps" on the current smartphones, and Hessian was a basic, high-level communication protocol used for smart phone-to-server communication. By mid-2008, I rejected the J2EE framework for the Spring framework. The Spring framework is an object cafeteria for Java. You can use as little of it or as much of it as you choose. From its initial release, XML configuration files drove much of Spring framework. Annotations that replace XML configuration answered this criticism. Personally, I suspect annotations since they spread the control in many source files, instead of in XML configurations, in known directories.

One of the Spring technologies I experimented with was dependency injection. This technology allowed one object to inject an object into a defined set of objects. This idiom is useful to inject logging into objects without clutter in the subject object's source code. Here, in the controlling dependency injection object, you could activate selective logging in subject objects. The injection would automatically display any input object and any resultant output object, thus creating a silhouette of coupling.

OpenVPN, where VPN is defined as a virtual private network, was started around this time. It allowed easy access to all the servers, such as multiple virtual machines running on a one physical server. Before this, tedious and complex Internet Protocol tunnels were necessary to access all the various physical and virtual machines.

Our next project at Matrix was MySQL master slave replication. There were several challenges that were encountered during this implementation. If a slave is offline, how do you catch up? How do you handle unique sequential identification keys? How do you isolate a test environment and then migrate that environment to production? For several questions, robust journaling of the transactions became critical. Switching from a potential production to a live production environment actually became easier to start. Once the potential release was validated, the synchronization took place, and we swapped the addresses of the virtual machines.

An e-commerce project existed before the beginning of my work at Matrix Consultants. In 2008, I took over the primary responsibilities for further development and continued support.

There was some initial refactoring to fix some obvious errors, and then came the addition of API interfaces like PayPal to purchase various items on the websites. The source code for e-commerce comprised a set of Java modules and PHP modules. Several vendor solutions were considered for the Java side, but too expensive, so the home-grown version continued to be used. For the PHP side, the solution was Ubercart. My biggest issue with Drupal was that they wrote it in PHP4, which made the system difficult to change. The Drupal developers had their implementation of what could be objects, but much of the source used top-down structural decomposition.

Shipping and taxation options were some of the development challenges that I faced. Shipping providers required that, when shipping an item, certain specific shipping rules applied. Vendors like USPS and UPS have protocols to activate the shipping services. These new protocols required an implementation in Representation State Protocol (REST), which superseded Simple Object Access Protocol (SOAP), a much more complex but older transfer mechanism not requiring HTTP access, only requiring base Internet access, not HTTP connections.

For shipping, because of the complexity of the logic before one-size and one-cost packages, I used a rules-based artificial intelligence application, Drools. Drools is a rules-based system and therefore a weaker AI application, weak when compared to a deep learning AI. It seemed ideal for all the shipping parameters that the various vendors required.

Another challenge was dealing with dealer inventory feeds for the dealer dashboard. The basic format of the information was all the same, but each feed had a slight variation in the format and for a discrete entity. Usually, the common format being a comma separated file, though they could be tabbed separated. Thus, each dealership had a slightly distinct set of entities describing their inventory.

When working on an E-Blast project, I considered it a spam/advertising/propaganda project. I completed it. This is the first project where I used JavaScript Object Notation (JSON) messages, and asynchronous JavaScript and XML (AJAX). This technology allowed you to send messages to a middle-tier server, and receive them at another, undesignated interval. In this project, I did not use any webpage keywords that were tightly coupled to the middle-tier application server. No JSP tokens, no PHP tokens, no EL tokens. The European Computer Machinery Association had standardized JavaScript, now designated as ECMA script, and made reliability possible. It meant that it required all the major web browsers to conform to the scripting standard. Well, almost.

In late 2011, I went to work for Grindr/Blendr. Changing jobs introduced me to several new technologies. The system allowed person-to-person connections using smartphones at any point on the planet that had a smartphone transceiver connection. These connections all used REST at the server end, which manages the traffic, and which then persists and retrieves data records in a database, MySQL in this case, that are specific to each user on the smartphone. The magnitude of these data-sets was mind-boggling. Each night, given a million messages times 2 gigabyte memory on a smartphone, presented a globally distributed database of 2,000,000,000,000,000 bytes, or 2 potential petabytes of data mutation in a dataset in a measured time period, perhaps one hour.

The messaging system was critical. The technology selected is RabbitMQ, written in Erlang. Erlang was specifically designed for scaled and distributed systems. Erlang and other languages like it, Scala, for example, have a highly structured sequential syntax, where a variable can only be assigned once in a module. Initially, this project had severe performance difficulties, mostly because of database latency. Performance analysis pointed the finger at Hibernate, the object-to-relational-database mapping tool. The middle tier had to handle the Apple Push and Notification Service (APNS), and the messaging in Google's Android API. Besides performance challenges associated with a relational database, two databases were in the mix. The first, MongoDB, was easier to grasp. The query language was in JSON and the results were a mix of text and image data. Thus, MongoDB allowed easy access to image storage and queries in a language with known structure. MongoDB has replication services that are easy to implement. The Redis database is what I might describe as an inverted index on steroids. An extremely fast, replicating cache store can exist in several database nodes. The commands to store and read globs of data are specific to Redis.

Then there was Google's Application Engine (GAE), which had an SQL-like query language called GQL. Under the hood, GAE used map-reduce technology. From a developers' standpoint, GQL did not support joins, so if you wanted to do something like that, it had to be done in the middle tier. There are tremendous advantages to the map-reduce technology. It supports a highly distributed system. But GAE was still a beta technology, often failing when critical information needed to be persisted. GAE is now a supported Google product.

The host for the middle tier and database back-end was Amazons EC2, also known as AWS or active web service, for this highly distributed system. AWS is like a fluid server that, depending on your requirements, could be configured with small or large amount of memory. It also had their version of MySQL or Microsoft SQL server. It was popular for highly distributed applications, since you could spin up as many servers as required. Of course, each instance came with a cost. But the ability to spin up several instances in different geographic locations with little or no side effects made system-scaling simple. Whereas REST was used to connect clients to the server instances, XMPP was used to connect the vast sea of mobile devices to the client. The advantage of XMPP is that is primarily a set of text messages.

We used IntelliJ, a top-drawer, integrated development environment for the entire project. We introduced Jenkins for automated testing, a periodic build tool. This package allowed a set of tests, in this case TestNG, as the encapsulating tool, with Jenkins that allowed test-driven development. Using Jenkins and TestNG, it rendered a report on demand that at least helped focus the "Scrum" each morning. The test-driven development allowed control of developing functionality, but was less useful when attempting to overcome performance issues. A shift in management and performance issues meant a hand-off to a newly hired consulting firm. Time to depart.

In 2013, after a spending time in Hawai`i working on a couple of my vanity websites, I went to work for Pricegrabber.com.

Comparison shopping was the business model of the company. My assignment had several components, the most important being a refactoring of the search engine keyword interface for Google and Bing search engine optimization. The core of the project had to do with keywords and ratings on these search engines. They proposed a contract that would last for three months. It lasted for more than a year. The Drools, rules-driven, AI engine was the heart and soul of the ad-manager. Several modules needed to be added to the core engine configuration to more effectively analyze the keywords describing the product. Most of the source for the ad-manager used Java version 6.0. The server was Tomcat, a reliable open-source server with J2EE plugins. The Drools interface allowed the managers, human beings, to load hints and rules into the Drools engine using a spreadsheet. On September 15, 2014, I departed the company and retired from corporate USA.

I still, until now, sometimes work with software. You can experience my software at johntredden.com. The source resides at https://github.com/jredden and https://github.com/southkonafarms.

ABOUT THE AUTHOR

A software engineer for forty-five years, John Redden is currently an organic farmer on the Big Island of Hawai`i. He has published articles in Brill Press journals sponsored by the Global Studies Association. *Atomic Baby Bible* is John's first book, though he does have three science fiction manuscripts and a fourth underway, set in an alternate ultra-tech universe.

Learn more at
www.johnreddenauthor.com